RSA: HISTORY, HARMONY AND HUMANITY
A suite of articles about Ray Steadman-Allen

RSA: history, harmony and humanity

A suite of articles about
Ray Steadman-Allen

General Editor:
Barbara Steadman-Allen

United Kingdom Territorial Headquarters
101 Newington Causeway
London SE1 6BN

First published in 2012 by
Shield Books
© The Salvation Army
UK Territory Literary Unit
101 Newington Causeway
London SE1 6BN

ISBN 978-0-85412-860-0

Cover design by Rodney Kingston

SHIELD
BOOKS
© The Salvation Army
United Kingdom Territory with
the Republic of Ireland

Printed by UK Territory Print & Design Unit

To Mum, whose consistent understanding of Dad's commitment to piano, manuscript, textbook and, more recently, computer, nearly all of which has been in another room, has actively encouraged the flowering of genius.

Contents

Foreword

Ronald Holz

NO other person, whether composer, musician, editor or administrative clergy, has had a greater impact on the development of Salvation Army music and musical culture of the past 60 years than Ray Steadman-Allen (RSA). He has been the guiding and leading figure in Salvation Army (SA) brass band music throughout these decades and in retirement has found time to enrich the entire brass band scene with significant and challenging works. Yet his influence ranges far beyond the brass band. His choral and vocal works have had an equal impact within the denomination, while his guidance of the SA music publications as Editor-in-Chief and his articulate advocacy in print and in speech of its musical mission have been of incalculable worth. In my estimation, he is the most gifted, prolific and forward-looking talent within 20th- and early 21st-century SA music. It is only right that we now have this book in which he, family members and distinguished musical figures of the movement combine to frame his remarkable life and work. I count it a great joy and privilege to pen this short foreword to such a worthy and admirable book.

Part biography and autobiography, and part Festschrift by leading musicians that examines his music and leadership, the book maintains a warm, human quality, so much like the man himself. We do not forget that his wife, Joy, has shared in their calling and ministries, and to have her input, as well as that of their two daughters, Barbara and Rosemary, makes for an intimate but far from sentimental portrait that balances the more technical discussions provided in Part 2. Nor are the humour and the 'lighter' touches feigned or forced. If you have ever met Joy and Ray, Barbara and Rosemary, you know they are a family that enjoys wit, fun and fellowship with others in gracious hospitality. They know exactly when and where not to take themselves seriously. That is also a great strength of this book.

RSA has studied The Salvation Army's music as deeply as anyone, and pursued his doctorate in music via its musical history. He was its first true musicologist, and as early as 1965, in his *Evolution of Salvation Army Music*, he declared succinctly the tension within SA music and, as a result, within his own creative life, that the reader must bear in mind. The very conflict of artistic and religious ideals – nothing new in ecclesiastical history – has, as usual, provided the stimulus of compulsory limitation in efforts to bring standards and new techniques to the service of traditional aims. I wonder to what degree he knew these words were prophetic of his own creative life just at a time when he was producing pace-setting works like the tone poem 'The Holy War', the Fantasia for Piano and Band 'Christ is the Answer' or the trombone concertino 'The Immortal Theme'?

Several years later in her unpublished thesis on SA music and worship (Trent Park College, London University, 1970) Joy preserved a quote from General Albert Orsborn that I would use now as a summation of RSA's philosophy – and aesthetic – while writing for and guiding SA music: 'We have no wish to be outcasts of the musical world but our music is and must continue to be functional as distinct from the merely artistic, aesthetic or impressionistic. Our message, our praise, our mission, our worship embody our function.' No better story enlightens this statement than Ray's account of Ralph Vaughan Williams's praise of the trombone solo 'The Eternal Quest', praise with a side comment that the work would be so much better if the [expletive deleted] little tune were removed! The tune and the associated text, 'Jesus is looking for thee', were the heart and in some sense musical source of the entire work.

As the reader joins the keen minds of Andrew Blyth, Dudley Bright, Paul Hindmarsh, Cliff Matthews and Dorothy Nancekievill in their more detailed assessment of RSA's output in various areas of SA music, I hope they will bear in mind those two quotes shared above. RSA wrote on demand and rarely with a freedom to just do whatever he wished to do. Therefore the title of one of his finest works, the sinfonietta 'The Lord Is King', summarises his entire creative life – his skill, his art harnessed to the mission of praising God and proclaiming the gospel.

I find it fascinating for Andrew Blyth, the UK's current Assistant Territorial Music Director, responsible for supervising music editorial work, to take us on a journey reviewing RSA's guidance of SA publications 1967–1980, as well as tasks taken in this arena both before and after these dates. What Steadman-Allen wrestled with back then may not be exactly the same as that faced now, but the lessons learned and the new territory opened made possible what happens today, especially in the expansion of musical styles embraced by the SA. Dudley Bright's study provides a fine encapsulation of RSA's compositional method, of challenges faced and problems solved. While RSA's brass band music has been given serious attention in the past, his vocal works, while highly valued, have not received the same attention. This is why the joint effort of Matthews and Nancekievell is so vital to the success of the book. That RSA's choral and vocal output well balances his instrumental music probably cannot be stressed enough, especially as words are so important to his creative work, whether setting them to music, in writing poetry, or basing his purely instrumental works on vocal models and sources.

Paul Hindmarsh completes the musical study with compelling insight into recent brass band works not specifically intended for the SA but now accessible to all. Interestingly, and not surprisingly, for the majority of them, connections to words and hymn tunes, and in some a connected narrative, were key to their inspiration and success. His study emphasises RSA's stylistic and musical eclecticism, a descriptor he and I embrace as a highly positive one in this post-modern age. For it has been Steadman-Allen's ability to assimilate many different aspects of modern musical life throughout his compositional life, ranging from the most esoteric classical music to the pop music scene, that has kept his output fresh and vibrant. We still have works of his to master and understand – what an achievement and legacy!

The appreciation that follows by RSA's friend Norman Bearcroft, who shared with him many exciting, high-water-mark events in SA music-making, and the representative series of personal encounters that follow, bring the human touch back into focus. I know many around the world who would and could have gladly added their own thoughts to the 'Encounters' portion, yet the sample contained here seems just right and balanced. The interview for the magazine *SA Bandsman* brings us right up to date and provides the proverbial 'icing on the cake'. We share once again in RSA's articulate, insightful thoughts on music, especially music of The Salvation Army.

I must add my own personal appreciation here. Ray and Joy have been of great encouragement and help to me on various levels ever since my wife, Beatrice, and I got to know them at Star Lake Music Camp in 1972. At that camp, the young staff members felt bereft and hurt in the midst of a difficult situation – the Steadman-Allens steadied us in the midst of that time of trouble. Our association goes back even further, for my father, the late Commissioner Richard Holz, brought Ray to Southern New England during the time of RSA's visit to New York for the premiere of 'Christ is the Answer'. Ever since then, whether I was seeking advice on research in SA music, or asking him to be a guest speaker and conductor at SA music councils, corresponding with him on a wide range of musical topics, or even inconveniencing them during retirement so that I could interview him but one more time, they were always gracious, kind, and of immeasurable help.

When I was privileged to write the notes to the YBS Band's award-winning CD *Alpha and Omega* (British Bandsman CD of the Year) directed by David King, I wrote to Ray about the project and he responded with characteristic wit concerning the title chosen, dearly hoping those who were to enjoy the superb playing by that band would not misunderstand the title! He himself was not 'A & O', even though there might have been some hidden flattery and word play on the part of the producers. Again and again, the humility of the man, his humanity, stand out to me, taking nothing away from the great gifts he has used so very well throughout his distinguished career. I commend this book to all who approve of the normal life becoming extraordinary when selfishness is conquered and submission to a greater good embraced. May this book be more than monument to RSA and his wife, Joy. May it prove a beacon and guide to others gifted and called to musical ministry and Christian service.

Professor Ron Holz,
Kentucky, January 2012

Introduction

THE opening of Luke's Gospel has come to mind as I have gone about this general editorial task; in many and various ways things have been written about RSA and it has been my intention in this book to compile an 'orderly account' from eyewitnesses who have walked across his path or accompanied him along it. It is not just a compilation of past publications, though; the book consists almost entirely of new material, each chapter being a newly commissioned article for this purpose. And Ray has taken this golden opportunity to record his own autobiographical recollections.

The book is unusual in its format and content. It is intended for a wide variety of readers, Salvationist and non-Salvationist, musician and non-musician. It is my belief that the book will fly on to the shelves of universities and colleges, not just because of its focus but also because of the calibre of both analyses and contributors. Correspondingly it will also be accessible for the lay reader because of its autobiographical and human element. That is partly why we have set it out in two main parts. But both belong together because the music comes from the man and the man is more than the music. Many of us with formal musical training will appreciate the humour of the title. History and harmony are standard music courses; each word describes the first two parts of the book.

Part One is 'domestic' – Ray's autobiographical recollections; Joy's comment on Salvation Army officership as a significant component of Ray's life; a celebration of their marriage; and our attempts as daughters to describe family life. The chapter titles of Part One are selected works of Ray's, acting as light-hearted (sometimes) descriptions of the different eras of his life. They are neither chronological nor the subject matter of the chapter! Part Two is analytical – Ray's editorial work, and evaluations and analyses of his compositional output. In giving him an opportunity to reply to what has been written independently about his work, we think we have created a much more dynamic read. Each contributor has sparked off in him new things to say that might otherwise have never seen the light of day. Part Three is an insight into the way Ray thinks – in all, a miscellany.

The idea for a book comprising several articles written by different people came from a passing comment made by my mother, Joy. She said: 'Your father isn't just one person.' It's true. He is supremely a creative and innovative musician but he is also pastor, preacher, *pater familias* and best friend of Joy, his wife. Theirs has been the right kind of marriage where one and one equal three, where mutual encouragement and respect have prevailed, where God has been central and in which each has given the other space to fulfil their individual potential. Into this family Rosemary and I were born and nurtured. It wasn't our choice (!) but we consider it precious.

Dudley Bright (Professor of Trombone, Royal Academy of Music) has written superbly about Ray's Salvation Army (SA) brass band music and Professor Paul Hindmarsh (professional music editor and arranger, lecturer and journalist) has paralleled that with an account of his non-SA band music.

It would be easy to paint Dad simply as a brass band composer, but he also loves words and their musical expression of them. Dorothy Nancekievill (Director of Music at Wells Cathedral School) in collusion with Cliff Matthews (Bandmaster at Gloucester and ISS member) and, in a different vein, Lieut-Colonel Norman Bearcroft (composer and past conductor of the ISS and the Canadian Staff Band) have reflected on his choral music. Dorothy and Norman are present and past conductors of the International Staff Songsters respectively. Maisie Wiggins MBE has commented as a soloist who has premiered works especially written for her, and Andrew Blyth (currently responsible for music editing in the UK's Music Ministries Unit) has explored the influence Dad had in his 34 years on the International Music Editorial Department, 13 as its Head. Doreen Rutt was a most valued member of the department in Ray's day, and was one of The Salvation Army's leading pianists.

In respect of that time, we asked composers Brian Bowen, Colonel Robert Redhead, Dr Ken Downie, Dr Howard Evans, Professor James Curnow and Lieut-Colonel Trevor Davis each to contribute a short word about their encounters with Dad as editor – experiences from the other side of the desk, so to speak. We could have asked so many composers. Forgive us if you are one and you would have liked to have had your say. We also asked James Williams MBE, well-known past conductor of Enfield Band, to write about his time as deputy bandmaster when Dad was bandmaster at Tottenham Citadel.

In order that Ray should not just be seen as a 'grand old man', we have recollected that he was in post as Head of the IMED when pioneers such as Joy Webb and John Gowans and John Larsson were at their peak in the area of contemporary communication. So both Major Joy Webb and General John Larsson have shared their experiences of working with him. To this day, Ray notices and evaluates contemporary expressions of faith in Salvation Army music making.

We want to thank every contributor who, without exception, has expressed his or her sense of privilege in being asked to offer their perspective on these different facets of Dad's life. Each has written carefully and humbly and we think this is a cracking collection of articles!

Although Dad has been recognised for his music in a number of well-known circles outside The Salvation Army, in various honorary awards (not least by the Royal School of Church Music in 2003 and Classic FM recently in its Hall of Fame), the Salvation Army context has provided and provoked opportunity second to none for creative and Christian development; how many composers would give their eye teeth for such instant 'feedback' in the immediate performance of their work across the world by bands and songsters held together by a common mindset and motivated by a common heartbeat? And how many composers have had the challenge of both writing expansively for Royal Albert Hall sized events and simple cameo-style gems for a morning or evening meeting in a local Salvation Army hall? For all the oyster-like aspects of The Salvation Army, we thank it for the precious pearls that have emerged.

Dad himself has written extensively, so this is not strictly a biography but a partial autobiography, and his ability to focus on the task has been eye-opening. He has included his earliest memories, things only he knows, and recollections of his time in Australia with my mother in the early 1980s. Just at the moment when most others sit back and contemplate retirement, Mum and Dad were appointed to Sydney as Director of Evangelism for the Australia Eastern Territory and Papua New Guinea, my mother also having responsibility for the Nurses Fellowship. After spending all their officership in and around London, they faced this extraordinary change with integrity and immense trust in God. They adjusted to a new way of living, ministered in a small downtown corps, travelled hundreds of miles to encourage outlying officers and got involved with the local alcohol rehab centre. But lest you should think Dad a saint having read our book, the family recalls a pet dog named Tinsel who had a great set of teeth, sometimes offered in a growl. The phrase 'tinsel-teeth' became a euphemism for those gritty moments that come in the normal cut and thrust of life and Dad has earned his fair share of the phrase. No, Dad is not just 'one person'!

Personally, I want to thank David and Linda Popple, whom I recognised early on as being just the right people to keep this project on track, wholeheartedly offering their home, their considerable time and their efficient admin skills in the pursuit of excellence in me and our contributors. We thank them for all the hard work and the friendship that has sprung from sharing this.

Rosemary and I are proud to present this 'treatise' with RSA as its focus and all of us on the team that have made this publication possible gladly give it both to you and to God for his glory and your inspiration.

Barbara Steadman-Allen
General Editor,
January 2012

PART ONE

History

Chapter One

His Guardian Care

[Chapters One to Thirteen are written by Ray himself]

'DAD, please can I have the temptation?' I must have been only six when I made this request so it probably startled my parents. As Salvation Army officers their 'quarters' occasionally stored overflow from the local hall. In this case, it was a brass baritone. I had attempted to blow it, with undesirable results. Dad had said, 'Put the temptation out of his reach' and that's what I thought it was called! None of us could have foreseen how large a part music was to play in my life.

I was born in The Salvation Army's Mothers' Hospital at Clapton, East London on 18 September 1922. It was within the sound of Bow Bells and so that makes me, I believe, a Cockney. I was dedicated to God with the names Raymond Victor Allen. My parents, Frederick and Gladys, were (or had recently been) stationed at Chippenham and I am named after a local Salvationist hero who, in 1921, had saved someone from drowning at the cost of his own life. From the same town, Ray Clarke, also a member of The Salvation Army and a former Secretary of the National Association of Brass Band Conductors, was named similarly. My dad came from Chatteris, Cambridgeshire, the Allens originally coming from Ireland in 1780. My mother was born near Swindon where, as a soldier at Gorse Hill, she met my father.

What I first remember are two lines from a child's book: 'They march around the nursery floor, my soldiers straight and tall.' My first certain memories are just flashes from Malta where my parents had been appointed around 1926. They were in charge of a Naval and Military Home in Floriana, which was still there when Joy and I visited but had passed into other hands. I can just visualise the large, dark and cool kitchen and the women who worked there. A more vivid memory is getting lost in the side street, the sun glittering on the sea and the women sitting at their doorsteps. Our voyage home to England was rough, hot and smelly. At some time we seem to have been involved in the Salvation Army hostel that once stood opposite St Pancras Station and is now the site of St Pancras Town Hall. There is a photo of me standing between square gate pillars that have lions on top. Probably a former mansion from the old New Road days.

3

The building was still there up to the 1960s. I took a chance cine shot of it during its demolition.

Following our return to England we moved to Leamington and Malvern where, at the age of six, the best I could achieve musically was to march behind the band 'playing' a pretend cornet, which was actually an old motor horn minus the rubber bulb. To think that Malvern was then also the home of Sir Edward Elgar! Somehow we missed meeting him. Photographs show Dad as the proud owner of a motorbike and sidecar, so I guess we got about.

We arrived at Birmingham Aston on a classically black, rainy night. I recall a fire and large fireguard draped with drying clothes, the only solution with heavy rain. In those days the band would march the new officers to the hall for a welcome meeting (the same night) but I don't think it happened on that occasion. Aston was important formatively for my development. Cloistered from the famous Villa football team but not immune from the smell of the brewery, I learned to ride a bike and bowl a hoop, spent hours at the local museum and had a Sunday school teacher ('company guard' in the old parlance) called Jack Lamb, who kept boys coming weekly by adding to his Bible lessons stirring tales of his soldiering experiences in the First World War. Most importantly, it was in one of my parents' meetings that I went forward with the compulsion that I needed God to help me be a better boy. There was a further appointment in another Birmingham centre where, sat on a wooden form in a gaslit hall, I consciously first listened to a band. It was Harry Kirk's 'Steadily Forward March' which has retained my affection. I also wondered how the bandsmen knew when to play or rest – first stirrings of musical curiosity!

Then we moved south to the seaside. Like good pastors my parents took their hearts with them but fell in love with Worthing. Everything seemed pleasant but then I was only nine. In 1931 the aeroplane was sufficiently a novelty for us to crowd into the Christchurch Road school playground to look up in excitement. That 11 November afforded my first experience of standing with my class for the two minutes' remembrance of the 'fallen'. Lead soldiers and miniature gardens were my hobby. It would have been trains but that passion eventually reached my brother who, later in an engineering life, built his own large-scale models.

I joined the children's singing company (junior choir), had some tentative cornet lessons and saw the pier in flames. In January 1932 my brother and sister, twins David and Vida, were born. One particular incident has made a lasting impression on me. Worthing Corps began in 1883 and suffered violent persecution. In 1933 there was a 50-year jubilee celebration, which Commissioner Charles Jeffries came from London to conduct. The early corps flag was to be preserved memorially in a glass case, to be displayed in the hall. The solemn moment of dedication arrived but the eminent guest confessed that, as a former member of the Skeleton Army, he felt unworthy to perform the sacred task and invited Commissioner William Stevens, a venerated former missionary, to come to the platform.

It was at school we went political! We were told about the US presidential elections and though I preferred the name 'Hoover' we had to write to some unknown American called Mr Roosevelt (harder to spell). How glad we were that Mr Roosevelt was the new President.

After the seaweed and warmth of Worthing it was back north, this time to Barnsley. A November 'change' and a rich time of development for me. The quarters was on the edge of a 'banking' (a great playground). I liked Yorkshire people, the sense of community and direct speech. This stood me in good stead decades later on holiday, when Joy and I went into a Salvation Army tea place. The corps officer recognised us and we chatted. Then from behind the counter came a lady, very Yorkshire, and demanded our order with a touch of rough humour. My wife could see the officer wondering how this would go down with 'colonels'. But Joy is a northern girl and had been the lieutenant in a Yorkshire mining village – the lady was delighted when she got as good as she gave. We were 'in'.

My first social encounter with Barnsley Young People's Band was its Christmas 'tripe supper'. I had fish and chips. The band leader turned me into a reasonably competent 2nd cornetist. My star achievement was the march 'Becontree'. Additionally I began piano lessons at sixpence a half hour (Lieut-Colonel Norman Bearcroft once commented that if it had been singing lessons my parents would have been robbed!).

What is now known as the eleven-plus exams came round and to my delight I qualified for the grammar school (a school unloved by former pupil and TV personality Michael Parkinson). Our uniform blazers were blue and my school house, Holgate, had a green shield on the breast pocket. From the moment I set eyes on a black-covered textbook, its red lettering announcing 1st Year Latin, I entered the academic world with delight. History lessons I don't recall, geography didn't enthuse me – but sciences and languages were just fine. I fear I was unpardonably pleased with myself; the downside was that school uniform was unfortunately highly visible to any local boy-gang looking for trouble. Plus I was now supposed to wear glasses. I hated them; it seemed I was the only boy at the Army with specs. So I tried to pocket them if my mother wasn't about. There were hints of a future difficult teenager.

My dad did a lot of pastoral visitation and occasionally I went with him, but I also went when he was collecting for the annual Self-Denial Appeal. The doorstep reception was probably no different from today but a clue to some economic fortunes may be gathered from my dad – after a rude rejection – muttering, out of earshot: 'New rich!' The Annual Appeal was followed by a divisional gathering. Corps targets were assigned and hapless corps officers had to stand and announce their corps result. One year my dad built a big target at which the officer 'fired'. If the target had been 'smashed' a light came on. Psychologically debatable, but times have changed. Guilt could be a great weapon, especially when the question was: 'Where were you last Sunday (or band practice)?' But somehow we remained enthused and thrived – mostly.

I must leave Barnsley nostalgia with a brief mention of the 'ghost dog'. Our dining room had two doors if you don't count the french door to the iron staircase at the back. One door led to the cellar. My mother was ironing and I was doing my homework when a greyish, almost transparent large dog came from the cellar door side, padded across the room and disappeared at the other door. I thought nothing of this for a moment then spoke up to my mother. But she hadn't seen anything. Creepy!

Until comparatively recently corps officers generally moved on after one to three years. This nearly always meant new schools. So when we went even further north to West Hartlepool on the English northeast coast I was a year behind in some maths but a year ahead in Latin. The advantage of the school was a music master who was a keen organist. He introduced us to the classics and rather took me under his wing. I loathed the gym but played rugby. I was also fond of cycling and once rode to Roker and back. Aside from schools, the making of new friends helped to create confidence, though I have sometimes felt that the comparatively short period we spent in any one community tended to make friendships a bit ephemeral. Nevertheless, I had some good friends at 'West' and elsewhere that I remember with affection.

As to my banding, I had been told by my previous band leader: 'Don't just say you play cornet but tell them 2nd cornet.' Sound advice about honesty! So I did, but Stan Hampshire, the band leader, put me on 1st anyway. Soon after arrival, Christmas came upon us with its stint of carolling for both senior and junior bands. The cold of the northeast coast must have affected me for, at a little place called Greatham, I passed out. While the piano lessons made reading easier I had problems with high notes. So, there being a trombone lying about at home, and my dad having been a trombonist, I gave that a go – equating slide positions with fingering – and it worked. Stan fitted me in and I owe him a debt for his judgment.

Our junior band was quite busy; we had one or two soloists and it fell to me to play the accompaniments. I regret that for one weekend band engagement, the cornetist and I were billeted together and practised at some unsocial hour with a portable organ! I mustn't forget singing company membership, still with unbroken voice. Joy and I seem to have identical songs in our experience, our favourite being 'We Are Soldiers Fighting for the King of Kings'. This song must have been the winner for that generation. Years later, in the late 1970s Joy and I were with Howard Evans opening the first Adult Music Camp. It was at a Butlin's holiday camp where the Army ran a holiday week. Norman Bearcroft, on stage, got the whole crowd singing that song.

Most corps had a corps cadet brigade for the purpose of training young Salvationists in various facets of Salvation Army activity, including Bible study (with marked papers), spiritual development, public speaking and so on. We met weekly in what must have been a shop attached to the hall. It was known as the Glory Shop. After class we would buy bags of chips. I benefited greatly from my time with this group.

The manner of my beginning to compose was as follows. School encouragement and Salvation Army involvement led to my developing rudimentary music creativity. Mozart and the classics were not unacceptable on programmes but piano solos were more or less expected to be 'Army'. So I began to transcribe band scores into keyboard pieces – learning instrumentation in reverse. From there it was a small step to trying my hand at real arranging with the help of a book and assiduous study of scores. I never completed any early efforts; lacking sound technical grounding and guidance I quickly ran out of steam and would try something new. Perseverance bore fruit. In the Army context, to be an aspiring composer was sufficiently 'different' to be almost an eccentric and not to be taken too seriously – even at home. This would be a suitable place, however, to say that in my formative efforts I later did receive encouragement from many directions.

Great Britain lived through the passing of George V (I recall muted tones from the wirelesss set: 'The King's life is moving peacefully to its close') and the drama of Edward VIII. Then in 1937 George VI was to be crowned. This coincided with my parents' appointment to Battersea, a Thameside South London district. At 14 going on 15, I was excited at the prospect. Our house in Simpson Street backed on to the railway. Without a bathroom, sixpence bought us a weekly clean-up at the public baths. Battersea hall was at the end of a market in the High Street. On a black table in the youth hall someone had carved 'Mafeking relieved'. The expected transfer to the St John's School was slow in arriving or perhaps never arrived at all. In the event I became bored with sitting around and was plunged into the adult world of work. It so happened that a number of Salvationists in the corps had jobs in various London Army headquarters and I became No 2 messenger boy or 'lad' in the Secretary's Department of International Headquarters in Queen Victoria Street. The tasks were largely running errands or helping around offices.

Promotion came quickly and I was elevated to No 1. Part of the job was office boy to General Evangeline Booth, which I knew even then to be an historic privilege. The General cared very much for retired officers and I would be sent out with a small parcel for someone. At other times it was buying her fish locally. I came to know the city centre pretty well. Her house, West Winds, was near Esher in Surrey and occasionally I took documents there. Sometimes she would be working late and when necessary I would stay on and take in a prepared tray of refreshment. She would ring for me to collect the tray and make sure about my going home. There was always a silver coin on the tray. The General's office was a kind of Holy of Holies, entered through green baize-covered double doors.

I kept music paper in the office and used spare moments to work on a few ideas. I had a forlorn hope that Eric Ball might come in and ask me what I was doing. International Headquarters backed on to Lower Thames Street with the river beyond. We boys would occasionally lark about on the barges during the lunch break. The International Staff Band rehearsed at lunchtimes and we would often sit outside and listen. Next door were the offices of the Salvation Army Assurance Society (insurance) which had a boys' band which I would dearly have loved to join.

Came the time to become a senior soldier, for which I was ready. By then I had become a boy scout and, during the Spanish Civil War, was involved with a big scouting presentation at Clapton Congress Hall in aid of the Basque children. My banding consisted of helping out on euphonium in the junior band. Transfer to the senior band in mid teenage meant a baritone. I still practised my beloved trombone at home.

I was excited when Battersea Band visited Chatteris for a weekend; Dad was leading the meetings in the place of his origins. Now and again we would have a 'special' (a visiting officer). 'Crimond' was becoming all the rage and the band was issued with manuscript parts. Quick to use home-grown talent, my dad asked me to arrange a couple of old-time congregational songs. One was 'He Was Found Worthy'. This exercise was the first time I had actually heard any of my efforts played. A milestone indeed. However, my creative efforts were not taken seriously: Dad wanted me to get a steady job in an office. Few in our Movement at that time secured a diploma in music and a young composer was a novelty to be regarded indulgently but not too seriously.

Many corps used to have a Saturday night meeting, usually some kind of programme with refreshments. Individual soloists were in demand and invitations came my way. Of significance was one from north of the river, Harlesden, which was reached by trolleybus. It was a link that eventually resulted in my joining that corps.

Came the time for my parents to move to Rugby. Would I go with them? I preferred to stay in London if possible. Songster Leader Will Sinnock of Harlesden had already found me a job as his assistant. He was cashier of the Road Guides Department of the RAC, located near Pimlico, and my job was to look after the Club's roadside telephone boxes (available to members), paying the bills and sending out charges to users (if they'd owned up). I enjoyed it. I made a friend who also lived in Battersea. Passing Battersea Park and over the bridge we walked to and from work at a fair speed.

Will Sinnock fixed me up to lodge with Bandmaster and Mrs John Lyons. This offered a choice of Tube travel or being picked up by car. There was a good number of young people in Harlesden Corps and this provided a happy social life. Six of us young bandsmen formed a small club, which met at each others' houses for billiards or table tennis. Supper was part of the routine and was invariably baked beans. Hence we became the Baked Bean Club. We would get together and play our instruments, even visiting other venues. As the other five were cornetists with me on trombone we contrived special musical arrangements, which was fun. The corps sergeant-major, a cine fan, would make movies of corps activities. I was embarrassed to see myself with the songsters at Hassocks stuffing myself with food!

One weekend we had a visit from a Brigadier Archie Burgess (of which more later). He was a wizard on the concertina and unlocked for me the mysteries of 'close harmony'. It was at this point that I began to appreciate the music of George Marshall (as did Wilfred Heaton and Ray Bowes). The music sections were strong and at last I began to complete pieces. Finally, I summoned the courage to submit a selection called 'Glory, Laud and Honour'. It was returned by the then Chief Music Editor, Colonel Bramwell Coles, who felt the final chorus was rather too trivial to sit alongside a noble hymn like 'All Glory, Laud and Honour'. When, years later, I succeeded to his editorial chair, I had to make similar judgments and offer experienced advice. It was ever my aim to be as encouragingly faithful as he was. Our 2nd trombonist and his wife were Beethoven fans and shared with me their gramophone evenings. The weekly pleasure of playing piano in a string trio also deepened my musical awareness. I began to build my own record selection – Bizet, Holst and two works influential for me at the time, John Ireland's Piano Concerto and Constant Lambert's *The Rio Grande*. The world of swing and jazz also had its attractions and I gathered the Glenn Miller discs as they were released.

The Second World War began on 3 September 1939. I was home at Rugby that day. In common with many others the Lyons family had received an Anderson shelter, bolted-together corrugated plates sunk into the garden. We were issued with identity cards, ration books and gas masks. A few people began to depart into the Forces. In the early part of 1940 our RAC department was rehoused in the squash courts of the RAC Country Club at Esher. At convenient points a bus would pick us up and bring us back. The club and its surroundings were very elegant and we enjoyed lunching in the dining room.

The Gas Light and Coke Company was having to replace staff and I secured a job in the spring of 1940. My first section was the Statistical Department and then I found myself in what seemed a crisis-driven scene, estimating the cost of materials for contracts. Finally, I moved to the wages section and would go out to the gasholders near the old Battersea Power Station to pay the wages. The route by bicycle was via Ladbroke Grove and Victoria Street. Massed daylight air raids began in September and one morning I had to dodge into a Victoria Street doorway to avoid falling shrapnel. Then there were the incendiary bombs and the disturbed nights. It was all pretty bad and had I been older I might have been more scared. One Sunday we had a landmine on or near the hall. So that day our meetings were held at Willesden Green. Just one more memory along these lines. Very early in June we were playing cricket on Wormwood Scrubs when we saw a northbound train packed with soldiers, many of whom were bandaged. From the bridge we waved down to them and only later did we learn that these were troops back from the epic Dunkirk rescue.

Chapter Two

Youthful Adventures

LIFE was the typical merry-go-round of middle-to-late teenage, and while I popped home to Rugby now and again, the 1940 London air raids caused my parents understandable concern and I was a poor letter-writer. Finally I yielded to insistence that I join my family on a permanent basis. Despite the risks, I didn't want the change and I liked that train journey from Euston via Wolverton and Bletchley, fare 7/6d return. My father knew the chief cashier at British Thompson Houston, a large firm which made turbines and had electrical projects. So a place was found in the Internal Audit office, again filling a post vacated by the demands of war. The job was largely checking pay slips and canteen takings and the calculation of percentages on large round slide rules. I still have my old conventional slide rule. A number of employees signed their payslips with a cross and it was fascinating occasionally to see the Christian name 'Verdun', linked with the First World War battle.

From time to time we had practice alerts and went to the shelters. The blackout was a hazard in a road with trees, and while Rugby was not raided, we saw the Coventry blitz: a huge red glow in the sky. Once a week I was a firewatcher at the local art school. This involved wearing a tin hat, making rounds and sleeping on the premises. Time was available for composition and out of that situation came 'The Bethlehem Story', a Christmas suite. It may seem strange in today's huge repertoire of Salvation Army Christmas band music, but in 1940 – at least in Salvation Army publications – there was only 'Adeste Fideles' (Goldsmith) and a 'Christmas Reverie' (Merritt). With the addition of a handful of similar items over the next few years I hope that I may be pardoned for claiming to be something of a pioneer in 'music for all seasons': Christmas, Harvest and Easter.

Rugby's deputy bandmaster, Eddie Dytham, who was not that much older than I was, became a great friend and aroused in me a love of Eric Ball's music. Eric has been an icon of practical, quality Salvation Army music, both vocal and instrumental. Eddie and I would play each other's pieces and I wrote two quartets. Other influences were seminal: Debussy, Constant Lambert, Delius, Albert Roussel, John Ireland. Prior to my parents being reappointed I worked my way through the Salvation Army Bandmaster's Correspondence Course, an excellent course combining theory, harmony, band training and conducting with Salvation Army music regulations and Christian doctrine. Higher education facilities being rare then, such a course met a real need and I later found the music content a solid foundation for music diplomas. But music, though important, was not quite everything. In common with most corps we had a club for youth called Torchbearers and I became the 'log keeper'. There were facilities for games, of course, refreshments and often a speaker. The evening always concluded with the lighting of a torch (specially made with a wick and some kind of lighter fuel) followed by a very brief form of words from John 1:7 relating to the 'Light' of God. It was an impressive if tiny ceremony. The Torchbearer groups continued through and after the war but gradually fell into oblivion. I was keen on this weekly gathering, and indeed had a period evangelistically afire – even speaking in the Saturday evening open-air service.

Routinely, in 1941 my parents were appointed to Bedford, famous through John Bunyan and *The Pilgrim's Progress*. The corps building was circular and though I only had time for a few visits I liked the place. However, it meant that once again I had the problem of housing. To my rescue came the Allen family (no relation) – Bandmaster and Mrs P. J. Allen and their two gifted daughters. 'PJ' has a published song to his credit. Doris played the piano and cello while Grace was an accomplished violinist, which inspired me to buy a viola and have lessons. Following its theft and return at Kettering we had the viola restored, and it is still played from time to time.

Chapter Three

Lord of the Sea

AT the age of 18, like all the young men of the nation, I had registered for war service (at Coventry). I quite fancied the Royal Air Force and had the idea of something in the wireless (radio) or communications area. At the interview a couple of searching technical questions sunk me without trace and I then had the option of army or Navy. Royal Navy sounded good so I opted for that, to my mother's horror! For some time there was no follow-up to the interview, perhaps because the BTH establishment where I worked was on a war footing. Now in May 1942 I received a letter to report to the naval training establishment HMS *Royal Arthur* and took the train to Skegness. The Navy had commandeered the Butlin's holiday camp there and turned it into a training camp. Kitted out and vaccinated, I was assigned to the Writer Branch, doubtless on account of office experience. My number: P/MX95854 – P for Portsmouth Division, MX for Miscellaneous.

Six weeks in boots, marching drills, handling a rifle, up and down rope ladders, saluting (very important), edible food and sharing a hut with another chap (in the interests of decency we had a board between us, down the middle of the bed!). During these weeks I sat the second Bandmaster's Correspondence Course examination, supervised by the Skegness Salvation Army officer. Musically I was nourished by the currently popular 'Warsaw Concerto' (Adinsell) from the film *Dangerous Moonlight*. The camp cinema was the first time I had ever seen a commercial film. Going to the 'pictures' was a no-no for Salvationists but it was so innocuous I wondered what the fuss was about. Then a weekend leave in nearby ancestral Chatteris to see my Aunt Esther, and off to a requisitioned school in Highgate for a course in Navy accounts, office procedures and King's Regulations. We lived on the premises and stood guard at nights.

Awaiting a posting in Portsmouth Naval Barracks I was made welcome by the Portsmouth Citadel Corps. While on leave in London I attended a Sunday afternoon concert by the International Staff Band – which I will now refer to as the ISB. It was at Regent Hall Corps in Oxford Street. For me it was a surprise event when Major Eric Ball was called to the platform to receive the baton of the

ISB from Colonel George Fuller. In those days Eric was something of an idol (in a non-worship sense!) and the atmosphere was electric. The proceedings were intensified when Eric – who could create a dramatic moment – went over to the gallery and called his mother down to the platform. Heady stuff for a young and impressionable Salvationist musician!

War service for me was in two main periods, the first in the Persian Gulf and the second in Scotland. Just prior to leaving England there was a 'Cairo Night' at Harlesden with Brindley Boon as elocutionist. Both band and songsters were on duty and I was with the trombones in naval uniform. I have a photo of this and possibly there is only one other photo of me in blues.

The posting was originally for Mombasa with journey by sea from Liverpool via the Azores and South Africa in a troop carrier called *Capetown Castle*. The majority of those on board were soldiers. In my kitbag I carried a trumpet, a ukulele and a small selection of music textbooks – including two volumes of *20th Century Harmony*, years later borrowed by Ray Bowes. We had hardly left Liverpool when we put into Belfast for a couple of days on account of lurking submarines. En route, one was sunk by our escort.

My first impression of distant Freetown, West Africa, was of mysterious black mountains with misty peaks. Boats circled the ship and offered fruit for sale. The native merchants had a formula: 'You throw money down, me throw up bananas afterwards.' To save washing, bare feet were encouraged but it was not popular. An Irish friend remarked: 'Out of ten people walking by, twelve of them step on your feet!' A few days later 'crossing the line' was celebrated with the traditional Neptune and court, the Marines being the life and soul. The victim was lathered with a mixture of dough, mustard and pickle vinegar applied with a whitewash brush. After being shaved with a wooden razor a hosepipe was turned on the shavee. We three writers had the job of producing the certificates, using an old duplicating machine and getting inky black in the process.

One day in Durban we went by electric train to Pietermaritzburg and had an introduction to apartheid. At its root seemed to be a concern about mixed births. Vans took us, clattering over dreadful roads, to a desolate camp where tents stood in mud. I was sent to work in the Navy headquarters and so had digs and tea in bed for three months, during which time – which included Christmas Day – the local Salvation Army and its people were most welcoming. As a bonus, I benefited from counterpoint lessons with the city organist of Pietermaritzburg. He thought my compositional style too impressionist and strengthened my foundations by a diet of Brahms and strong basses. Then a small group of us were assigned to the Persian Gulf. To Iran via Bahrain was by Dutch oil tanker (great pork chops!), when we had to cut engines by reason of Japanese activity. Some tense moments. Thence by minesweeper, an Arab dhow, going round the sheik's palace in Bahrain and finally taking ship with Indian troops, eating really hot curry.

Khorramshahr, HMS *Euphrates*, was our naval base, still bearing bloodstained signs of the Ghurka assault in 1941. Our daily routine was simple; the heat prevented afternoon ledger work so we did a solid morning and some later on as necessary. Nearby was Abadan, then the home of the Anglo-Iranian Oil Company with a largely British colony. Homes were open to us and I not only joined their little orchestra but, with Navy colleagues, provided items on their programmes. Our padre tried to organise a group to visit Old Testament sites but disappointingly it came to nothing. My 21st birthday was celebrated quietly with a tin of ice-cold Australian peaches. Leave was in Tehran – tents in the British Embassy, wiener schnitzel in the Polish centre where Chopin's music was played. We fraternised in cafeterias with British, American and Russian troops. It was good-humoured; politics and the cold war lay in the future.

Camp life went on with spasmodic visits from groups of entertainers, and I had two unpleasant bouts of malaria. I took the examinations for Writer Petty Officer. The invasion of Europe began on 6 June 1944, and we followed its progress with news coming through the radio and some newspapers. We came home via Baghdad (crowds, we were told, were for a public hanging), through Palestine (saw a sign, 'Galilee' – exciting!) and Alexandria (another Christmas Day and my overcoat stolen).

On arrival at Portsmouth Barracks in January 1945 I found myself promoted to Petty Officer, sent on leave and put in charge of a pay office, housed in a characterful early 19th-century Scottish country house, Tullichewan Castle. The house was requisitioned for WRNS training and Combined Operations and located in Balloch, Dunbartonshire, near Loch Lomond. Demolished in 1954 it is now the site of a housing estate.

There was organising to be done and soon routines were established. Glasgow proved a fascinating city. It was in that city that I gained my Trinity College Licentiate Diploma (with Phillips Prize) in brass band conducting. Sir Granville Bantock had come up from London to conduct the examinations. We had a long talk, during which he gave me his card, on which he wrote 'Introducing Mr Ray Allen, trombone', and said: 'Look me up when you come out.' But he died soon after, and his associates at Paxton's were not interested; professionals were returning and it was no time for unknowns. Still, I have the card to this day! At that time I had aspirations to go in for film music and actually got a commendation for a BBC competition orchestral piece. But my work was to be elsewhere.

A crowd of us used to go to Paisley where I learned to ice-skate. In addition to setting up a band to provide light musical support for a variety of camp events, I started a mixed choir and taught a little music as well as playing for the Sunday services.

The International Staff Band visited Glasgow and I was delighted to hear them play my 'Bethlehem Story'. My first march, 'Gladsome Morn', was already published. During that period there was an opportunity to travel to London for a music weekend in Eaton Square where we enjoyed appreciation classes by a number of the city's music personalities, including eminent conductor Sir Adrian Boult, who subsequently wrote to me on another matter. Long train journeys could be dreary, the compartment lit at night by a solitary blue bulb, packed with people, mostly smoking or sleeping in corridors. VJ Day came in September, and we closed HMS *Tullichewan* in June 1946, following which I went on demobilisation leave.

Chapter Four

Gone My Care

BEFORE demobilisation, I had called at Colonel Bramwell Coles's office near King's Cross. Colonel Coles was the chief music editor, in title Head of the International Music Editorial Department (IMED). He received me in his usual gracious manner and the conversation turned to the future. Eric Ball had left active involvement with Army music in 1943 – I had been stunned when I'd read of this in Iran – and there was a vacancy. I was offered an editorial position and I was over the moon! I never dreamt that one day I should occupy Colonel Coles's editorial chair. Work in the IMED began in October. It basically involved preparing manuscripts for print, including adding sol-fa to vocal music and checking proofs. My first job though was to add the bar lines for an arrangement he was making of 'Soldier, Rouse Thee', which was recorded by the cadets of the Warriors Session.

The IMED offices were on the second floor of Salvationist Publishing and Supplies Ltd, Judd Street, off the Euston Road and close to St Pancras and King's Cross stations. The offices felt old-world and I still feel nostalgia for the brown-grained paint, the hammered piano, the suspended green-shaded lamps and the dangerous unconcealed electrical wiring on the ceiling. Indeed, the very books and artefacts, dating back to the department's 19th-century beginnings, had an aura of history. There was a pedal organ reputed to have come from the old Grecian Theatre and used in Richard Slater's day. In the late 1970s we loaned it to the International Heritage Centre exhibition, then reopened in the building. A receipt was of course obtained. Later, when we were in Australia, I received a letter from the person in charge of the International Heritage Centre asking me what had happened to the organ, as they had a note of its loan to me! I soon clarified that and when we returned to the UK I enquired about it. It seems two gentlemen had called and taken it away, never to be seen again.

Adjustment to civilian life was not difficult. I had a settled and enjoyably challenging job with opportunities for composition. As, fortuitously, my parents had been reappointed from Halifax to Harlesden I was able to live at home with the resumption of former friendships, and with my new job came a surprise invitation to join the ISB. I had played trombone and piano solos during a weekend in the Channel Islands with the legendary Major Bernard Adams as a co-soloist. I almost tremble when I think about it! However, I have surmised that Bernard, as the deputy bandmaster of the ISB, may have made the suggestion.

Familiar surroundings were not a guarantee that life would just resume where it left off. I was by no means the same person and a few relationships were put under strain. I had retained strong links with Harlesden Corps and the sergeant-major had kept up a praiseworthy newsletter correspondence with all the corps service personnel throughout the war. There had been a hint that, on the retirement of the bandmaster, I might become his successor; but on my return it was not to be, as my father was the new commanding officer. The issue was in danger of becoming emotional and so it was timely when Colonel Bramwell Coles suggested that I conduct a few practices with the band at Harrow, a corps which had developed strongly from its more rural origins. Of course I confirmed that Bandmaster Fred – who had done stirling work – was fully in agreement with the arrangement and I eventually transferred to become first the band instructor and then the bandmaster. The colonel and his wife soldiered at the corps and four of his sons returned to the band from war service. It was the Coles family's war involvement which we have to thank for the march 'Victors Acclaimed'.

Harrow was a friendly corps; I had lessons to learn about management but generally there was support. At Harlesden, some time before, the recruiting sergeant – a lady who, with her husband, was kind to my parents – had suggested that I consider the possibility of offering for Salvation Army officer service. Sometime around 1947 I was producing publishable music and Colonel Coles had indicated that, in his view, I would be of more use to the Army if I were an officer. I suspect he had in mind the gap left by Eric Ball. Again that challenge! I considered this avenue of service carefully and prayerfully; the way of lifetime service was opening.

Perhaps I might mention two works I wrote during this period: a euphonium solo, 'The Ransomed Host', featured by a Scottish soloist at the Royal Albert Hall, and a suite for piano and small brass group, 'The Three Gardens'. Premiered in an ISB programme of new music and still in manuscript, it points up the forward-looking willingness to experiment on the part of the new bandmaster, Major Bernard Adams, who had the courage to give new ideas an airing.

That year saw the first official British Territorial music camp. It was held in the old Hadleigh Farm Colony property and catered for 40 to 50 boys. I use the word 'old'. It was where, at the turn of the century, men received training in farming skills before being helped to emigrate to Australia. The ancient huts were nearly derelict and the boys used to swing on the gas pipes. I was privileged to be a staff member – the youngest – and like Eric Ball at Star Lake ten years previously wrote a camp march, 'Hadleigh Camp', which was duly copied on site and played at the Regent Hall the following weekend. The week's repertoire had to be from those published in the *Triumph Series*. Larger-scale works were only permitted after Dean Goffin came on the scene. Technical progress was amazing and the last devotional meeting memorable. Again, a privilege came my way: to give my testimony.

Brigadier Albert Jakeway and Senior-Captain Charles Skinner were also in the department. Charles taught me chess in the lunch breaks. It must have been about this time that I was invited by Brigadier Archie Burgess (he of the concertina and close harmony at Harlesden) to meet, at his Palmers Green home, the legendary Colonel Arthur Goldsmith. Colonel Goldsmith was a composition pioneer who had been a colleague of Frederick Hawkes and Richard Slater, 'The Father of Army Music', before the turn of the century. Nervously I played to him my 'Bethlehem Story'. It was on my part a test of nerves, on his an object lesson of greatness in encouragement. Ahead lay August 1948 and the International Training College.

Chapter Five

The Lord is King

LIKE many others I cannot quite recall entering the International Training College, a huge campus in Denmark Hill opened by General Bramwell Booth in 1929. As I was living in North London, it was probably just an Underground and bus ride – or was it a tram? I hadn't foreseen my official reception, which proved to be more on the lines of an official reaction. Just prior to my entry, I had been borrowed by the prestigious Chalk Farm Band as pianist for its tour of Sweden, a long-standing fixture. When, ultimately, I was notified of my training commencement date I discovered that I would not return from Sweden until a day later. Bound by my earlier commitment I advised the training authorities of this unfortunate clash of dates. As it happened there were other late arrivals due to such reasons as release from the services.

When I arrived I was informed, not to my surprise, that I was a day late. 'Yes,' I said, 'you have a letter about it.' So they sent me home for a day. I more than suspect that Lieut-Colonel Will Cooper, who had to deal with this matter, was not too thrilled by having to do so. A former naval man, he was strong on keeping one's word, but justice had to be seen to be done and he too was a man under authority. All of us developed an immense respect, even affection, for this inspirational leader. And, to test my priorities, because I had been in the ISB (or because I was late?), I couldn't join the sessional band until Christmas!

For the 1948 intake there were approximately 300 student-cadets of which 100 were men. Each session has a name, and in our case it was Peacemakers. By a long tradition, each session also has its own song. Originally a 'verse and chorus' affair, the sessional song took on anthem proportions when Eric Ball produced 'Torchbearers' in 1933. I had the honour of setting Will Brand's words for ours. The chorus is quite epic and runs:

> We will go forth as architects of Peace,
>   Her walls, her palaces to build again;
> Her temples, wherein man shall find release
>   From fear's unquiet servitude and pain.

We will go forth, but armed against her foes,
As men of old who built anew with sword in hand;
Peacemakers, healers of a people's woes,
With God's commission, and at God's command.

Although the training session then was only for nine months it was tightly crammed with study and hands-on activity, so this account is perforce somewhat sketchy. There were separate house blocks for men and women cadets, each with one room, and tiny flatlets for married couples. At that time there were no children in the college. Our academic assignments were Bible, doctrine, sermon preparation and SA procedures. We also had daily tasks like brass polishing or cleaning. Meals were communal with the continuing rationing of butter and sugar. On Wednesdays and alternate Sundays we went in 'brigades' to visit corps, returning to cocoa prepared on a rota basis. The remainder of Sundays were in-house devotional meetings and a monthly 'spiritual day' which was high-powered and usually led by top leadership. At Easter, groups were sent out on 'campaign' and similarly to collect during the Annual Appeal. Friday was the day off after a morning of assigned jobs. On Thursdays the whole session marched down to the Camberwell hall behind its band. My future wife, Joy, carried a flag, a responsibility of which she is justifiably proud as she had that privilege for the whole session. On the vocal side there were male and female choirs and in Thursday's evening gathering the whole session became a choir. During those prayer meetings we were also assigned to 'fish', ie, move among the congregation to stimulate 'seekers' with spiritual commitment in view.

So much for the routine. Now the story can become more personal with a touch of romance. The role of sessional pianist – accompanying the session as a choir – came my way, which I enjoyed of course. Joy tells me that in the first rehearsal she had spotted me at the piano and decided that her marital future was with me. I very soon agreed! To pursue that theme for a moment, my glasses were broken at one time and so on the Thursday I sat as near to the trombone section as I could get. A voice behind me, from the direction of a portable organ, said: 'Don't listen too hard.' I made a closer inspection of the organist – and that was it! Made in Heaven!

Of course, officially there was a great divide between men and women cadets, but these things happen. Quite a number of marriages arose out of that nine-month period, though I am glad to record that the cadets were well aware of why they were there and behaved with integrity. More was known than couples suspected. Joy and I shared a spot in close proximity in the Bible class. Our tutor was the redoubtable Will Cooper, who observed: 'Jacob served seven years to have Rachel as a wife and got Leah. So he served a further seven years before he could marry Rachel' (Genesis 29:16–28). Then, taking off his spectacles (as was his habit) he looked over at us and said: 'And some of you think nine months in the training college is too much?'

Now and again I borrowed Joy's accordion for some evangelistic enterprise. It was always returned with a little written 'thank you' or a bunch of violets. One unexpected encounter: at lunch with tables for a dozen or so someone would go out to the kitchen and refill the water jug. One day I went out and there was Joy – from her separate dining hall – on the same mission. It seems ordinary now, but under our restricted conditions such an encounter was unbelievably special.

It will be obvious that, in a body of people, there has to be a wide variation of personality, temperament and character. Salvation Army officers, while they have counterparts in other priesthoods, have a unique role by virtue of the evolution of the Movement. The officer is first of all committed to the task and can be relied on to perform it with imagination, awareness and compassion. He or she is also to be well grounded in the Christian faith and Army method, something of an entrepreneur with business acumen and more besides, like handling the disappointments and setbacks which come with the job. 'Job' is an inadequate word for such a lonely vocation. So training has to try and inculcate such concepts together with discovering and assisting the student to self-discover potential strengths and weaknesses. Well, at least it's an ideal!

The session included many individuals and characters, but I will mention only one, as his story (here abbreviated) has special interest. I refer to Major Peter Muller who was then of course Cadet Muller. Peter had been a German prisoner of war. He had attended two or three churches but always there were guards and a feeling of separateness. One Sunday, in the street, he was approached and invited to an Army meeting. His first thought was 'What will I do about lunch?' but that was also on offer. He didn't go the first week, but saw the person again, who said, 'We looked out for you.' So he went, found acceptance and eventually entered the training college. Personal kit was a problem but a corps lady provided clothing from her late husband, which fitted him perfectly. We kept in touch.

Much of what we learned was on the job – collecting, house-to-house visitation, selling Army literature in public houses, preaching with preparation. We were thrown into the deep end and Camberwell must have had a long-suffering population. In my own case I have stood – with embarrassment – in a busy town displaying the placard 'I'M A FOOL FOR CHRIST. WHOSE FOOL ARE YOU?' Or again, I have been dropped off to give a solitary witness to a bus queue (which boarded the bus while I was in mid-flow). Others have similar stories and it may well be that other approaches now operate.

At Christmas I made it into the band. We had a fine bandmaster in Captain Albert Drury and when I had found time to write a devotional selection, 'In Quiet Pastures', he graciously gave leave for me to rehearse the band in it. Which we did al fresco under the huge old mulberry tree in the quad. None of us could guess that it was a piece of music which would circle the world in blessing and still survives. This paragraph is an appropriate moment to mention my close college friend and excellent cornetist Ray Munn who, as a captain, served with distinction in what was then the Congo.

With such a crowd and a busy programme, incidents were endless. I was one of a brigade sent to Liverpool Walton, a warmly welcoming corps. For campaign Saturday nights, some kind of dramatic presentation was standard. For Walton's benefit a creative brain had devised a version of *The Robe*, the novel and film where the centurion on duty for Jesus' crucifixion secures his robe and becomes a believer. So that was our Saturday evening drama. More often than not such presentations ended with an appeal and a few cadets around the piano soulfully singing something like 'I'll Follow Thee, of Life the Giver'. A bench was rigged up on which hung 'the Robe'. At the climax the centurion (me) was to enter, kneel and push his sword point into a convenient knot hole in the floor. The spotlight on the upright sword hilt would produce the shadow of a cross on the cloak.

That was the plan. Rehearsals went well. On the night, the hero entered, done up more or less like a Roman soldier. He knelt. Tense atmosphere. The crowd was really eating this up. Not many Roman soldiers seem to have worn spectacles so our hero has shed his. And, peering desperately at the floor, couldn't find the knot hole! Sing your way out of that! Brindley Boon would have said: 'It all breeds character.'

Through the whole period we supplemented in-house worship with Spiritual Days, often led by visitors who could be powerful speakers. Solemn occasions marked the end of the session. There was a Covenant Day when we confirmed our calling and its implications. We were fortunate in having the legendary General Albert Orsborn to lead it, taking as his theme 'Ever... Never', based on Leviticus 6:13: 'The fire shall ever be burning upon the altar; it shall never go out.'

The Commissioning weekend began with a pageant and a full day of rehearsals at the Royal Albert Hall. It caused a bit of a stir among the saints when the theme song was 'I'm Riding Along on the Crest of a Wave' from a Ralph Reader Scout Gang Show. The Commissioning itself was a full-day affair, also in the Royal Albert Hall. First came the actual Commissioning and later in the day we received our assignments – with a variety of reactions. As I stepped forward the ISB played the fanfare introduction of my 'Hadleigh Camp' march. The weekend concluded with a devotional day at Camberwell with relatives. My parents were there, as were Joy's. She had joined the college from Hastings, but the family originated from Stockton-on-Tees, where both of her parents were highly respected local officers. From a young age she had always known she would be an officer and I am sure her folk were very proud that day.

I had hoped to be returning to music editorial work but received early notice that I was to be made a cadet sergeant-major for the following session: the Standard Bearers. This was an honour, though it meant a further year at Denmark

Hill. Just to help things along Joy was appointed to the mining community of Thorne in Yorkshire. We have made our own a devotional chorus which I recorded for her 21st birthday. It runs:

> All my days and all my hours,
> All my will and all my powers,
> All the passion of my soul,
> Not a fragment, but the whole
> Shall be thine, dear Lord.

This chorus makes a final affirmation in my later selection 'By Love Compelled'.

Chapter Six

By Love Compelled

Cadet Sergeant-Major 1949–1950

MY denied hope to return immediately to the International Music Editorial Department was due to departmental history, which had made the leadership uncomfortable with what they may have seen as a short-term professional arrangement. It was now policy to go through the normal processes, including a year as a corps officer. In the event it was a valuable experience. In my case, the first commissioned year was as a cadet sergeant-major with a clear job description of personnel regulation with responsibility for the Special Service Brigades. There was a sergeant for each of the six men's and nine women's brigades, together with a sergeant-major, an assistant sergeant-major and a young people's (YP) sergeant for men and women. The YP and Special Service Brigades were made up of selected cadets and changed every so often.

The session was seen away and we returned to empty rooms. Previously, I mentioned a between-sessions campaign. During the 'break' – ie, the time between the May commissioning and the new intake in August/September – the men sergeants and some sectional and house officers were formed into an evangelistic campaign party which toured the West and Wales for ten days. We went to Cardiff, Swansea and the valleys. We would sing, undertake open-air meetings, contact people and conduct meetings. We wore black berets. Douglas Kiff's accordion was invaluable. The sergeant group was then sent for three weeks to various corps for observation. Norwich Citadel was my assignment. I was met at the station by the corps officer, Major Leslie Boniface. Two days later he was taken ill and died which was, of course, a traumatic time for all concerned. I was living in the quarters and naturally I needed to support in every way possible, including at the corps.

When the new session, the Standard Bearers, arrived at the training college, the sergeants were on a kind of crowd control duty, seeing that people got to examination rooms and interviews and generally answering questions. Other than the changing Special Service people, the sergeant-major did not have a permanent brigade of his own but acted in a supervisory and liaising role between the administration and the sergeants. My assistant sergeant-major was George Wright. He was a sturdy character whose parents were in hostel work for the Salvation Army Social Services. He usually drove our minibus.

My Special Service Brigade was made up of cadets from differing brigades and membership lasted some weeks. Then George and I would get a new batch. It was intensive evangelism. We did all sorts: visited social centres and the Campfield Press, spent days out doing street visitation, preached at Speaker's Corner in Hyde Park (and learnt to handle hecklers – though we did not get too many, and the regular man would step in if needed) and went to Soho. Soho was quite special. We did this on Saturday nights when London's West End was full of folk on a night out. We stood in a ring and normally waited until the escapologist had finished his act; we got into our act before his crowd melted, and away we went. We made great contacts there. Many people with real problems would be open to our ministry. We would often have seekers kneeling in the ring. This was excellent training for our Australian appointment many decades later. A favourite excursion was to go to Bethnal Green, where Brigadier Alice Sigsworth worked among deaf and blind people. The lads loved her famous meat pies.

The sergeants had their own classes, Church history, regulations and so on. Midweek they took their brigades to a corps, complete with basket and provisions. In the dining hall the sergeant-major took a turn with house officers presiding at dinner and tea, seated on a dais – 'The Throne'. The food was fair but we got sick of some sloppy fruit pudding they kept serving and there was a mini-mutiny. So I took up a portion to the Training Principal and put it down in front of him with appropriate words. My Navy life had ingrained into me standing up for one's 'men' – not that I ever had many!

February brought the Self-Denial Appeal again and I went up to Aberdeen. Collecting in the city shops I found the Aberdonians very generous. The corps youth adopted me while the music sections staged an evening programme to help me reach my 'target'.

Sheerness and Marriage

Some time earlier I had proposed to Joy on a day in Esher. It was a special day of course and one which I commemorated by a setting of 'God be in my Head' with a tune I named 'Esher'. Longed-for May came and I was commissioned to Sheerness, Kent, together with Lieutenant Frank Wingfield, a fine man whom I have since been unsuccessful in contacting. Joy and I became officially engaged and she was brought down from Yorkshire to Dartford, also in Kent. An engaged couple is supposed to have appointments reasonably close so that the pair can get to know each other better. We did have days off to share, and met once at Chatham where we saw *Lilac Time*, with music by Schubert, at the now demolished Empress Theatre, and climbed to the memorial. Peterborough was the venue for another wonderful day.

I gained a dog which was really Joy's. Its name was Vic (my second name is Victor). When her commanding officer moved, leaving her alone in Thorne, she had bought it as a puppy from a farm. When Joy came south to Dartford, on the day that I was due to go to Sheerness, I received Vic. As he and I ran up the road outside the college gates Vic managed to get his lead wrapped round my legs. Of course I fell flat – just as a tram was passing. What a lemon I felt! An unpromising start to a dog-man relationship. But he was a great dog.

There were others also travelling to the Canterbury Division. Joining us at the station were Senior-Captain and Mrs Ernest Barnes and family. Who was seeing them off but the well-known dance band leader of the 1930s and 40s, Henry Hall. Henry was Mrs Barnes's uncle. After the First World War he had been a member of the staff of the Music Editorial Department and had been a bandsman at Nunhead. He wrote the marches 'Nunhead' and 'Sunshine'. The trio of 'Sunshine' became 'Here's to the Next Time', his regularly-heard radio signature tune.

Sheerness, on the Isle of Sheppey, had a distinguished historical record as a naval town. There were a number of villages on the island. I was fascinated by the number of old wooden houses into which my visitation soon took me. Most of them have now gone. The corps at Sheerness was compact, and our gas-lit quarters was 49 Maple Road, backed by a canal which rather encouraged livestock. The hall was, and still is, in the main road. Frank Wingfield and I led indoor and open-air meetings, sold Army papers in the pubs and visited conscientiously. One of the pubs was by the railway station. The station itself is now rebuilt after a train ran into the buffers causing major damage.

My predecessor had resigned and married a local girl; they lived in the town. One of my bandsmen was on the deaf side and sometimes got the number of the song instead of the tune. We found out the hard way. These days, if similarly afflicted, I would be more sympathetic! I gravitated to conducting rehearsals and sometimes needed to conduct on Sundays as well.

Joy came and helped me at Self-Denial time, as did my mother too. Frank started a boys' club and had a rapport with young people. Our divisional commander (DC) was Lieut-Colonel Bertie Rolls, a Friar Tuck of a man who had also been my parents' DC at Battersea. My uncle Charles had also been the Canterbury DC and it was nice to see his signature in the corps books. Music composition provided a change of pace and I think it was at this time that I worked on 'By Love Compelled'. I have already referred to Brindley Boon, a man of many gifts who had been on the Salvation Army scene before the war. Older than I, he was possessed of an incredible memory for people and events and could tell you what his last conversation with you had been about. He was an editor, songwriter, brilliant raconteur and author. He and his wife were stationed at nearby Sandwich. Independently, both of us decided to take our Sunday schools to Maidstone Zoo and, unexpectedly meeting there, spent a happy day.

Official approval to marry came through and then farewell orders arrived. I was to take up an appointment as editorial assistant in the International Music Editorial Department. My mother and other ladies worked to leave the house spotless.

Our Wedding and First Years of Marriage 1951

I shall never live it down – I went to my wedding by bus! The venue was Regent Hall Corps in London's Oxford Street. Much of the day is a dream. I recall going into the hall and speaking to Joy's mother. The weather was good. The ceremony was conducted by Colonel Norman Duggins, Executive Officer of the ISB. Will Brand and Colonel Bramwell Coles had collaborated on a wedding song performed by a group of songsters from Hanwell led by Sam Hooper. Major Fred Grant played the organ. Joy had been plagued with a cold but it vanished as she came into the hall. She was a lovely bride, holding a white songbook and a spray of lily of the valley. In those days, the back wall of the platform was covered with the names of pioneer Salvationists of Regent Hall, now painted over.

The ceremony was classic 'Army' with the reception at the Polytechnic in Regent Street. An announcement there that I would be rejoining the ISB came as surprising news. There was time to spare before we boarded the coach for Boscombe – arranged by my in-laws. Over the road from the Polytechnic was a Quality Inn. We had been too excited to eat much in the reception and were suddenly famished. So we tucked into mushrooms on toast. The next thing I remember is Joy and me sitting side by side in a Royal Blue coach both struck dumb: what had we done? Then arrival at Bournemouth. Mrs Walker met us at the door. Harold was the deputy bandmaster of Boscombe and its 'top' solo cornet player. We spent time mooching round the many antique shops and, predictably, went to a band programme at Boscombe Corps. I take full responsibility.

The Army had indicated, surprisingly, that there would be no provision of quarters as our home. The Movement was still suffering from postwar housing shortages. Fortunately, Joy's parents helped us to secure our own home. For some reason, I thought only of living reasonably near Harrow Corps. The prospect of resuming bandmastership may have been tempting. I doubt the wisdom of this kind of thinking.

Travel to the office was from Northolt station to Marylebone, a walk through to Baker Street and then on the Underground to King's Cross. We had a park or recreation ground behind our house, which was good for walking Vic the dog. Once he rolled in something disgusting and we had to bath him, which he hated. Then he immediately did it again! The corps hall was reached past South Harrow Tube station and up the hill. I vividly recall cutting through there deep in contemplation of Schoenberg and his 12-note system.

Following my return to the office I resisted reappointment to the ISB. My former time had been a learning curve, but apart from the adjustments of newly-married life I planned to deepen my technical expertise with a serious course of study to secure a music degree. The matter died and though I was briefly in the shadows I was commissioned to write a trombone solo for Maisie Ringham in connection with the ISB Golden Jubilee celebrations. 'The Eternal Quest' was the result. I only mention the above experience because the solo bears the mark of inner conflict appropriate to the music, which has survived as a 'winner'. Dean Goffin wrote his superb 'Symphony of Thanksgiving' for the same occasion.

Chapter Seven

The Scarlet Jersey

HARROW Band graciously re-established me as the bandmaster. It was a good working band, with supportive local officers, and they were more or less patient with my musically venturesome and evangelistically eager-beaver demands. I think I would have been embarrassed to be a bandsman in my band during one of our weekends away! We were campaigning in my quiet little ancestral Cambridgeshire town of Chatteris and were asked to undertake a promotional march. As a band we had developed singing – inspired, I expect, by the ISB – and impulsively (rush of blood to the head) reverting to my old training college sergeant-major days I struck up a chorus. Who sang? I did – solo! The monastic silence was powerful. That I then followed with: 'Come tonight and the band *will* sing!' rescued nothing. What's the too-frequent political defence? – 'Lessons to be learned!' I was old enough to know better but made some management mistakes, like telling the band, just before we went on to the platform for the salvation meeting, that I was going to change the band around. Wow! My ideas might have worked but my psychology and timing were hopeless.

Amsterdam invited me as a guest to the Musicians Councils. It was my first overseas invitation and an experience I enjoyed. It was a thrill to conduct united bands in the historic Concertgebouw. They presented me with a book of Dutch national songs. This early visit inspired a 'Netherlands Rhapsody' and a festival march 'The Netherlander', which was locally acclaimed as having caught the national spirit and was recorded. Long after my retirement an editorial successor put it forward for publication; it was rejected as insufficiently creditable to me.

Barbara arrived in the April of 1953 and Joy's parents came to stay. Joy and I walked round the block to induce the birth. Barbara was actually born while I was at the Sunday afternoon open-air meeting. My father-in-law, Harry Foster, met me outside the house and had some fun asking me to guess whether we had a boy (whom we would have called Berric) or a girl. I went up to see mother and daughter, expecting the traditional, Hollywood-style post-birth scene of pale languor. Not a bit of it! Hardy northern girl that she is, Joy was sitting up in bed eating a roast beef dinner. Of course we were as poor as church mice and where were we to get a pram? Thank you, Lord – somebody at the corps gave us a maroon one which we had refurbished. Not many weeks later we moved house to Hide Road, Harrow. It was Joy who found the house. An elderly couple were selling; it still had the criss-cross air-raid tape on the windows.

I now went to work via Harrow-on-the-Hill. Colonel Bramwell Coles and family lived not far away. As well as studying I was writing busily. We had acquired a grand piano and I entered for a brass band composer's competition with a piece called 'Neptune's Diadem'. It was performed on the radio and I was sure they'd lost the last page! I came second to David Stone who wrote, I think, a more popular type of piece. Subsequently the first two movements and a modified third appeared in the Salvation Army journals as 'Lord of the Sea'. Miriam Richards added words to two of the movements and both were published as songs: 'Christ Brings Peace' and 'Water's Edge'. Ideas often come when I am out and about; the tuneful second theme of the last movement came to me while walking home through the park gates.

We had Dartford Band visit us for a weekend (Joy's old appointment) and as bandmaster's wife she went down to the hall to help with a welcome tea. I found what I took to be a bucket of porridge in an airing cupboard at home and put it to heat on the fire; it caught fire – it was fat! I got on my bicycle and in panic did an Olympic spurt to the hall to tell Joy. She responded: 'Have you called the fire brigade?' No, I hadn't. A car took her home and we phoned. The fire had just begun to lick at the bathroom floor so they tore down the kitchen ceiling and, though they made a right old mess, they extinguished the fire. Then it was a matter of insurance. A young man called and the form-filling began. 'Ray Allen,' he says to Joy. 'Was your husband in the Navy?' 'Yes,' says Joy. He continued: 'And was he on the *Tullichewan*?' 'Yes,' was the answer. 'My wife knows him – she was a Wren there.' So our claim went through without a hitch!

There was a mild brush with the law. One dusk, when I was on the way to band practice (by Harrow School), an over-zealous police constable ordered me to stop and spin my bicycle wheel. His manner did nothing for police relations and the light was working!

Joy was taking elocution lessons and had developed a link with the Poetry Society. It was a fulfilling period and she gained her Licentiate diploma at Trinity College, London. She also kindled in me a love of poetry for which I am eternally grateful. When shopping we would give ourselves sixpence each and roam Woolworths. Woolworths was then a different style of store, the counters were laid out fairly flat with loads of cheap things on offer. They actually ran on 'Nothing over 6d'.

Lieut-Colonel Coles retired in 1952 and, as he and his wife were soldiers of the Harrow Corps, we had a tribute festival at the corps. Staff Bandmaster Major Bernard Adams came and Harrow Band was on duty. We played two or three of the colonel's compositions. 'The Hill of Calvary' was one, but our big piece was

'Man of Sorrows'. Perhaps not an inspired choice nor an apposite title! What fiend seeks to infiltrate performances on such high-profile occasions? Ask John Bunyan – our good intentions went astray! Poor Colonel Coles! We should have stuck to 'Victors Acclaimed'; after all, he wrote it as a family celebration.

Change But Not Decay

Colonel Coles was succeeded by Lieut-Colonel Albert Jakeway. He and his brother Vic had been pillars of the prewar ISB as the Bb bass section. When Eric Ball relinquished bandmastership of the ISB in 1943 a number of caretakers had filled the position, including Jakeway, but ultimately the baton passed to Lieut-Colonel William Stewart, a former ISB solo cornetist. Jakeway then took on Rosehill Band. The Assurance Society had been evacuated to 'Rosehill', a building in Reading, as a wartime expediency and the band was made up from its staff. Here too Ball and others had helped with the leadership. After Jakeway took on the band it developed into an all-star unit with a cult following. I had the pleasure of travelling with the band when they played in a prison. Sadly, Rosehill Band was deemed to have ended its purpose and was closed down to the deep regret of its members, its fans and certainly its conductor. So change was in the air.

I gained my BMus Degree externally at Durham in 1952 having worked my way hard through an excellent correspondence course under Dr Ben Burrows of Leicester. The Durham professor was Arthur Hutchings and I had to supplement the written and oral examinations with a string quartet.

At Harrow we were great friends with Percy and Lily McLean. He was deputy bandmaster. They lived in a wartime prefab. After a day of three open-air and two indoor meetings we used to go there for Sunday supper. If I overate, Joy would kick my ankles. Percy ran the male-voice party. The most vivid memory we have of them is singing a song called 'Jerusalem' (not Parry's) unaccompanied, the second verse of which – being started too high and steadily rising – yielded successive declarations of 'We long for thee, we sigh for thee' which became more and more strangled and falsetto the higher it got. These lines, coupled with the strangled falsetto, made it extremely difficult to keep a straight face.

I acquired a 'Teagle' two-stroke motor which, attached to the back of my bicycle, rotated a roller pressed on the rear tyre. It was a most effective piece of engineering and worked well until the classic situation when I broke down. No petrol! Christmastime, with a balaclava helmet, I would ride off to carolling. A shortage of good cornets meant me taking Percy McLean off trombone and temporarily giving him a cornet; also Wally Beard, the band secretary. They were very supportive, but I began to feel the strain and learned that Stan Raikes of Hammersmith – who had led the wartime Cairo Red Shield Band – was available. So he transferred and took over the Harrow Band. Coincident with that, three excellent cornetists transferred in, which improved things enormously. Of course Stan got the credit! To my surprise I missed the band more than I had expected and must confess to an emotional moment when I stood outside the hall and listened to their first rehearsal under Stan. He chose Eric Ball's 'The Old Wells'.

In the wider music world there was a good deal going on in the realm of 12-note techniques and it captured my imagination. I have always regarded these early married and family years as a happy and creatively progressive period. Our grown-up children now tell us that they remember my return from the office as a ritual with their parents having a quiet, exclusive half hour together.

Bandmaster of Tottenham Citadel Band (1955–1959)

Rosemary was born in 1955. The midwife must have decided to get rid of me, as she sent me on my bicycle for a gas and air bottle. On return I found a new baby daughter. Someone had lent me a tape recorder and we have Joy commenting and Barbara singing her own song to the baby, while Rosemary makes baby cries. I had given up Harrow Band in the early part of the same year. It was a surprise to be visited at the office by the corps officer of Tottenham Citadel (northeast London), Captain Leslie Hendry. He was accompanied by Vic Jakeway of the same corps. It appeared that a successor to the Tottenham Citadel bandmaster, Ernest Edwards, was sought. I was immensely complimented of course; the band was regarded highly, it broadcast regularly and had made a number of records. Mindful of my former bandmastering experiences, I was a little hesitant and we talked it out at home. It was an irresistible opportunity and I agreed. I was prepared for those who might believe that I had given up Harrow with the knowledge of the Tottenham invitation, but that was not the case. I suspect no one knew the emotional pull I experienced. I retained a deep affection for my former band, had visited them all from time to time and helped a number through problematic periods.

Here then we were living at Harrow and committed to putting in full service at a corps some distance away, but so many city Salvationists did the same for a variety of good reasons. On band practice evenings I would leave the office, take the Tube to Manor House and a bus to the home of Vic Jakeway and his wife for tea. Every Sunday we took public transport to Baker Street where James Williams, the deputy bandmaster, with his wife Elsie, picked us up in his bronze VW Beetle. The Williamses were gems to us. Gordon Youngs, our bass trombonist, was a great band secretary. Right from joining the corps team we enjoyed friendly comradeship.

My first Sunday with the band was an experience. In fact all our firsts were experiences! Former Bandmaster Ernest Edwards was at the Sunday morning open-air meeting – scare number one. 'Ernie' had been the bandmaster since 1938, had an awesome reputation and maintained a first-class band. Here was I, untried at such a level (E.E. was fine to me and soon transferred to worship with his in-laws). The open-air meeting concluded. We formed up for the march and the band struck up George Marshall's 'The Liberator'. Those three opening quavers! The sheer sound, precision and drive! There is at least one railway bridge in Tottenham. We had a sprinkling of military and ex-military bandsmen and they could blow! When going under a bridge it became a wall of sound. In the summer months we would hold our afternoon open-air meeting in the main road, sweltering in our stand-up collars. As the Southend-bound coaches and cars passed us, the people would sometimes wave and inevitably someone in the band would make the ironic remark: 'They're not happy!'

Quite a number of corps people had meals at the hall and arrangements were made for us to have Sunday dinner at the Crossways Army Home for Unmarried Mothers. About four people left the band at the same time as Bandmaster Edwards. It may be that they felt it a good time to put aside the busy commitment, or were unsure of the future. But new people came along. In fact, there was often someone waiting; though as the band was 25 players, we did have moments when key positions were not filled. With a few military musicians absent on duty, especially in the summer months, numbers could be tight and there were times when it was a problem. Our Sunday afternoon meeting was well attended with many visitors, usually with an international sprinkling. So of course they expected a full band and programme, even on a bank holiday!

We had a wonderful time at Tottenham. Weekends away were naturally highly pressured in view of the expectations. My first experience of the coach journey home: totally hilarious. Wisecracks and impersonations of current radio comedians would have made a show in their own right. Though obviously not without strain, the band's programme was exciting. I can still hear James Williams saying in my ear, just before a broadcast: 'Relax.' Or if we had a problem when others were within earshot, he would whisper: 'Keep smiling.' I owe James a lot. The band had made records under Ernie and I too had that responsibility. One call in this direction was a last-minute request and we put down Harry Kirk's 'The Penitent' and a brass quartet with Eric Ball's 'The Victory of Love', these being part of our repertoire at the time.

The flow of new music was good but we also chose material across the board, not just 'the latest' as is sometimes the norm. We ran a series of music from various decades from the 1920s to the 1950s. For the first concert Colonel Frederick Hawkes was invited and the band played his march 'The Warrior'. His impromptu speech was brilliant; I only wish it had been possible to record it. Also, on 24 February I improvised on one of his tunes at a similar event in Croydon. He later sent me a book, *Foundations of Musical Aesthetics*, inscribed and signed 'To Captain R. Allen a small token of gratitude'. Writing of improvisation, of which I was fond and played publicly on programmes, I once improvised on Eric Ball's setting of his own words 'A Song of Courage' – in his presence at Tottenham. Later the song became the theme for his new band work with the same title. I have often wondered if my piano solo reminded him of the song, inspiring the band composition.

Naturally, having a top-class band was a help to composition. During the Tottenham period I wrote, among other items, 'Rhapsody on Negro Spirituals' for James Williams and the march 'Silver Star'. I was surprised when the band shuffled its feet at the end of our first play-through of 'Silver Star'. Later I was told that this is the military band way of applauding. I felt honoured. It was toward the end of this period that I wrote the first version of 'The Holy War'.

It was not all band. There was a good songster brigade and young people's work as well, so Joy was involved. We needed to be nearer and moved house to Lower Edmonton, which at that time retained its rural character with shops encircling Edmonton Green. Occasionally Joy and I passed each other in trolleybuses coming from and going to the Army. Once we were able to wave to each other! We saw the young men – students or military bandsmen – become married couples and families. I had the joy of conducting their weddings and dedicating their babies to God. We used to have parties at home: a whole gang from the band with wives or girlfriends. None of us was particularly affluent and the food was mostly in the baked beans bracket. They would eat sitting on the stairs and generally make their own fun. It all helped to cement relations. Sometimes the younger set seemed to have no homes to go to and on one occasion I threw their coats in a heap on the floor and said: 'Goodnight, I'm going to bed.' They knew me and took it well.

Ivor Snell came to live with us. He and Bram Gregson (they are now both in Canada) were an incredible euphonium section. I include three Ivor stories. He went in for a correspondence course which offered 'no pass – no fee'. He felt that it was taking too long to complete and asked for his money back. He was told he had to work through the course first!

He had a decent job and a motorbike (on which Joy sometime rode pillion) and decided to take his driving test. I had just passed my test (the instructor had a colourful vocabulary for other drivers) and Ivor decided he would do his. He had driven jeeps in Singapore and reckoned he only needed a brush-up course. I lent him my *Highway Code*. Back from his first lesson we asked how he had got on. 'Argued with him,' said Ivor. The day of the test came. Ivor said: 'Ray, where's that *Highway Code* book you lent me?' We located it and pressed it into his hand. Down the stairs he came, running his fingers through the pages: 'Know that, know that, know that...' He arrived back home a little subdued. 'How did it go, Ivor?' we asked. He replied: 'I knew I'd failed when the examiner, in a kind of cold voice, said, "Will you kindly get this vehicle off the pavement."'

In those days we were young enough to rustle up a bit of supper. One evening I had been making minestrone soup and began to feel tired. Joy, in the next room, had no idea of my fraying at the ends and was amazed when I ungraciously said: 'Here it is, I'm going to bed.' Her response was: 'If you're not having any,

I won't have any either,' and back on the unlit stove it went. We stumped up the stairs a trifle frostily. Then Ivor came home. We could hear scraping in the kitchen. It seems that he thought: 'How nice of Joy and Ray to leave this for me.' Joy asked: 'Are you hungry?' 'Yes,' I replied, and we stole downstairs to egg and chips. Enough stories! Ivor is a lovely person and we kept in touch. He became euphonium player and deputy bandmaster of the Canadian Staff Band.

In 1957 I directed the first East Midlands music school at Grendon in Northamptonshire. With me were Ray Bowes, eventually to become my successor, and Hector Main who tragically lost his life on a boat.

Some Personalities (1955-1959)

On 14 January 1956 Bandmaster George Marshall was promoted to Glory. His life story is a matter of record. Suffice it to say here that his mining accident on 13 August 1918 put him permanently in a wheelchair but did not affect his promise as a composer. There had been 'outside' items published (I once saw a march called 'The Cyclist') and he joined the Music Editorial Department as an extra-mural editor and proofreader. Also he taught music theory, *The Musician* carrying a regular advertisement which read: 'Bandsmen, get on top of your music.' He was still on the IMED staff when I joined and departmental members tried to call to see him if 'specialling' in the area. Joy and I visited him in his bungalow up in Sunderland. Barbara was with us, and when we arrived unannounced his wife, Jenny, was not home to open the door. We peered through the window and George indicated where to find a key. We had not been sitting there chatting for long when Barbara – used to the social niceties of 'visitation' – asked: 'When do we get a cup of tea?'

George Marshall had a distinctively modal harmonic style (appreciated by Wilfred Heaton, myself and no doubt many others) and was a meticulous proofreader. When sent some pieces to edit he was capable of drastically rewriting parts of them. I wish I had been able to spend more time with him but distance prevented it. A legacy to be administered by and used at the discretion of the current Head of the International Music Editorial Department came through during my headship. We purchased a memorial piano, funded an LP recording of his works and arranged for inscribed copies of *The Oxford Companion to Music* to be annual prizes at the Territorial Music School.

Dean Goffin was appointed to the UK in 1956 not too long before 'The Light of the World' surfaced. At the 1956 Bandmasters Councils General Wilfred Kitching announced that he was bringing in a young officer to succeed Music Secretary Lieut-Colonel Ernest Rance 'who will do wonders for the British Territory and our musicians'. One or two 'hopefuls' may have had their own reactions, but when Dean Goffin came from New Zealand he did a first-rate job, especially in establishing the annual festival at the Royal Albert Hall. He was generous to me and we maintained a friendly relationship.

Colonel Albert Jakeway, my mentor, retired in 1958. I had grown to have an affectionate regard and respect for him. An outspoken man with a strong sense of fairness and loyalty, he came from Keighley in Yorkshire and had a heart of gold. He had been a young officer at South Shields when George Marshall was writing his first pieces and would talk about those early days. As a departmental head he fought his corner and could be prickly with what he saw as leadership interference. He never really got over the closing of his beloved Rosehill Band. As his assistant, I found him supportive and encouraging. Perhaps few are aware of his pastoral contacts with ex-prisoners.

The colonel had always been gentlemanly to me and my music sometimes intrigued him. He was interested in newer techniques and would call me in to analyse my 'side slips' and clustered chords. It has been fascinating and educational to experience the diverse but effective way in which the three of my predecessors handled the work and outreach of their department.

It was in Jakeway's time (1958) that Ralph Vaughan Williams wrote for the Army his 'Prelude on Three Welsh Hymn Tunes'. He came to Judd Street for a special performance of it by the ISB before the then Music Board. The official invitations included me but somehow no one had mentioned it so I missed out. He is a composer with whom I wish I could have studied and I have always regretted not seeing the great man.

The composition of the 'Prelude' arose from Vaughan Williams chairing an ISB festival in Dorking, where he lived and still conducted the Leith Hill Festival. Philip Catelinet had previously premiered and recorded the RVW Tuba Concerto, allegedly giving some assistance in the scoring of the 'Prelude'. At Dorking, Arthur Rolls had played my 'Eternal Quest'. Vaughan Williams was generous about it and commented that it was a good piece except for the hymn tune! (That's how it was told to me.) From a musician's standpoint he had a point; the included song 'Jesus is Looking for Thee' is somewhat sentimental in musical terms, whereas it is the evangelistic 'heart' from an appeal angle. The work provides a telling illustration of the two levels of Army music: artistic and evangelistic – perhaps a subject for a deeper discussion. The great man signed published score copies for departmental members, collected from his London home by Michael Kenyon. Sadly, my copy has disappeared.

Colonel Albert Jakeway was succeeded by Lieut-Colonel Charles Skinner who taught me to play chess when I first joined. Charles was additionally the ISB's deputy bandmaster and a close friend of Staff Bandmaster Bernard Adams. Skinner had come into the department when Eric Ball left. At that time he had qualifications and aptitude for accounting and was set for a 'career' in finance. However, he had already made a mark musically with published work and as a competition winner, so he was naturally seen as someone competent to fill the vacancy. Musicianly and thorough, he was a first-rate editor and was particularly gifted as a songwriter. We are indebted to him for his beautiful setting of 'Let

Nothing Disturb Thee'. He eventually moved back to finance, returning again as our IMED Editor-in-Chief. By that time Leslie Condon had joined us and our reputation as composers was growing.

More Creativity and a Nightmare

Tottenham Citadel Band continued to have an influential ministry and it was during this period that I wrote the march 'Silver Star', gaining the military applause of shuffled feet after our first play through. For James Williams, our star soloist, I wrote the 'Rhapsody on Negro Spirituals'. For the Royal Albert Hall festival in June 1959 I was asked to write another trombone solo for Maisie Wiggins. At the time I was still under the RVW spell, and it shows. The task took through the spring, and during it I went to do a night for the Bearcrofts who were at Gosport, having a revival. I went by train and bus and on the bus I was working out details of the solo. It was a three-movement concerto called 'The Immortal Theme'. For its day it broke some new ground, including a 12-tone opening motif. The night before the performance was due I had a dream, or more truly a nightmare, in which the piece was being played and General Kitching rushed on to the stage shouting: 'Stop, stop!' Of course, he had never been known to do such a thing and the dream really arose from my nervous tension. What actually happened was that the General complimented me on it the next day (at the Councils) and invited me to speak on it.

Chapter Eight

The Holy War

THE year 1958 had afforded me a busy tour in Norway, accompanied by the music secretary of the time, Major Haakon Dahlström, later the Territorial Commander and a devotee of his fellow Norwegian, the late Colonel Klaus Östby OF, composer and former Swedish music secretary. The usual tour pattern was a visit to a corps, a band practice, back to a billet and off again early the next morning by bus or ferry. In Stavanger I met a pitiful little man who had been badly treated by the German Gestapo. Also present was a boy named Björn Thorsen who married in England and with whom I later became close friends.

The Norwegian visit led to Joy and me being invited to go again to Norway in 1959, this time as guests of Oslo III Band. We were hosted by a lovely young couple who were kindness itself, but every mealtime there was religious music playing. After a day or so I asked: 'Do you have any other music?' They then confessed that they had borrowed the records and actually they liked Glenn Miller, a liking we shared. So the music changed! At this time I developed a craze for oil painting.

It was about now that we changed our name from Allen to Steadman-Allen. Tottenham Citadel Band broadcast fairly frequently and, as its bandmaster, my name was heard on the radio from time to time. There were two Ray Allens in the public eye – one was a singer, the other a ventriloquist. So occasionally there was confusion and mixed communications. I had long mourned the absence of 'Steadman' from my name; it went back to 1839 when my great-grandfather married Mary Ann Steadman in Somersham. The Steadmans have been a large tribe for many years, rooted in Soham. My grandfather, father and an uncle had been given the name but it had missed my generation. The 'Allen' confusions gave me the opportunity to do something about it and we changed our name by deed poll. I have mentioned this because, over the years, the name change seems to have generated interest, judging by the times I have been asked about it. There is a slightly funny story linked to the change. I am told that in a concert a compère introduced a song of mine 'written by that well-known duo Steadman and Allen'. Just incidentally, Joy and I used our time living in the Midlands to visit Soham and found a few of the clan. One is a Salvationist. Small world!

Returning to the restlessness, there were factors and maybe a reaction from an over-taxed creative life. As Peter Skellern put it: 'You're burning your candle too bright.' Someone in authority commented: 'What would suit you would be being national bandmaster in Italy' (there was one small band, in Rome!). Dean Goffin had been brought from New Zealand to be National Bandmaster (a new title) under Lieut-Colonel Ernest Rance. Rance retired and Goffin became the new Music Secretary for the British Territory.

I was then appointed to succeed Dean as National Bandmaster, but I am afraid that I reacted unfavourably. Editorial and creative work was my aptitude; travelling about the country was not a role I now regarded as apposite and there was a touch of – let's be honest – unjustifiable pride. Three years earlier I or perhaps Leslie Condon would have jumped at it, but we were younger and for that task at that time Dean was the best choice. It was then put to me that my duties would be to develop the musical youth side, an inspired idea about which I was more enthusiastic. But I pointed out possible administration problems in that the Bands Department had no jurisdiction over the youth – which came under the Youth Department. I suggested a better approach was to make me Music Adviser to the Youth Department. But that was not possible. It was evident that Dean needed an assistant and I was picked for it. As it was 'that or nothing', I admit I displayed what they now call 'attitude' and accepted the latter – nothing. With a great deal of sorrow and regret Joy and I decided to relinquish our officership. Norman Bearcroft became the National Bandmaster. The youth idea never materialised – it was never a serious proposition – and Norman, who proved ideal for the job, was launched into an influential life's work.

What were we to do now we were no longer officers? An opening came: the Beckingham brothers had bought music publishers Wright and Round, and needed a managing editor. Would I take it on? It was a fair and timely offer and we went. But where were we to live? Locally advertised was an upstairs flat in a Cheltenham farmhouse. We read of it and took it. It was situated in a car-breaker's yard and had four rooms which sloped so that a ball would run across the floor. We were surrounded by old, rusting cars and buses. The girls loved it as a playground and remember it fondly. Joy got a job teaching drama and passed her driving test so we were well and truly mobile.

Wright and Round 1960
Wright and Round had been a long-standing brass band music publisher based in Liverpool. The Beckinghams, three brothers with former local Salvation Army band connections, bought the business and transferred the stock from Liverpool to a kind of hangar/garage on a Gloucester trading estate. When I arrived, on a cold morning, there was an oil stove to combat the low temperature and draught. There was a storeman called Matson, an ex-theatre percussionist. I began by cataloguing the music stock.

There were enormous stacks of brown paper parcels containing scores from early decades of the century. A system was organised and the company moved to a premises in Conduit Street, Gloucester. The routine was pleasant and conducive to composition. I arranged a suite of Tchaikovsky music with the title 'Holidays at Klin' together with the 'Wyedean Suite'. Also I produced the *100 Hymn Tunes for Brass Band* which is still used. Naively – and no doubt due to my Salvation Army conditioning – I did the set as the 'editor' and lost out long-term by omitting to establish any personal sales royalty basis. Just prior to leaving Tottenham Citadel I had completed and in rehearsal played through 'The Holy War'. I have a tape of that first reading. During the Cheltenham period I revised the work into the present published form.

Part of the job involved going to band contests in connection with a trade stand. Fortunately Jack Beckingham was an enthusiast and so he and Matson would often go. I had my first experience of adjudicating, which I can't say I have ever really enjoyed. It was an 'own choice' in the Forest of Dean. There are a number of villages there with bands. The decision lay between a band that had tackled a somewhat difficult piece with moderate success and one that I felt had the edge but with an easier piece. My verdict had a mixed reception – and then my newly acquired car, with passengers, ran into a signpost in the fog on the way home! Fortunately I was driving slowly.

Life in Cheltenham

Our family Sunday worship needed to be considered. We were, of course, no longer officers. Joy supported, but naturally I was concerned that she was included in the consequences of the move. Things are different today. There was a small family to clothe and feed and, with all the goodwill in the world, pastoral care can be patchy. What shone with Christian love was the attitude of the Cheltenham bandmaster and his deputy, who came round to visit us. Deprived of our ministry, corps and band, it was 'streams in the desert'. Terry Camsey's parents had a fish and chip business in town and they were kindness itself. We would go for a weekly bath and a meal. On one occasion we washed up and put the crockery (lovely set) on the draining board which tipped up and all was smashed. We just had to put it all in the bin and plan to replace it the next day. When Mrs Camsey came home she couldn't believe her eyes!

I was invited to go down and conduct the band practice, which I did, but found some embargo on our Salvation Army public activities. So we became temporary Baptists, where I taught a Bible class. We occasionally worshipped in Cheltenham but more frequently attended meetings at Gloucester or Bristol Easton, where the Boardmans were stationed. Leslie Condon brought Woolwich Band to Cheltenham for a weekend and we of course billeted him. On the Sunday afternoon I was invited to conduct his band in my little *Triumph Series* tone poem 'The Great Crusade'. Arriving at the passage which includes 'Never quit the field', I suddenly realised what the words were and turning to him (he sat near) hissed something. He grinned back.

The New York Staff Band came to Oxford for a one-night festival. Joy and I took our sore hearts over and poured them out to their bandmaster, Richard Holz. He was sympathetic and it did us good to share. Leslie Condon was the sole contact with my old department, apart from receiving my newly published arrangement of Bach's 'Bist Du Bei Mir', minus the arranger's name. The warmth of fellow Salvationists was the reality which warmed our spirits.

We lived reasonably comfortably and chose a new house which we saw built. There was a degree of pleasure in being able to select and afford new household goods, so we were 'all right' – but it wasn't right and we missed our ministry. Unknown to us things were happening; the Lord was doing a little nudging. Firstly, we had been to a Baptist service. It was mid-September, because as we shook hands with Mr Millington, the pastor, afterwards, he said: 'What have you wished for yourself for your birthday?' I gave some kind of reply and he came back with: 'What about a little obedience?' He knew our story. That was *my* nudge. Then we had a letter from Commissioner Emma Davis: 'What's this I hear....?' As a girl Joy had worked for her in the north. Commissioner Davis had been away in Australia and the Pacific on an extended tour and had only recently heard about our situation. We went to see her at her home in St Albans. The conversation that followed proved our desire to return, and only shortly after that there was a cordial letter from the Chief of the Staff offering reconciliation. Would I be prepared to go back to the IMED? Would I! For the best of reasons all went smoothly, I suspect to everyone's relief.

On the day we received official reinstatement I chaired an evening festival at Cheltenham Salvation Army. Things had relaxed by then but no one yet knew of our re-acceptance. So it was a very sweet experience when the opening prayer expressed concern for our future. I peeped at Joy, and while – in the circumstances – we could see the humorous side, the prayer had a caring honesty which touched our sensibilities.

Following our official reinstatement while still resident in Cheltenham, we decided to go in our officer uniforms to Gloucester for the Sunday afternoon. They had a visiting songster brigade. We sat near the back. Retired Bandmaster Reg Button, a dear man, happened to turn round in his seat near the front and spotted us in full regimentals. Raising his hands he cried: 'Praise the Lord!' which rather defeated any ideas we had of slipping in quietly. On returning to London we followed the Skinners into 117 Maidstone Road, New Southgate, where we spent ten happy years.

One sad note was that, during the years of our absence, my old boss Colonel Bramwell Coles had come from his retirement home in Canada for a family visit. Taken ill, he had died, unbeknown to us. When at a later date we learned of this, of course we hastened to express our sympathy.

(Left) The funeral of Chippenham Salvationist Ray Tinson, after whom Ray Allen was named.

(Below) Ray on holiday in Bexhill with his father Frederick.

(Below) The whole family in Worthing – Ray with his parents Frederick and Gladys, brother David and sister Vida.

(Above) The family in
Rugby, 1942.

(Left) The 'Baked Bean Club'
at Harlesden in 1940 –
five cornetists and one
trombonist (Ray) –
in uniform and out of it.

(Top) The men of HMS *Royal Arthur*, Skegness, May 1942.
Ray remembers his service number: P/MX 95854.

(Above left) A writer in
the Royal Navy, 1942, and
(above) in the Persian Gulf,
1943.

(Left) At the piano, 1946.

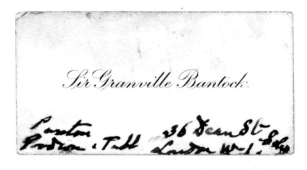

(Above) The card from Sir Granville Bantock. On the back is written 'Introducing Mr Ray Allen, trombone'.

(Left) Cartoon used in *The Musician* when Ray was in the International Staff Band, 1946.

(Above) A 'stolen' moment together for Ray and Joy at the International Training College, Peacemakers Session, 1949.

(Above right) Sergeants' campaign in Wales, 1949.

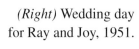

(Right) Wedding day for Ray and Joy, 1951.

Chapter Nine

My New Day

SLIDING back into the departmental programme was smooth and generally welcoming. To the best of my recollection the first year was unremarkable and more a time for getting used to a new district – Bounds Green – schools and corps, which was Wood Green. As a divisional centre it was sizeable and Joy was soon co-opted. In 1962 I was sent as a delegate to the International College for Officers (ICO) at Sydenham. It was the worst of winters: thick snow. The session lasted ten weeks, leaving Joy with the two children. It was a tough experience for her and, of course, I had the telephone as the only contact. I reminded myself that the overseas officers were even further away from loved ones.

The ICO brought together a group of officers from varying appointments around the world. Sometimes it could be a group with work in common like editorial or public relations. Lectures on aspects of the Army were given; the top leadership, departmental heads and specialists visited and made their contribution. Additionally there was doctrinal and Bible input and a lot of praying and sharing. We made visits to Salvation Army institutions, the Campfield Press, Coventry and Canterbury Cathedrals and the London sites of early-day Army history. There were also corps visits and trips to any big Army event that happened to be on in town.

In 1962 the Territorial Commander of Denmark, Commissioner William Cooper, invited me to his territory for a personal tour. He evidently hoped that a visit from someone such as I, still fairly young, could offer some inspiration to his musical forces. Postwar Denmark was poor and there was no question of air travel. My journey was by sea to Hamburg, then by train through to Denmark via Flensburg. I enjoyed it all. At that time the Army in that country seemed unsophisticated in its expression and it was a pleasure to work with the musicians, some of whom became permanent friends. I would particularly mention Bandmaster and Mrs Stanley Hansen of Copenhagen Temple and Bandmaster Erik Silfverberg, whose compositions have enriched the Army. Denmark is a fairy-tale country for the little sightseeing I could fit in, including Hans Christian Andersen's house in Odense. In Copenhagen there is the imposing 'brick cathedral'. More sobering were memorial places in the city where resistance people or hostages had been shot during the war.

That was the era when we started taking black-and-white cine film, the Danish visit ending with charming shots of Christmas at home. Erik Leidzén died in that year. He had visited our band practice at Tottenham when I was still the bandmaster and we had prepared 'The Cross'. Complimenting us on the playing, he laid down his baton and spoke to us on the theme of his band piece. It was an unforgettable experience and yet again I wish we could have kept a record of what he shared. A giant. Subsequent to his promotion to Glory, I felt constrained to write a band piece as a kind of memorial tribute, though not sad, called 'Toward the Golden Shore'; it features some of his songs. A copy of his encouraging letter to me is included in Ronald Holz's excellent biography.

What a full year this was! We took the family to Holland, Belgium and Germany. Probably at an older age we might not have had the courage! All four of us went with a ridge tent in our Morris Minor 1000 (UAD 288) and had a wonderful time. We camped in Amsterdam, along the Rhine and in Cologne. We hit the autobahn at rush hour and couldn't get off the Düsseldorf road for a long time. From there we visited Bonn and Beethoven's birth house. Then Brussels – where we lay in our tent and listened to our neighbours saying how many countries they'd rattled through in x number of days. Being interested in military history, I took off on my own to visit the battlefield of Waterloo. I had a slight exchange with a pub landlord – who didn't speak English – about paying to park the car. We had an excellent meal in Brussels but driving home through the city was an experience for us. Predictably we lost our way but eventually we found a kind motorist who led us at breakneck speed. Home via Ostend.

Christ is the Answer (1964)
Early in 1964 I went to the USA Eastern Territory and Canada on a six-week tour. I was scheduled to play the piano for a concert in New York. I wrote a piece for piano and band to play with the New York Staff Band. It was called 'Christ is the Answer'; this was subsequently given official release and has since been used from time to time. The piece pays tribute to the New York Staff Band soloists of the day. There is a little story here: the chorus I featured, 'Christ Is The Answer', is by a US Salvationist – hence its inclusion. Working hard on writing the piece I began to weary of this chorus and said to Joy: 'I don't want to hear it for a long time.' Shortly afterward we visited a corps and, while standing in the open-air meeting, heard the leader say: 'Now we'll sing a chorus: "Christ is the Answer"'!

Travelling via Seattle I visited Vancouver – what was then Mount Pleasant Corps. I then billeted with the Pindred family in Toronto and visited Calgary (receiving the traditional stetson hat), Edmonton (the Rockies and swimming in the warm springs) and Brantford (which ran its own Salvation Army radio programme). Joy had typed my notes, and at the head of each page it invariably read 'Joy likes maple syrup'. I took some home, of course! Also there had been a night when I spoke of having brought 'long johns' as a guard against the cold. But the buildings were all so well warmed I never felt cold, and so offered them for sale in a public meeting to the mirth of the crowd. Lest all this reads like a frothy jaunt I hardly need add that – as with all such campaigns – the primary purposes were never in doubt, the preparation prayerful and the workout exhausting but spiritually founded.

The Salvation Army Centenary (1965)

The Centenary of The Salvation Army was of course a big event in our world, with a series of gatherings, festivals and so on. The Crystal Palace grounds (in London's Upper Norwood) were taken for a huge international parade. It was a beautiful sunny day and the place was thronged. Unqualified to march as I had no official involvement in the parade, I was nevertheless not going to be left out. So I got myself in front of the bands and no one queried it! All our family was there; we picnicked on the grass together with myriad others. The original Crystal Palace, home of the Great Exhibition of 1851, had been a venue for Salvation Army events for years before its destruction by fire in 1936. I faintly remember coming there by bus (circa 1929) from Birmingham on my father's knee and can just about recapture a sense of glass, ironwork, indoor plants and crowds.

Dean Goffin, planning the centenary Royal Albert Hall festival, was generous in involving me personally. First the ISB premiered 'The Holy War' and with the ISB I played the solo piano in 'Christ is the Answer', the piece I had written for New York the previous year. The event is recorded in Brindley Boon's book *Play the Music, Play!* It was a thrill to receive a standing ovation for both works. Dean Goffin was in charge of all the music and was first rate. There was a performance of *Messiah* with Dean conducting. There was a Service of Thanksgiving with notable personalities and top Army leaders in Westminster Abbey. Bernard Adams and Charles Skinner had solicited a special fanfare from a teacher at one of the music colleges – Richard Arnell – and I transcribed Vaughan Williams's 'All People that on Earth do Dwell' from Elizabeth II's coronation service.

There was also a huge rally in Trafalgar Square with a band and the Joystrings, with General Coutts at the helm. We had never experienced anything like this and never have since – it was just fantastic. At that time the Joystrings were a novelty that had received publicity and were consequently in the public eye. This group had begun as a training college outreach under Captain Joy Webb. With the popularity of the Beatles, UK rhythm groups were proliferating. The Joystrings had a hit single, 'It's an Open Secret'. They did pioneering outreach, though eyebrows were raised when they were featured in the Blue Angel Club. The UK Army leaders were naturally very proud and the group had a tent during the Centenary celebrations where they signed autographs.

As a grand finale there was a meeting at the Royal Albert Hall. That meeting was a great occasion, with General Frederick Coutts leading. All four of us went forward to the mercy seat in the prayer meeting. Commissioner and Mrs Henry Warren (who had known Joy as a girl) said to each other, 'Army music is in good hands.'

Musicals

The musicals of Captains John Gowans and John Larsson are well documented. *Take-Over Bid*, the first, had been the result of National Youth Secretary Brigadier Denis Hunter's inspiration and commissioning of Captains John Gowans and John Larsson to write a musical. The venture was successful and was followed by a series of musicals. Apart from the value of the musicals themselves many of the songs became congregational favourites and have been incorporated in the Salvation Army songbook. On one occasion in the 1970s I was invited to lead the song 'How Much More' during a 'Day with God' in the Westminster Central Hall. Almost as soon as the opening lines were being sung people began to come forward to the mercy seat. It was an unforgettable experience.

Festival of Light

I have described the Festival of Light in a poem (see Part Three). It was an ecumenical march to Hyde Park and was both a protest at the way society values were declining and an evangelistic witness. The Salvation Army was represented by Joy, our girls and me, Wesley and Margaret Harris (Regent Hall officers), some other Salvationists and a youth band. There was an opposition crowd lining the route which, while not entirely threatening, was rather intimidating. We were at the front, watched over by a police sergeant. Some men from a London-based Christian businessmen's organisation carried a large wooden cross. After it was over we came across a lonely, ordinary-looking young man who looked a little pensive, almost bewildered, but had something about him. I asked him if he had 'people', thinking he might be with an identifiable group of Christians. Indicating the crowd he said: 'They are *all* my people.' It was a reply which caught our imagination and reminded us of the Author of our faith.

More Changes and Tranås Music Camp

In July of 1966 the Goffins were reappointed to New Zealand. We bought Dean's car in which we took ourselves to Tranås Music Camp in Sweden. Tranås Music Camp was not run in opposition to the territorial one at Dragudden but the charisma of the band's name, and possibly the guests they invited, brought an interesting cross-section of students from other countries as well as Sweden itself. At that time Gunnar Borg was the Tranås bandmaster and a compelling figure.

All four of us went in 1966; Barbara had her trombone but Rosemary, aged 10, was too young and had to be content with a tambourine, which left her feeling a little out of things. The week finished with a campfire. We had some holiday and stayed at the Army hotel in Stockholm. It was in connection with the hotel and official expenses that we were given the phrase which has remained in our usage ever since: *Frälsningsarmén betalerrekning* ('The Salvation Army will pay the bill').

In preparation for overseas visits I tried to assimilate a basic vocabulary of terms for practices. Waiting while everything is translated can be a nervy experience for all concerned, and in rehearsal immediacy of comment is vital. It was for a visit to Sweden that Joy decided to recite two poems – in Swedish! She was helped in pronunciation by Lieutenant Gunnar Granholm, the assistant officer to the then Captain John Larsson at Hillingdon. She conquered that all right and her performances were well received. That is, until, just before an outdoor occasion, someone said to Joy: 'The poet's here.' She just about went to pieces! Even so it had amazed me how many folk could understand and speak English.

Hendon

At some time we transferred from Wood Green to Hendon in response to an invitation for me to be the songster leader, following Muriel Yendell. Rosemary and Barbara joined the youth sections and Joy became the songster sergeant. Roland Cobb was our bandmaster. We had a comfortable relationship with the corps folk, although Joy maintains – with affectionate humour – that when you are a sergeant no one in the brigade is your friend! Subsequent enduring friendships have of course disproved that. She was effective and took time to sort out things, which was helpful us all, including me. Muriel's high choral standard was maintained and it was great to be able to plan and contribute to the weekly meetings.

There were of course opportunities for 'specialling'. Joy and I remember the comedy of an evening at Southall where the local brigade sang 'Bound for Canaan's Shore', which has a silent syncopated pick-up beat at the commencement of some chorus lines. Our two girls, on the front row, distinguished themselves by nodding on these beats so that the effect was (nod) 'Bound for Canaan's shore', (and nod) 'Bound for Canaan's shore'. Alas, Southall Corps, which contributed notable personalities to the Army, has – like others – succumbed to a metropolitan floodtide of population movement.

Chapter Ten

The King's Minstrel

1967 In charge of the Music Editorial Department
IN the spring of 1967 Colonel Charles Skinner, the Head of the International Music
Editorial Department and my boss, was appointed to National Headquarters to
work in Finance. Charles's going left a vacancy for a new Head. In apprenticeship
and service terms I was a natural successor, but successions are not necessarily
automatic and I had the added drawback of having spent time out of officership.
There was a period of about three weeks during which we waited and wondered
while keeping the departmental programme moving. There was, of course,
speculation. My friend Major Brindley Boon had been rumoured as a possibility
for the role, but in the end they appointed me; it indicated trust and I appreciated
it. Prior to retirement, Brindley's final assignment was, as Colonel Boon,
masterminding the amazing 1978 Congress.

I welcomed the opportunity and my first task was to bring out piles of
rejected manuscripts that had been filed in cupboards. I felt that contactable
contributors would prefer to have their work returned even though they might
be disappointed. It must be understood that for our form of journal publication
a fair stockpile of various styles, subjects and grades had to be kept in hand to
balance consecutive issues.

Over the years rejections inevitably brought disappointment, though I always
sought to be gently explanatory, remembering the loving care and labour which
had gone into the preparation – plus the fact that these people were exposing
their inner thoughts, often with more creative desire than technical ability or real
inspiration. It was still comparatively rare for most of our contributors to have
had the benefit of academic training and many were self-taught; many too (as
today) just put it down as it came and relied on us to shape it up. Within limits,
one tried to encourage. But sadly there had to be those times when received
material was just unacceptable, either in quality or in being unsuited to Army
needs and purposes.

On the subject of rejections, non-Army contributors sometimes failed to
align their creations with the Movement's purposes. I have received indignant

reactions from those who, possibly stung by our inability to appreciate their magnum opus, played the patronage card by telling us: 'This was given high praise by Professor X' (or some MusBac or diploma holder), with the implication: 'You morons, not to value my jewel!' Then again, perhaps the Army brass band as it was heard in the street did not always project a helpful image for our departmental public relations.

There was fun with some received items. I recall a tape which, when we got near the middle, offered a mouth organ with a few bars of 'suck-blow'. There were occasions when salvage was justified. I suppose all editors will have funny stories of letters received; on one occasion we were taken to task about the old chorus quoting from Psalm 23, 'My cup's full and running over'. Wrote the correspondent: 'I have to tell you that in our church the Lord's Supper is always celebrated with decorum.'

I did try to be helpful in principles and technicalities and suitability for Army usage, and I have since received a number of acknowledgments from young composers of the 1960s and 70s who have now reached their own place in the scheme of things. I suppose my work in those years represented actual, personal, creative expression and pushing out boundaries, plus helping budding composers and writers to develop their skills and gear their thinking to practicalities and gospel purposes.

In the pursuit of these I must occasionally have seemed stodgy and conservative. I know that is what the composer who sent me 'Sally Sleigh Ride' thought. If only he could have looked into my file of topical items I occasionally wrote as a safety valve, under the general title of *Hymns for Rat Racers*, he might have taken a new and more accurate view. I have a distaste for the use of the term 'Sally' as it has seemed to trivialise 'salvation' and what a cost that has represented, both divine and human. We have needed to watch titles which have come our way such as 'Bacchanalian Dance' on account of their connotation. Even *The Magic Flute* seemed at variance with what we stand for. Yet, at the end of the day, titles are quite secondary to the music itself and often meaningless in musical terms.

Apart from the routines of editorial work – issue choosing, score editing and preparation, proofing, Music Board meetings – it was a privilege to be at the heart of the Salvation Army music world with its creative opportunities and global contacts.

Home and Away 1968–1969

In 1968, Barbara had been at Wycombe Abbey as a boarder since 1965 and Rosemary began at the City of London School for Girls. We recall an open day at her school where a Latin class sang in that language the Beatles song 'Yellow Submarine'. Rosemary also took part in a performance of Britten's *Noye's Fludde* and played trumpet in various events.

We went again to Scandinavia, first to Sweden and then to Denmark, where we had a break in Copenhagen with Stanley and Amy Hansen, who were local officers at Copenhagen Temple Corps. The Danish bands, especially the youth, were being encouraged to explore the more up-tempo, rhythmic and slightly swingy idioms. Erik Silfverberg was highly influential in those areas and has made a fine contribution to the Army's music.

Joy and I were special guests at the Chicago and Atlanta music camps. We were used to the general pattern of taking small groups in theory and conducting studies, together with band and choral rehearsals. The electronic age had not yet dawned and the curriculum was less diverse than it is today. Part of my assignment at Chicago – and the traditional one – was to rehearse the top band, which also included many Chicago Staff Bandsmen who served as instructors. My breath was almost taken away when the request came up: 'Can we run down "The Holy War"?' In the event we did more than 'run it down'; the band took to it very well and gave an excellent account of itself.

A new cultural experience came our way when we joined a session eating roasted sweetcorn, something I had not done since Navy days as a guest in a South African home. We found that Dean Goffin had shared similarly on a previous occasion. Major Ernest Miller, the Music Secretary, was a genial host and took us around Chicago. We were fascinated to be shown where the St Valentine's Day Massacre had taken place in the prohibition gangland days.

Atlanta proved to have a different character, perhaps at that time a little less sophisticated, which appealed to us and brought out the best in us. Joy was given plenty to do, which was quite her cup of tea. We found that the US Civil War was not forgotten in the South. Looking at a cyclorama depiction of a battle scene we heard a lady exclaim: 'My grandaddy was there!' That statement seemed to bring history into the 'now' and has been one of my favourite Easter sermon illustrations. We left for the airport very early in the morning, in total darkness. That is, until every light went on and the whole camp sprang out to sing us on our way.

Barnet (1970)

We moved house in the autumn of 1970. For some time we had wanted a quarters with a garage and learned that the widow of Colonel William Charles was leaving Barnet. Barbara had already transferred to New Barnet Corps. Bill Charles had been the flag bearer for the ISB; a big, tall man, he had also been the Property Secretary. Their house had, I gathered, been designed or purchased for their retirement. We liked it, and on holiday we received a phone call from IHQ to say we could move in if we wished. That was fine, but the removal was set for a date when I would be in Australia. So we received help from Ray Bowes and Robert Redhead, both of whom were working in the IMED.

On moving-in day the man next door was working in his garden. RB hove in sight (uniform and glasses) carrying something or other. 'Morning,' said Alec, the new neighbour. 'Morning,' said RB and went on into the house. A little later RR turned up (uniform and glasses). 'Morning,' said the neighbour. 'Morning,' said RR and entered the house. Later in the day, the neighbour spoke to Joy and referred to those two. 'Oh,' said Joy, 'my husband is in Australia.' What an introduction! Maybe he wondered what kind of a set-up was going on next door!

Australia was an interesting but tiring six-week assignment which took in Queensland, the Sydney area, Melbourne and a night in Hobart, Tasmania. Unlike subsequent trips for other people it did not take in New Zealand. For the most part it was standard: music events, practices, councils, seminars, that kind of thing. I conducted the Melbourne Staff Band's 80th anniversary celebrations. Later on, in 1980, when we were stationed in Sydney we led the 90th and then in 1990 went from England for the band's centenary.

The new journey to the Judd Street office went via Baker Street. Walking past the Royal Academy of Music and not taking sufficient care, I tripped on the steps. The porter emerged and helped me inside. That was the one and only time I've ever been in that august establishment!

Rhythm Groups and New Composers
I fully expected that, like all my predecessors save one, I would retire as Head of the International Music Editorial Department. The production of music had been in place for nearly 90 years and unless there were major changes there seemed to be no reason why that should not continue. The 1960s had been good years. We had enjoyed the excitement of the centenary and our music sections were healthy. The earlier Gowans-Larsson musicals had made a huge impact, as had Major Joy Webb's Joystrings, and corps 'rhythm groups' were springing up, with some amazing titles like The Bill Booth Revival Machine and The Clean Heart Engineering Company. I had shared discussions about the newer Anglican and rock styles at Musical Gospel Outreach meetings. Yet the wind of those newer idioms and fashions of religious expression in Britain was still just a light breeze.

There was still uncertainty as to how best to involve 'rhythm groups' in corps worship. Although some groups had a mature approach, others seemed not to help their own cause where their insistence on no uniform (inappropriate 'gear') and general attitude was perceived as teenage rebellion – and sometimes was. Perhaps sometimes it was not so much rebellion as the difficulty of being accepted. It was a problem for some leaders fitting such groups into an established format. Were they just being outrageous? We can evaluate the strengths and weaknesses more easily with the benefit of hindsight. So for a while there was something of an undercurrent revolution until there was official recognition complete with guidelines. I regard the designation 'worship band' as an unfortunate choice, in parallel with 'Christian music'. Although people know what the terms mean they can carry a connotation of stylistic exclusivity. The label has been, for me, somewhat insensitive. It led to our traditional brass bands asking: 'What are we, then?'

Jumping ahead, my first day as *Musician* editor, as late as May 1983, brought me a challenging phone call demanding to know why groups were not featured more highly in the Army press. In response the paper ran double-page spreads with action pictures. My only stipulation was that the coverage should include personal testimony. The fashion for long hair under the band cap came and went, not without some casualties. Printings of the Joystrings songs in the 1960s had ceased, groups preferring either to evolve or import their material. The shelf life of popular religious song is short in most cases, as is a good deal of traditional Salvation Army output.

The 1970s were noteworthy for the appearance of a new generation of composers, particularly in North America: Himes, Curnow, Bulla. Edward Gregson was already making a significant mark in Britain and there were other new voices.

Joy Joins the God Squad

Barbara had begun at a teacher training college to train as a science teacher. Then Joy joined the 'God Squad'. I should explain. Now that Barbara was undergoing teacher training, Joy secured official permission to take a course at the same college. Initially she studied drama since she had a diploma in that area already. Discovering that Sunday rehearsals were expected, she transferred to the Religious Studies Department: the 'God Squad'. The popular view of Christians (aided by the media and TV dramas) seems to be of humourless killjoys, slightly unequipped socially (or downright bizarre), who quote from the Book of Proverbs in the *King James Version*! Be that as it may, I gather from my wife that the coffee break of the Religious Studies bunch was usually an hilarious affair. Readers will mostly be aware that being a Salvationist involves being teetotal. Imagine, then, her taking friends to a concert at the college, and as they enter the Students' Union a voice is heard: 'And the usual for Joy?' There is a legend that she had a weekly chemistry session and they used to follow her round picking up broken glass.

Star Lake 1972

I have never lost my sense of excitement – plus a degree of apprehension – on receiving an invitation to be a 'special guest' at an overseas music camp. It can be a step of faith on both sides. One goes expecting to work hard and give oneself hoping that it will be successful for everyone's sake. They have probably been having 'guests' for years and you are the next in line. There has never been a time when the invitation has failed to include Joy with me – which has been appreciated. Also we have been glad when Joy has been used – though on one nameless occasion someone said to her: 'What are you going to do? Have you brought your knitting?' We have certainly made the most of every opportunity and have made many friends.

The year we were at Star Lake, 1972, we began with the largest pizza we had ever seen. Changes of personnel at Star Lake had put an extra burden on the staff but it was a happy week and we have maintained links ever since. A memory is of the then Captain Wiggy Simons, responsible as some kind of master-at-arms people-manager, whose rallying cry was: 'Come on, you guys!' He took us home to meet his father, a veteran of the old New England Staff Band who plied us with his speciality, clam chowder, and regaled us with tales of the Army past. He was an eyewitness of the time when the legendary march king John Philip Sousa had written 'The Salvation Army March' for an Army celebration. Dear Wiggy, gone to be with the Lord, represents so many thousands of our Movement who have spent themselves unstintingly.

The Trumpet of the Lord

The excellent music sales department at Salvationist Publishing & Supplies Ltd included a wide selection of recorded music – at that time LPs. North American agencies had produced attractive gospel song arrangements for choirs and brass groups. We were in the mid-musicals era and I had directed a songs record of *Jesus Folk* and was given the go-ahead for a set of arrangements with an album title *The Trumpet of the Lord* (the title of one of the songs). In addition to the choral group we had nine brass instruments and a rhythm unit with piano. Robert Redhead, Brian Bowen and Ray Bowes joined me in contributing arrangements. It was a pleasant change to have a variation of pace from our traditional requirements. We then did a second album, called *Sound the Battle Cry*. The rehearsals were at Judd Street after the building had closed for the day. The security man used to get fidgety towards 8 pm, rattling his keys.

Music Editorial Department 90th Anniversary

All kinds of interesting things were happening. The year 1973 saw the 90th anniversary of the International Music Editorial Department. As the Music Department it had begun in 1883 under Herbert Booth, but soon Richard Slater became its chief assisted by Fred Fry and Harry Hill. Men soon to be household names joined the staff: Frederick Hawkes and Arthur Goldsmith. Hawkes became the second head followed in succession by my first chief Bramwell Coles, then Albert Jakeway and Charles Skinner, who moved into finance – and then it was my turn. I don't recall too much of the 90th anniversary, but there was a celebration festival chaired by the Chief of the Staff, Commissioner Arnold Brown, at Regent Hall where a bound set of Chopin's works was presented to Doreen Rutt who had given long service in the department for many years and latterly copied innumerable band parts for Leslie Condon and me.

Major Howard Davies (now a retired divisional commander) is an excellent composer in all fields. In addition to a sizeable input of attractive music, he also wrote a musical on the life of Commissioner George Scott Railton, *Soldier Saint*, which he staged at Regent Hall in 1975. I first met him during my 1970 Australian visit and was greatly impressed. Although it had apparently been planned for some time, it came as a surprise to me when the Robert and Gwen Redhead were appointed to Canada. I then remembered Howard Davies and enquired as to his availability for the department. In addition to his choral and band work he has contributed powerful congregational songs. We were so glad to welcome him and I believe he, Muriel and his family enjoyed their time in England. While in the UK he was able to visit the home of his ancestors in Blaina, in Wales. Also he was a keen photographer and amassed a collection of pictures of the city of London.

In Canada, the Redheads gave stirling service and Colonel Robert eventually became the bandmaster of the Canadian Staff Band. They received further appointments which brought them back to Britain and then retired in Canada. Work colleagues do not automatically become friends but generally the music editorial teams developed quite a close bond.

Welsh Hospitality

On a more domestic note, our younger daughter Rosemary had a place in Swansea University but, in her second year, accommodation was a problem. We hunted for a place without success. Joy, as ever, did her sums and found a tiny cottage in a row of Victorian workmen's cottages in Ystalyfera. It became a little bolt-hole for us, benefiting from the kindness and hospitality of Morriston Corps, particularly Songster Leader Eric Lear and his wife Nancy. We retained that cottage until retirement, making it available for holidaying Christian associates including people from the Navigators – strong inter-varsity evangelists. Though we lived in New Barnet we continued to worship at Hendon where, for a period, I was songster leader and Joy the sergeant. Then Joy felt she could be more help at New Barnet Corps where she joined Barbara and became the songster leader. In due course I followed to share a place of worship.

The Founder's Home

Barnet was historically interesting. A Wars of the Roses battle had been fought there and The Salvation Army's Founder, William Booth, had lived at nearby Hadley Wood. We sometimes took visitors to see it. It was at Hadley Wood that Herbert Booth (youngest son of William) had sought the songwriting help of Richard Slater, who must have lived reasonably close. Possibly inaccurately I often imagined Slater walking along the footpath by the railway line. That historically-recorded evening had seen the completion of Herbert's song 'Grace there is my Every Debt to Pay'. My weekday walk to Barnet station passed the former house of Commissioner Theodore Kitching, father of General Wilfred, and I often thought of his song which has enriched us: 'How Wonderful it is to Walk with God'.

Glasgow Musicians Councils 1975

The same year Joy and I travelled to Glasgow to conduct musicians councils. We – and, I hope, they – had a good time. I wanted to make a point about songwriting – the importance of the words we sing, their depth of experience, their scriptural basis and so on. I touched on the pitfalls of errors such as mixed ideas or metaphors. It was a subject theoretically familiar to all, but as a former songster leader I felt it worth consideration in a not-too-heavy way. To illustrate the possibility of singing words with ideas which are not entirely understood, I concocted some verses to a familiar tune so that reading the music wasn't a problem. By the time we'd finished, the point had been made – we should understand what one is singing about. I'd put together many well-known religious phrases and made them rhyme but – although respectable enough – they were mixed-up ideas and wrong references and therefore nonsensical. Here are the four that got the most smiles:

> Shepherd divine, thou hast called me to be
> A fisher of men till thy glory I see.
> When in the storm and the loud waves roar,
> Feed me with manna till I want no more.
>
> Help me, Heavenly Father, as I seek the lost,
> Come just now in power as at Pentecost;
> Then within the battle's heat, when the foeman stands,
> I will be as helpless clay in the Potter's hands.
>
> Like the woman at the well, off'ring me to drink,
> Washed in the all-cleansing flood never will I shrink.
> Like the boy whose loaves and fishes fed a multitude,
> Let me ever follow thee o'er waters rough and rude.
>
> When my feet would go a-straying, pilot me to shore,
> As a bird beneath her feathers, open thou the door.
> As in penitence before thee here I bow the knee,
> Come thou mighty Rock of Ages, roll right over me.

Family Faiths

Barbara decided that, after all, she should be pursuing a music career. Birmingham University was happy to take her, but an A level in music was required. The local evening class A level course had closed for lack of subscribers. So it fell to the parents to help. Syllabus in hand, I set a programme of work and Joy supported valiantly, encouraging when depression set in. There still remained the question of paying for Birmingham. The episode is included as an example of faith, and we prize Barbara's letter to God. It sets out estimates of costs and hoped-for income for work (she cleaned). She secured a Countess of Munster grant for which she had to give a trombone recital. A figure came out from the calculations. Her letter concludes: 'Dear God, What are you going to do about it? Love, Barbara.' She eventually became Head of Music in a Guildford school, then offered for officership and was accepted as a candidate. Things took an unlooked-for turn and she is now a vicar who – we are told – runs her church like an Army corps. But, as my grandfather used to say: 'That's another story.'

'Share your Faith' Campaign

Sometimes, for a national or international campaign, leaders required a new song or chorus. For the 'Share Your Faith' campaign there was a competition. Eventually there were two semi-finalists. My task was to go along to IHQ and present the pair of songs to a tiny team of two judges. Both I knew; one was the International Literary Secretary, a colleague-friend. I made for the piano, but there was no singer – I'd forgotten to organise one. I thought: 'Here goes, Ray, do your best.' Modestly I admit that my school had regarded me as a boy soprano – probably because I could read music! On this occasion I did my best and finished the entries. There was a silence. Had I blessed them? In the midst of a busy, draining day, had I brought a gift of spiritual refreshment? Had I lifted their hearts heavenwards? Then the lady spoke: 'Bruce Tulloch has a nice voice.'

North London Youth Band

Around 1977 I took over the conducting of the North London Youth Band from Lieut-Colonel Ray Bowes. It was a happy time for me as I had missed working with an instrumental group on a regular basis. We normally practised at St Albans and enjoyed quite a busy programme. Both our daughters were keen members and I believe that membership of such groups greatly helps to retain young Salvationists at what can be a difficult or rebellious period of their lives. They were a generally talented crowd. One member was Dudley Bright, who has contributed to this book.

General Arnold Brown

General Erik Wickberg retired and Arnold Brown, his Chief of the Staff, was elected to succeed. It might be thought that such changes did not affect things very much. However, the Head of the International Music Editorial Department traditionally had access to the Chief of the Staff and the General (through channels) which doubtless went back to Slater and the Founder. Thus some administrations were less personally remote than others. Throughout his term of office, General Arnold Brown continued to be particularly keen on all things pertaining to Army music and, through his departmental heads, Norman Bearcroft and I (Norman being the British Territorial Music Secretary) made full use of music's potential.

For the retirement of General Wickberg there was a suggestion that a band selection of his favourite songs be put together. The task came my way – it called for little creativity beyond technical processes. Someone asked me what I was writing. I replied, 'Musical knitting.' For, of course, such an item – for a single occasion – had no subsequent value and one knew this when working on it. Many years before I had written a Fantasia on 'Crimond' for a visit by Queen Elizabeth II. The ISB played it, I suppose – I wasn't there – but I never saw it again!

As a precursor to the 1986 edition of the Salvation Army songbook, a committee was set up to choose 100 songs, eventually published in 1976 under the title *Keep Singing!*, together with a band tune book. This brought me in closer contact with John Gowans, who hitherto had only been known to me as the author of the popular Gowans-Larsson musicals. I learnt to respect his mind and warm personality and contact was renewed when he and Gisèle retired to Rochester in 2002. All four of us went to Chatham Corps and we enjoyed a good deal of fellowship.

'We Believe'

Soon after General Brown's accession I found myself in the fairly unaccustomed conducting role for a series of Salvation Army radio programmes using hymns and various corps bands, plus a TV carol concert involving the famed Roy Castle. I also began to plan a book, *Colour and Texture in the Brass Band Score*. Then two centenaries came along, both of which required music – but for different reasons. The year 1978 celebrated 100 years of Army bands, for which there were three Staff Bands in London: ISB, Melbourne and Canadian. This kept me busy with composition: 'Daystar', played united, and 'On Ratcliff Highway', inspired by a *War Cry* illustration of Whitechapel Band marching through East London's dockland area, which was premiered to great effect by the Australian band under Colin Woods. Also being celebrated were the Doctrines of The Salvation Army, for which the General asked me for a musical setting. That statement of belief has the solid biblical foundation of its heritage and is robustly worded. But lyric text it just isn't! I had no stomach for concluding a festive musical work for a glorious chorus, ending with 'the endless punishment of the wicked'. Handel and Elgar, to name but two great oratorio composers, would have blenched. So John Gowans came to my rescue with a beautifully shaped verse and all was well. Almost.

For the occasion Norman had organised a huge chorus from Wales and the West and had travelled around to rehearse 'We Believe' – all the usual routine for congresses. There had been a complete performance at the beginning of the

Congress and it was intended to perform it again at the end. However, things did not quite go as planned. Just before the Sunday evening meeting, the General said to Norman: 'I'm afraid we'll have to cut "We Believe".' He was apologetic but the programme was overfull. The congregational singing of some of the refrains is on the official LP, but otherwise the work – beautifully printed and published – has sunk without trace.

The International Staff Songsters

When he was Chief of the Staff, Arnold Brown put to me the possibility of a permanent 'up-front' singing group, but on an ad hoc basis, without resource funding or official backing, pulling together people from London corps. I didn't see it getting off the ground though it was a thoroughly attractive proposition. Just a few years later, when Norman Bearcroft returned from Canada and Arnold Brown was General, he called Norman and me to discuss the official setting up of what became the International Staff Songsters. We talked it through and it seemed a worthwhile venture on that basis. Norman had successfully carried through the formation of the Canadian Staff Band when Commissioner Wiseman was his territorial commander, so we knew the problems and Norman's determination. Joy and I were under notice for a change of appointment so it was almost a foregone conclusion that my friend Norman should have the post of leader and we were happy for him, looking forward to news of the developments.

So far as I knew, Norman's expertise had been more in the instrumental field than choral but, supported by his new choir members (some of whom, trained vocalists that they were, had firmly-expressed views!), he carried it all through superbly and made the unit very characterful and popular. They could range from difficult anthems, through tender songs to music-hall-style numbers such as 'From the General down to Me'. In common with other composers, I was personally grateful for the opportunity to write for the ISS pieces that were rather more stretching than those geared to *The Musical Salvationist*, the standard quarterly choral publication which generally had to be averagely usable and cost-effective.

During the latter period of the 1970s I worked on my book *Colour and Texture in the Brass Band Score*. While it was not a textbook, I aimed to produce a book with copious music examples dealing with band instrumentation, technique and resources. It is in two parts: the first covers instrumental colour, lines, ensembles, special effects and percussion. Part Two has to do with various textures, thematic treatment and idiom. It was published by SP&S shortly after our move to Australia and has since been reprinted.

Shortly before Christmas 1979 we were informed that we were appointed to Australia, leaving in the New Year. Lieut-Colonel Ray Bowes would be my successor.

Chapter Eleven

Southdown

Farewell

THE office staff, that January day in 1980, were sympathetic and I had a degree of emotion in finalising my clearing up. Those who know me will also know that I tend to create piles of paper. However, Joy and I were now psyching ourselves up for pastures new. Visas had been collected from Australia House; I endured the long queue next to David McCallum, a star of *The Man From Uncle* TV series. Our Welsh cottage had a few stored items and a Barnet playschool round the corner housed more. Our beloved grand piano was stored at Salvationist Publishing & Supplies, Judd Street.

Our leaving for the airport was spectacular! We gratefully accepted a Barnet corps member's offer to take us in his car. Our own car, a tangerine Skoda coupé (originally chosen by Joy), had been passed on to Barbara. Early in the morning, Ernest turned up at the door in full uniform, his car immaculate; in front, on either side, small Army flags in embassy style. There was more. Jamie King, a young and enthusiastic Barnet Salvationist, appeared bearing the corps flag. Slowly the small procession moved along Warwick Road until Station Road was reached. Jamie waved goodbye and we were on our way to Heathrow.

We arrive in Sydney

Plane travel for that distance was uneventful, the passing of time marked by a series of food trays and a stop at Bombay. We dozed, ate, arrived at Sydney, collected our bags, checked out and were hit by the heat. Met by the helpful Army airport major we said: 'It's hot in here!', to which he replied: 'That's just the air conditioning – wait till you get outside.' We'd left UK in winter; in New South Wales January warms up through February and March achieving temperatures in the high thirties. That year it reached 40C with pavements shimmering in the heat.

Our address was in Baltimore Street, Belfield. At that time THQ officers' houses were sited in south or west Sydney. For obvious reasons the coastline prevents a 'Sydney east'. The north shore, nearer the ocean, is noticeably cooler.

Our first year was a time of adjustment, organising unfamiliar responsibilities, checking out resources and the reliability of co-operation. The new quarters was a bungalow – one of a cluster – which was fine for the two of us. What we had not experienced before was the community-committee style with 'gardening bees' and an officious woman whom I upset.

From hearing the much-used phrase 'whingeing poms', we soon encountered a certain degree of cynicism regarding immigrant Brits who, in the nation's experience, had brought their problems with them. So we were determined to be positive. We were made to feel welcome but we were aware that we could not take acceptance for granted; it was necessary to prove ourselves. In any case we'd come to work and serve.

Following our initial blending into the system, a few changes and a move into a pleasant home near the sea, we should place it early on record that we made, rather than found, our niche and look back on our Australian experience and Army service with affection.

We must have forgotten how bare some Army quarters can look, and of course we had brought only a few personal items, especially as we had been assured that our stay would be brief. But we were rather unprepared for austerity. There was an up-and-over garage (which somehow got dented before we moved out). 'Your car's in the garage,' we were told. That sounded good – coming from a 'back-room' editorial chair to having an official car! The distances we would have to cover were admittedly well beyond a bicycle. But we were built up for a fall! A green Holden automobile entered our world, a vehicle of which we had never heard. It had a gear lever on the dash and one needed three hands to operate the controls. Added to this, the previous owner, a nice man but a muscular giant, evidently had no problems. Now I wasn't at all frail but I wrestled with the steering wheel. One way and another we began to have a bit of reaction. We missed the kids, but we would not whinge, we told ourselves resolutely; like the apostle Paul we would be 'more than conquerors'.

After we had a chat with the Chief Secretary, Colonel William Cairns (a cultured officer), and had met again our territorial leaders Commissioner and Mrs Leo Ward (I had former contacts with him at IHQ), we inspected our office and went home. We had about ten days of orientation during which time we mostly sprawled, lightly clad, in front of the second-hand fan provided (together with an old TV) by an Army charity establishment. It was a much-appreciated opportunity to get our bearings.

Before I launch into a description of our lives in our new context, allow me just to say that we fell in love with Sydney. It has its variety, as does any city, but is a photogenic place. We particularly liked to stroll in the Rocks, a residential area going back to the early 18th century. A visit west to Old Sydney, with its colonial associations, was of great interest, showing life as it was then complete with military redcoats and convicts.

The Office, Evangelism and the Nurses' Fellowship

The Australia Eastern Territorial Headquarters is situated in Elizabeth Street, Sydney centre, in a building since replaced in about 1990. We had a couple of wooden partition offices with two desks, phones and a filing cabinet. This was for Joy and me to share. I had been appointed Secretary for Evangelism (and Music). It included Papua New Guinea. Joy was the Secretary for the Nurses' Fellowship, a post perhaps not ideally suited to someone with no medical links or experience. It looked as if the Evangelism part was open to personal initiative. In the original planning there was an attached travelling evangelist, but a breakdown somewhere occurred and I think I only met him once. In general we were free to go out on the road for corps visits and tours, supply literature and see that appropriate material was available for counselling at the big meetings. The 'out on the road' aspect was a wonderful opportunity and became our salvation. Of the music side I will comment later.

We Explore the District and Join the Local Corps

There are a lot of Sydney suburbs and some seem relatively small. Our suburb, Belfield, was neat and tidy, mostly bungalows with red roofs and handkerchief gardens. Belmore was nearby, together with Lakemba, where there was a supermarket, and Campsie where our corps was. The streets are on a grid system. Coming out of our cluster of dwellings, we turned right, up to Albert Street, over the railway bridge and straight on into Lakemba Street. The supermarket was of a no-frills variety, humid and smelly. There were a lot of Lebanese living in the area; the next street to us had a Lebanese convenience shop using the term 'mixed business'. Sydney has an excellent book of street maps which we found invaluable.

We had said that we would attend the corps that belonged to where we lived. Campsie, the shopping centre, had a traditional, hard-working corps with quality officers in charge. There was a singing company (junior choir) with a few little girls – which functioned on anniversary occasions and usually to a taped backing. On our travels we tried our best to promote the value of using an established singing company in meetings, introducing youngsters to the routine of regularly taking part, but changes in traditional practices are not imposed and need grassroots enthusiasm.

Corps people were friendly, with an elderly woman who sat behind us and – we think in an attempt at humour – managed to wind me up most of the Sundays we were there. The Campsie Sunday evening open-air meeting was impressive. The Salvationists stood not far from the War Memorial in the main road. The band had a macebearer and the bandmaster a silver whistle. The participants included a large number of comrades, including the songsters. It was one of the little procedural unfamiliarities that the men and women stood separately, but it was an excellent public witness. We became friendly with Major and Mrs Gordon

Hoskings, caring corps officers. The Australian Army seemed superficially the same as at home. But there were differences we had yet to discover; we were the ones who had to learn to adapt.

We welcome a new Departmental Secretary

Initially we had a young lady secretary who left to get married. We were then fortunate in securing the services of Major Joy Meehan. On the eve of departing for missionary service she had been diagnosed as having multiple sclerosis. She could get about with a stick but somehow a satisfying niche could not be found, so we asked for her. She fitted us like a glove and was very happy in the work, especially that of the Evangelism Department. She was competent and dedicated and we looked after her in various ways beyond the official relationship.

The Realm of the Music Department

It must be confessed that initially I did not want the 'music hat' – in *The Musician* there had been a certain amount of negative criticism about the music the International Music Editorial Department was publishing, to which I had been given no opportunity to reply. I needed a break so I had requested another appointment. Australia had been the result. With one exception my predecessors in the IMED had all retired from the editorial position and I had envisaged the pattern applying to myself. Indeed, the leaders were very reluctant to move me when the department was operating smoothly, and it would be false modesty to deny that, in that task, I was wholeheartedly accepted. With hindsight it would seem that my need for a break came across as a request for a transfer, which is the way it works. In the course of an interview discussion there had been the thought that the Literary and Music Editorial teams might be merged, with a possible supervisory role for me, and that any break would therefore not be protracted. Furthermore, I had requested that any change, even if temporary, would not involve music. It did not take me long to realise that, for obvious reasons, I was inevitably typecast!

We talked with the Territorial Commander – in his home – and I told him that I had particularly requested no music in whatever they gave me and that I was rather dismayed at the Music Secretary part. 'It won't be quite like that,' he replied. I felt ready to come home again. I have always felt that it was a rather woolly assignment, and that there was no real need for us. We had left the girls thousands of miles away, and for what purpose? So we were constantly unsettled; no fixed term and International Headquarters in London was vague. From their viewpoint they had accommodated me – not the easiest of appointments for them to make. Doubtless we were not the first to have such human feelings but we discovered that the experience was good for us, gave us a different kind of ministry and was, without doubt, Heaven-blessed.

New South Wales's Music Forces

The music side was virtually all organisation and administration. I conducted occasional rehearsals and we had some excellent corps music sections of which there were perhaps a half dozen larger groups in the city area: Sydney Congress Hall, Hurstville, Dulwich Hill, Earlwood, Petersham and Campsie. Then came quite a number of lesser-sized bands and songster brigades. Elsewhere there were, of the bigger aggregations: Wollongong, Brisbane City Temple, Ipswich, Mayfield and one or two more. Smaller units were scattered about the territory. Support for us was quite good once we had their confidence. It seemed to us that the Australian style was to give us a warm welcome and then wait to see what we would do. Not so abrasive as the ex-Britisher who said to Joy: 'What's Ray think he's going to do, then?'

Generally we found music sections co-operative. The Sydney Congress Hall Band traditionally acted as the territorial band and its bandmaster, Barrie Gott, was very helpful. There was a 'No 2' band at the Congress Hall, run by Vita Terracini; of Italian stock he had an officer brother who had been the Music Secretary and was now in a wheelchair. While the SCH band was smartly efficient, the No 2 band, no less self-respecting, had its own style. It consisted of young people and band reservists or those who did not feel able to take on the more exacting commitment of the other band. Both got on well and pursued their own way of doing things. Sydney also had a territorial women's choir.

The Nurses' Fellowship

This has now been renamed Medical Fellowship. When Joy became its secretary for the Eastern Territory it had people in Papua New Guinea as well as New South Wales and Queensland. Joy wrote a periodical newsletter and kept in touch with the members. She would convene meetings in various places. Also she initiated, encouraged and undertook fundraising. Vital medical and maternity equipment was purchased including items for Papua New Guinea. Four incidents come to mind as I write.

There was a couple in north New South Wales; she (I will refer to her as E) had been a candidate but they were both out of the Army. E vowed she would never rejoin. She came down to Sydney on a visit and, as a nurse, she wanted to see who was sending her the newsletters. Joy took her out for coffee and then they went on to the Salvation Army shop as Joy needed a new uniform hat. 'Try one on,' she said to E, who did and bought it! 'What am I doing, buying this?' she exclaimed. Then later one day G, her husband, who had become a recruit, decided to go to a meeting. During the prayer meeting they both knelt at the altar in reconsecration. We heard later that they had got into uniform and were fully involved.

A SANF weekend conference was held at Collaroy. Prior to this a man with an English accent had telephoned me at the office. He told me he was from Derby

Central Corps and had a good testimony to give. Could I fix him up with some corps for him to share his story? I did. Briefly, his story was that he had been a hard man, a member of a South London gang, but had become a Christian and he was now the band colour sergeant. This proved to be true enough. He was visiting his sister and we arranged for him to tell his story at a few neighbouring corps. Joy invited him to the Collaroy conference to share his experience.

For the last of Joy's congress weekends there was the usual SANF dinner and gathering (at The People's Palace). The statistical officer was a clever man who played the bagpipes. Joy invited him to play his pipes at the dinner. He began by joking that he'd had a cold and that he'd rubbed Vick on the pipes! Marching up and down, his playing was fine but the character of Army choruses in that idiom, fixed scale and drones, was most unusual to our ears, especially with the chromatic notes of the originals. It made for a jolly occasion.

Once there was a meeting convened some little way across the city which Joy had forgotten. We were relaxing at home when the telephone rang and a voice asked about her presence. In panic we leaped into the car and raced through the suburbs. Got there – not *too* late!

Joy felt that her supportive role was worthwhile, albeit she was not a medical person. It was, up to then (apart from corps appointments prior to her marriage), her only actual official appointment, and one which she enjoyed.

We Get Down to Work
We of course intended we should get on with what had been entrusted to us and do our best. There was the annual congress looming and a showground venue had been chosen. Fortunately, I had worked with Dean Goffin and Norman Bearcroft before, so we organised a massed choir, got out music and I went around rehearsing. Also I discovered that I was enjoying that side of things. On behalf of the Territorial Commander the Music Board was happily standardised. Soon we began to discover whom we could trust and whom we could rely on, buzzing along quite well. Joy was getting to know her Fellowship people both close at hand and as far away as Papua New Guinea (where we never were able to go). As well as organising group meetings, fundraising and sending news or personal letters she made contacts when we visited an area.

As we developed our ministry, one of our biggest fulfilments and most valuable contributions to the territory was our 'campaigning'. We would secure approval from a divisional commander to visit his division and set up a ten-day itinerary. This could include music practices, seminars, meetings or whatever they wanted. At the heart of it were our visits to the corps officers in their quarters. There we could talk with them – no official portfolio, no party line, just genuine interest in them, their families, their work and their problems. As time proved, we gained their trust. They would open up; we would try to counsel, to encourage. Though we seldom could do anything practical, it seemed to help them to share. We remained totally confidential. On one occasion at a small but thriving outback corps we found an officer who had no idea how to manage his books, so after the open-air and evening meetings we had a go at teaching him.

The Pommies' Palaver

To Australians the British are 'Poms', which term, I understand, arises from the days of convict transportation. The Sydney Congress Hall bandmaster's parents hailed from Sheffield where Fred Gott had been the bandmaster. He and his wife Jean had emigrated years before. They were warmly friendly to us in true Yorkshire style. Fred ran the band at Auburn and was divisional bandmaster for the West Sydney Division. They introduced us to the 'Pommies' Palaver' which is (or was) a monthly gathering of British expatriates in a church hall which had Union Jacks and other nostalgic memorabilia. There were refreshments and a speaker. It was a club with quite a religious input.

Our Transport goes Upmarket

Another word about the car. When we arrived at Baltimore Street they had said: 'Your car's in the garage.' That car (and its problems) has already been mentioned. The THQ garage was in the basement, approached by a ramp. Although we got used to it, at first it seemed steep and a little nerve-racking. The temptation on exit was to rush at it, whereas a gentle ascent in a low gear worked well and safely. We had arrived in January, a cruel period of heat, and the car not only had steering which required steel muscles, but it was also upholstered in plastic which got very hot so that one sweated profusely.

I began to develop aches and pains and, one morning, I was parking the car in the basement when Joy got in the lift. Unknown to her, it had in it people who 'mattered'. Someone said: 'Where's Ray?' Although we had determined not to complain, Joy frothed over and shot out: 'He's parking that car and I shall never drive it!' A little later the Staff Secretary, a decent soul, popped into the office, did not look at Joy but said to me: 'There's a car downstairs you could have. It's a lady's car.' It turned out to be a little silver Mazda 323, which we loved, and even talked of bringing it home to the UK. Not long afterwards the Staff Secretary asked: 'How many kilometres has that car done?' I said: 'About eighty thousand.' 'Oh,' he replied, 'we should change it – we trade them in at sixty.' So we had the pleasure of choosing a brand new Chrysler (which I later crashed and they wrote it off – but that's a later story).

The Centenary September 1980

The Centenary of the Australian Salvation Army was understandably a very special event and broad plans had been made before we appeared on the scene. I not only found that we had involvement in happenings in Adelaide, which seemed a thousand miles away in another territory, but that, as Music Secretary for the Eastern Territory, I also had the job of planning a tour for the Enfield Band and the Swedish String Band, both of which groups were travelling in our territory prior to taking part in the celebrations down South. Of course, my previous experience had never before included such organisation. I did not know the geography, the character of towns, distances or resources. I shared the issue with the Chief Secretary and co-opted a retired officer and previous music secretary, Lieut-Colonel Gordon Spillett, to take over, which he did admirably. I remained nominally responsible but the colonel's calm approach, experience and organising skills were a godsend.

Committees and Planning

It should be explained that Australia was once a single command. No doubt due to expansion and geography the command was divided early in the 1920s and a degree of rivalry, generally good-humoured, exists between the Eastern and Southern Territories. I had visited the Southern Territory in 1970 and received the warmest of welcomes. I believe that the people I have met and served with are no different a cross-section from any other. But in the course of the Centenary celebrations, and even in the planning, it was essential not to become over-sensitive to cross-cultural differences. Commissioner Arthur Linnett, the Territorial Commander in Melbourne, had been my opposite number when he was the Literary Secretary at International Headquarters and I was Head of the IMED. He was a kindly man and I found this previous relationship helpful.

On arrival at the Southern headquarters we found a large group already gathered for the planning conference. Much of what was discussed was over my head and, at that date, I had no idea what was expected of musical representation from our territory. Evidently there was to be a Centenary Village with various aspects of Army work; someone suggested an art exhibition, which was agreed. As a newcomer it was all unfamiliar to me and I assumed, perhaps erroneously, that everyone there knew what I didn't. One worried that help, co-operation and a sense of common cause might not extend to the Australia Eastern Territory. I did gather that there was a working committee in Adelaide masterminding it all, though others were possibly equally at sea. Perhaps I'd misread the signs. On return to Sydney I found that my apprehensions were shared.

So much for the committee side of it. The final results were excellent, so some central team did a first-rate job. It transpired that in one of the Centenary Village marquees there would be allocated spaces for the Eastern Territory to make representative presentations of various aspects of the work, music among them. There was simply no resource for this and the location was a very long way away from Sydney. So I wrote to Ray Bowes in London and asked for photocopies of manuscripts and other relevant memorabilia. Ray did us proud!

I then found that the Southern Territory had allocated me non-musical duties: seating, microphones, stage-managing, about which I had not been notified and which failed to take into account duties I already had, connected with our charges, Enfield Band and the Swedish String Band. These duties put me in totally different places from the Melbourne allocations, so sometimes they were unworkable. I suspected that General Arnold Brown had envisaged their co-opting my services in some kind of associate music directorship, an impression later confirmed. But the planners must have thought differently. So I saw to chairs, oversaw microphones, gave out announcements and acted as stage manager. Somebody had to do the equivalent of feet-washing! Although I also wore an Evangelism hat, those areas were already in hand, so it was swings and roundabouts. Joy was involved with a Nurses' Fellowship dinner and that was sufficient. We were quite happy, however – there was enough to do and see.

A Few Preliminaries
Still in Sydney, and some days before Centenary kick-off for which we were all due to travel to Adelaide, we were in the office tying up a few ends in connection with Enfield Band and the Swedish String Band, who were touring in our area en route for Adelaide. There was a message from the front door: a consignment of Enfield brochures and records had been delivered, addressed to me. That was the first we'd heard about it. Now what? I think they had come across from New Zealand. No one had warned us about this huge consignment. We had no idea at that moment how to handle it all, so we just forwarded it south. Had there been some notification way back? We shall never know.

The Swedish String Band arrived, a smart group led by Colonel and Mrs Lennermo. The conductor was their daughter Karen. I had met the Lennermos before when they accompanied a Swedish string band to London for the 1965 Army Centenary. On that occasion, in the Royal Albert Hall, Mrs Lennermo referred to Leslie Condon and me as 'you boys'. I have always enjoyed the unique sound of the string band with its tuneful song material.

Joy took the string band under her wing; she has a soft spot for Sweden. They duly arrived for a welcome meal. A few corps excelled in catering teams. Joy created something of a sensation as – remembering the music camps from our visits – she said grace in Swedish. They visited various centres, Joy travelling with them. Enfield Band visited Canberra where the audience was embassy staffs, civil servants and influential people, an excellent public relations opportunity. Bandmaster James Williams kept his programme fairly light.

The Centenary Events
Every one of these nine events has an interesting aspect, and if human frailty occurred it was outweighed by the surge of celebration that was going on among the rank-and-file Salvationists. Immense gratitude is owed to the spadework of the Adelaide team. Adelaide is not a big city and resources were doubtless somewhat difficult. They did well.

The Three Band Festival

I only include this little incident because it cemented mutual respect between Sydney Congress Hall Band and ourselves. The bands involved in the festival were front-rank: Melbourne Staff, Sydney Congress Hall and the British visitors from Enfield. Additionally, there was the Hawthorn Timbrel Group. But it was the seating of the bands that created an instant problem. I was virtually in charge of the staging and just about everything else. No one had told us this until just before the event. We would get a phone call: 'Did you know you are on duty at X or Y?' No we didn't. We had initial instructions as to where and what but alterations popped up spontaneously. So off we went and found that the Melbourne Staff and Sydney Congress Hall Bands had already settled themselves either side of the front of the stage. When Enfield Band arrived, Sydney's Bandmaster Barrie Gott immediately sized up the situation and said: 'We'll sit at the back – they can hear us any time,' which was magnanimous in the circumstances. I was relieved; crisis averted.

Later, all participants, including the string band, were having tea. I said to Joy: 'I think I'll get another cup of tea.' As I passed by a table a voice said: 'Colonel, can we have a word?' It was a group of Sydney Congress Hall bandsmen. I replied: 'I know what you want me for.' They said: 'Well, what do think about the seating?' Here was the problem. For acoustic and visual reasons bands regard rear stage plus curtains as disadvantageous, which is very understandable. I was their Music Secretary; but I was also an Englishman and previous bandmaster of the band that became Enfield, so I had many friends therein. I looked at them and just replied: 'If your bandmaster has shown himself to be such a gentleman, I think you should follow his example.' Whether or not this carried their judgment at the time I'm not sure; I rather think it might have. All I know is that from that time on and until we came back to the UK the bandsmen were wonderful to and totally supportive of us. The festival was very good and, despite its placing, the Sydney Congress Hall Band acquitted itself excellently. No harm done. An encouraging sequel was that we found a place to go in for refreshments and discovered it full of Sydney Congress Hall people who overwhelmed us with their friendly warmth.

The Half Night of Prayer

The prayer gathering had a healthy attendance and was the last time I saw and spoke with Dean Goffin. He was there with his wife Marje as Territorial Commander of the New Zealand Territory. I had no official involvement (no chairs and microphones to set up) but spent some time sharing in part of the prayer period. Having been a friend and colleague of Dean's back in the late 1950s and 60s I was glad to see them both again. Dean has made a very special contribution to Army music both in person and as a composer. Not only is his work skilful but it also has that desirable quality our Founder referred to as 'reaching the heart'. As Territorial Commander of the New Zealand Territory, Dean was knighted in 1983.

The Centenary Village
A Centenary Village was a happy inspiration. It was a spread-out exhibition park made up of marquees which contained presentations of various aspects of Salvation Army outreach and service. Many Salvationists and retired officers are painters, so there was also an art exhibition. In one of the tents, labelled 'Music Ministry', there were about four trestle tables. Three were empty and initially bore large signs saying FOR THE USE OF THE EASTERN TERRITORY. The General was due to come round very shortly.

I had, as mentioned earlier, secured from London a good supply of photocopies of band and songster compositions, manuscripts and the paraphernalia of printing. It was the kind of material we kept in the Music Editorial Department in London for our own purposes or exhibition loan and it was only a short while since we had put on a show in London's Oxford Street linked with the Army's centenary of printing. I was glad that I'd had the forethought to ask Ray Bowes for material and that he'd provided so handsomely. We spread out our exhibits, had a look at table four with its supply of Army periodicals and went to look at what else was on offer.

Round the Gum Tree
The Australian Salvation Army was begun in Adelaide by two expatriate Salvationists from the UK (John Gore and Edward Saunders), who had somehow found each other in 1880. We gather that it was the result of both men being in a church service when one shouted 'Hallelujah!' We celebrated in a great circle round the actual gum tree with a re-enactment and a real horse and cart. A service of thanksgiving took place with traditional Army songs. What was interesting to us was that descendants of the original men were there, including an officer and his wife from Sydney, Major and Mrs Watters. This event had a unique historical interest. It was also a very hot day indeed.

Commissioner Denis Hunter
The top leadership was of course heavily involved. Commissioner Denis Hunter, being the International Secretary for the South Pacific and the Far East, had prominent responsibilities. We had known and shared with him and his wife Pauline on a number of occasions. Enjoying a short walk in Canberra we suddenly came upon Denis wandering, as Wordsworth would say, 'lonely as a cloud'. So we took him under our wing for which I am sure he was grateful.

On the occasion I am reporting Denis led an indoor meeting of the rally kind, supported by various music sections including Enfield Band (who played 'On Ratcliff Highway' brilliantly) and there was a little Army family of string

75

players that was sweet and played beautifully. My role was the usual one of doing the announcements, and during the meeting Denis said to the crowd: 'On this occasion I am going to ask the colonel to *sing* the announcements.' What a challenge! So I sat myself at the piano (music at last!) and began a kind of impromptu operatic recitative, which concluded: 'Don't be late for the fête and don't dally for the rally.' Being spontaneous and ad lib it went down well, but I was flattered to find it not only one of the happenings that people spoke about but that it was also included on the official Centennial tape recording!

The Nurses' Fellowship Dinner
The Nurses' Fellowship was for all medical Salvationists and flourished in both territories. A dinner for the Nurses' Fellowship was a joint venture with the Southern Territory. Their secretary was Mrs Major McIntyre, and Joy and she got on very well. Some 200 people sat down to the meal which was graced by both Territorial Presidents of Women's Organisations.

The Tattoo
The Tattoo was an outdoor performance by various units – an admirably inclusive idea having the elements of a show. We weren't able to attend, however, having another commitment.

A huge audience enjoyed the spectacle and the smartly marching bands. The visitors – Enfield Band and Bandmaster James Williams – opted for a simple point-making reminder of the main gospel purpose of Salvation Army bands by following its march with a traditional formation of an open-air ring and playing 'Tell Me the Old, Old Story'.

The March and the Rally
Salvation Army troops marching with bands and banners can be an impressive spectacle. By tradition it was headed by top leadership. We hadn't envisaged non-Salvationists such as American-type cheerleaders joining in, but it was colourful.

The march preceded the big rally, which took place in a sports stadium. General Arnold Brown was in charge and on his instructions I had the privilege of directing the music and united bands. It was most inspiring and exciting to be at the centre of the great wave of congregational singing and sound. The General, always at home with a crowd, was on top form.

Postscript
Many people caught a tummy bug at the end of the event and came home with it. I succumbed and felt terrible, but despite this I completed my reports for the Army press. For Joy and me it was yet again a reminder of what a wonderful, self-sacrificing Movement we belong to. In retrospect, the whole project must

have done much to unify the Salvationists of a vast continent where sheer geographical distance can inflict isolation. In some ways, early in our Australian service, along with the spiritual lift we received, the Centenary experience afforded us a useful exercise in understanding cultural and mindset differences and helped to establish us with our own Eastern Territory people.

British Musician Visitors

Lest this heading seem nationalist, there was an ongoing tradition of bringing musical personalities, mostly officers, to Australia and New Zealand. I had been one of them in 1970. From our viewpoint any Brits brought news from home and were a link, which those who serve away from home will very well understand. We had two visiting musicians in our time. The first was Captain Trevor Davis, then the National (British Territorial) Bandmaster. The standard itinerary was usually open rehearsals at a few centres and guest involvement in a weekend's musicians councils. Trevor did most effectively all that was required of him. A warm and urbane gentleman, he has a disarming, friendly manner, which was well appreciated.

There was one unusual incident worthy of note. Joy and I had a close interest in the Alcoholics Rehabilitation Programme in Booth House, not far from the THQ. In the course of Trevor's visit I encountered a sad case. Owen's sorry story was that he had been a former bandsman in the Southern Territory. Following a period of driving some distance his wife took a turn at the wheel. Within minutes they crashed and she was killed. He was unable to forgive himself and took to drink. Finally he had got into an Alcoholics Anonymous programme. On the Sunday afternoon Trevor was conducting a music clinic in the Congress Hall. I had left the hall for a few moments and was outside. Owen (whom I did not then know) stopped by and asked if I believed God could save him. Naturally I gave a positive answer and took him into the hall where Trevor was working with the band on a selection, his back to the audience. Owen made his way to the mercy seat but Trevor, of course, could not see him. Commissioner Harry Warren, who, in retirement, acted as assistant officer, and I took Owen into the officers' room. Owen found his way back to God and began to make good. The last we heard was that he had gone back south and resumed his Army service.

During his free time we took Trevor to Cronulla, the 'birthplace of Australia' where Captain Cook came ashore. There is a monument there, though I have heard some political extremist has advocated its demolition. During our time there some schoolchildren came by and one dropped a pair of glasses down a drain. So there was I, groping into the hole, with Trevor hanging on to me. We rescued the glasses, and somewhere there is a photo of the incident.

Ray Bowes, my successor in London, was the second visitor. He was en route for New Zealand with two or three corps visits and a musicians councils in Sydney. As Music Secretary it was my role to support him and drive him to his engagements. The visit was not without incident. There was an evening with local musicians in the south of Sydney. Part of the proceedings was a meal and question period. For starters I had given warning that Ray only ate plain fare. 'Nothing spicy or exotic for him, please,' I spelt out. But because everything was curried and spiced up, poor Ray went round saying: 'I haven't got anything.' So we arranged that he should select a few items which we would help him with and we fed him later.

Then came the question period. That passed off satisfactorily except for a woman who asked about the arrangements for the two LP records *The Trumpet of the Lord* and *Sound the Battle Cry*, many of which were mine. I had brought copies to Sydney. The lady had been to London and wanted to secure some of these arrangements. She had been directed, she said somewhat derisively, to Leslie Condon, who was unable to see her as he was busy. So what about it? What's the problem? Can we have them? Ray was a little uncomfortable as, although he knew these arrangements, and indeed had done one of them, he could not be expected to know, off the cuff, the whereabouts of non-published manuscripts which went back before his time. So I interposed. I understood her raising the issue if she was in London but explained that I was the originator of these sets, and that, had she referred it to me, her Music Secretary, I could have supplied her. She never followed it up. Perhaps I have a strange effect on some people. It was in that area that I was rehearsing one of my massed-item pieces for a forthcoming congress. A woman on the front row said, 'I don't like this piece.' I responded immediately and, I am afraid, a little snappily, with: 'Then don't come to the congress!' But she was there!

I Crash the Car

The other incident in Ray Bowes's visit concerned my car crash. I had taken Ray, together with our Band Inspector, Len Collier, up to Mayfield, a two-hour drive north. The evening event went well and I went round to collect Ray from his billet. There was some delay in getting away and I began to get agitated as we had an evening fixture in Sydney. We eventually left and were on a winding two-lane highway. A map, placed on the dashboard, slipped off and I bent to retrieve it just as we arrived at a nasty bend. I hit the side of a truck carrying two big concrete blocks, ricocheted into the car behind and, the car being automatic drive, shot back into the truck. Out for the count, I came to in hospital having bashed a knee, sustained a cut eye (stitched) and a damaged nose. My uniform was wet with blood. The passengers were apparently all right but the car was a write-off.

Those are the crash facts. A local policeman was heard to say that he was surprised the driver got out alive. I saw the car in the pound some time later with the front stove in. Now here's the sequel. At our end we were discharged from casualty and, by a mercy, Len had a sister living nearby so we got to her house.

A phone call was put through to someone in Sydney. It was still the forenoon. We were told that the area divisional commander would drive across to pick us up and take us back to the city. Bear in mind that there was an evening fixture, the tea and first meeting of the musicians councils weekend. We sat on and sat on in the hospital. Of my two passengers, Len wasn't too bad, while Ray had no visible injuries but had bruised ribs. My damage has been mentioned. We were all in misery and desperate to get away. Our guardian angel driver arrived, accepted some refreshment and off we went. Lunchtime approached. I think food was the last thing we wanted, but with the best of motives, we were all guided into a place for fish and chips. Apart from needing to get home I was worried about the evening fixture.

Back in Sydney, Joy had a phone call from the Chief Secretary: 'Joy, Ray's had an accident, he's been to the hospital but don't worry, he's all right.' A little later another phone call, this time from the Territorial Commander's wife: 'Joy, would you like me to come round and sit with you?' It was very caring of them, but Joy thought: 'How bad is this accident?' I got home and was put to bed with a little soup. Later we made it to the evening fixture. By this time I had a Technicolor face and really looked dramatic. The word had of course got round and I was swamped with sympathy. My friend Ray Bowes, in discomfort but nothing physical to show (and anyway he wasn't *their* Music Secretary), felt the absence of sympathy and reacted with: 'And I've got to go on to New Zealand for another week!'

There was a kindly sequel. A little later Joy came over to me and said: 'Would you like to have a week in a caravan?' Yes, I would! It turned out that one of the Scotney family had offered his caravan, the Chief Secretary had agreed and a delighted Joy handed me the key. Such generosity and thought was not uncommon among some of our people and was a quality we appreciated. As a footnote: Ray, being the forgiving gentleman he was, never mentioned this incident to me again, though I did to him. Ray was promoted to Glory in February 2010. When I had the privilege of offering a tribute at his Thanksgiving Service I felt he would approve (and would have chuckled at) my public referral to the incident.

The Scotneys

Just a paragraph about the Scotneys. In 1970 I had met Harold Scotney in Sydney; he was then the Band Inspector and had published band music to his credit. His brother Hubert had been Chief Secretary in the UK and was a retired commissioner. With his wife he lived in a bungalow quite close to us. Occasionally Commissioner Hubert Scotney would ring our doorbell well before breakfast. He would be standing there to visit, immaculate in his summer outfit. I had a keyboard for which he made and delivered a wooden stand. He maintained a vital interest in the international Army and it was good to sit in their 'lounge room' discussing relevant issues. Probably because I felt rather uprooted from the IHQ centre, I relished both answering questions and being invited to share my views. When the Commissioner was taken seriously ill and awaited the Home Call we visited him in hospital, read and prayed with him. We think we were almost the last people to visit him. His wife Florence was very good to Joy. They had lost a daughter who would have been Joy's age and Mrs Scotney 'adopted' her. I was interested to learn that when Herbert Booth had visited Australia for one of his preaching tours she – as a young corps cadet – had played the piano for at least one of his meetings. After her husband died, Mrs Scotney moved into a residential home where we continued to visit and befriend her. It was their son who kindly loaned the caravan. He or his brother also had manuscript paper printed as a gift for me. It was this brand of kindness that enriched our lives so frequently in Australia.

We Benefit from Experience and a New Address

Into our second year (1981) we had got our bearings, established a personal programme and had learnt how best to use our situation and environment. Our departmental secretary, Major Joy Meehan, made a great difference to the working day and by this time was a friend as well as colleague. Though the tasks carried their own stresses and concerns we were at peace in the office. The major was wholeheartedly in what we were doing and it took a load from our shoulders.

Then we changed house. Up to then we had not enjoyed the facility we had been given, but when a senior officer and his wife retired we were able to move into their detached bungalow in the Botany Bay area. We had heard that the Army was going to sell it as it was on a main thoroughfare to the airport and, at peak times, the city and airport traffic was busy and noisy. This had not worried the previous occupants; I was told they were hard of hearing. As former London-based people, traffic was no problem for us. We asked and received. At the end of the road was the Pacific Ocean where we could swim in a special shark-free enclosure and enjoy the beach; we even swam at night in the summer. There was a good shopping centre round the corner, and a decent garden – it was Heaven! Even so, Britain called me and I would sit with Joy looking out over the Pacific and say: 'I'd swap this for Thornton Heath any time!' It was in this bungalow that my inspirations flowed freely and where I wrote, among other pieces, 'My New Day' and 'At the Edge of Time'. The territorial leaders, Commissioner and Mrs Howard Orsborn, looked in shortly before we left. The Commissioner asked a few questions and saw the garden. We thought: 'They'll move in when we go' – and sure enough it became their retirement home for a while.

Havens and Relaxing Breaks

There was a major on THQ by the name of Stella Green. Through her we became acquainted with Charles and Doris Thornley, who kept a small hotel or guest house in Toukley, upcountry and in a waterfront area. From time to time we were able to take a day and relax there. Later the Thornleys sold up and bought a farm in Richmond in the western suburbs of Sydney. Like so much of that part of Sydney there was history dating back to settlements and convict transportation in the early 1800s. Richmond Church is dated 1820. When we returned for a visit in 1990 the Thornleys took us for a holiday. Then we stayed at their Richmond place for a day or two. It transpired that Charles had discovered that a ruined structure on his property had been a courthouse from the old days. They found clothing and artifacts.

Another quiet retreat we found (also through Stella) was Oxford Falls, off French's Forest in North Sydney and not known even to some of the locals. It is an area of flat rocks with water and waterfalls, very soothing, solitary and far from the busyness of the city, though only minutes away. We would picnic there.

This all sounds as if we spent our lives in relaxation! We worked hard and found breaks important to keep fresh, and as we recharged our batteries for body, mind and soul, we could plan our tasks. Apart from the caravan week we never had a full holiday in Australia. In 1980 Barbara came out to us; in 1981 we went home to the UK for Rosemary's commissioning; in 1982 it was her wedding. So we were always saving up for these trips! However, our official journeyings took us about a good deal which made our work yield interesting visits.

En route for England in 1982 we were given a 24-hour whistle-stop tour of Hong Kong by the local officers commanding. I had sent uniform suit measurements from Australia and was whisked off to a tailor where there was a fitting by what seemed a crowd of Chinese. We saw an Army school and were taken into the steamy, smelly lower city where The Salvation Army has work. We also caught a glimpse of the Chinese border.

Institutions and People

St Peter's was a large charity shop complex. It was based on the US style of collection – repair and resale. The establishment employed quite a number of people. We sometimes spent time (and money) there. The people in charge were Major and Mrs Gordon Abrahams. Gordon was a big, pleasant man.

The William Booth Institute (WBI) was a sizeable social centre with an alcoholic rehabilitation programme. Located in Albion Street it was within walking distance of THQ, not far from Central Station. Many of the staff had been on the programme and we learnt how much of a day-by-day struggle alcoholism can be. We enjoyed and occasionally led one of their weekly meetings. A number came to faith during or after the Alcoholics Anonymous programme and the testimony parts of the meetings were quite special. The sharing was free of Christian jargon, was down to earth and from the heart. To give a relevant gospel talk was a privilege and a challenge. I used to love this work and Joy tells me I had a rapport with the people. On our first Christmas, being away from home and our family, Joy suggested we offer our services at the institute. Major and Mrs Lingard, the officers in charge, were pleased to welcome us. We had thought that helping out would free us from moping about our family back in England; in fact we found that our presence was timely and we were able to be supportive. Part of the AA programme was to send the clients out to an Army farm upcountry. We visited it; there was a pig farming project going on.

A number of the folk on the programme used to attend the Sunday evening meeting at Sydney Congress Hall and occasionally witnessed. Seekers often went forward to kneel at the mercy seat. When we were back there in 1990 we led the Sunday evening worship and a goodly number were there from WBI. Some went to the mercy seat; it was a wonderful occasion for us. Our prayer song was 'O the Deep, Deep Love of Jesus' and I had the pleasure of conducting the band in one of my devotional pieces.

Downtown King's Cross was notorious for its nightlife and sex trade. There was an open-air ministry in which we sometimes were able to take part. One tiny incident demonstrates the caring attitude of the social wing of The Salvation Army. On this occasion Joy and I were walking to the office along a main road. We spotted a man lying in the gutter, well under the influence of alcohol. We got him to his feet and helped him to one of our hostels nearby. He was in a poor state, filthy, ragged and smelly. We took him into the hostel and the officer immediately took him over, saying: 'Come in, my friend, and let's talk about it.' We have a huge respect for all aspects of this work.

We transfer to Paddington Corps
We felt the need for closer involvement at community level and transferred from Campsie to Paddington, an old inner-city corps with a single Dutch officer, Captain Herbert Swans. It was not a traditional centre. We became soldiers 2 and 3 – No 4 was a Filipino girl. The congregation was people from around the community: all sorts, flotsam and jetsam and the aged. When Herbert first went to the corps just a handful turned up to the meeting. So Herbert determined to do something about it: a meal and a meeting. He became a well-known figure downtown and would beg all the food. People at first came for the meal and an afternoon meeting. In due course that order reversed and folk got saved. But Herbert was the despair of the administration: he would not make soldiers – he said, 'They are trouble!' He had a pastoral affinity with dropouts and the gay community, and at Christmas arranged a hot dinner for 400 in the Paddington Town Hall.

Our service was to wash up and help in the meetings (I played the organ) and we both counselled. We would leave home about 2.30 pm and return home around 6.30 pm. I remember fixing a fuse for a dear old lady so that she could boil her kettle. The quarters was partially under the hall and smelt of Herbert's ancient dog. When we left for England Herbert found a flag somewhere and had everyone sing every verse of 'God be with you till we meet again'. There was a farewell cake and we were given a book in which there were cards, greetings and photographs. Herbert was definitely special for that work. Eventually, however, long after we had come back to Britain, he was appointed to a conventional corps and we lost contact. Paddington Corps was closed. It was not a corps in the accepted sense but a centre which specialised in downtown ministry and did a tremendous outreach in the best of Army traditions. These days that kind of ministry has been developed. We loved it. Incidentally the district, which is rich in the period style of iron balconies, has now shed its former type of residents and gone 'upmarket'.

Referring back to community involvement, I was once co-opted to serve meals in a large hospital when a strike was in progress. Also, for some reason which escapes me, we have a photo of me there with an enormous teddy bear. No, not won at a funfair – probably a charity collection. Talking of funfairs, we did once venture into one near Sydney Harbour Bridge, Luna Park. I incautiously mounted some large, swinging boat thing and spent the whole time praying to get off again! In a search for something quieter we went into one of those circular-experience, action-panorama installations. It turned out to be one of those speeding car effects – just what my stomach needed! We gave the rest of the tickets to some children.

The Limelight Department Film
When Herbert Booth (youngest son of the Founder) took command of Australia in 1896 the Army had a Limelight Department with 300 slides and a magic lantern. Herbert anticipated today's multimedia resource by developments which, using a cast of 600 people, produced 120 still and moving pictures on 3,000 feet of film. The pictures were coloured by professional artists. With the aid of the pictures, he lectured on the persecution and courage of the early Christians. Subsequent to leaving Australia he continued to give the illustrated lecture in many parts of the world. Some 80 years later writer and broadcaster John Cleary researched and worked on the film in Melbourne, which we were privileged to view when he travelled to the Sydney headquarters to share his results.

Some 'Specialling' Engagements
The specialling engagements we undertook would be far too numerous to list. I mention just a few that come to mind.

Glen Innes: we flew there in a tiny plane which landed in a muddy field. *Mudgee*: a tiny but active corps with an efficient little band. It was here that after the evening activities we helped the young corps officer to understand a little more about keeping books. *Sapphire City*: in the Saturday night open-air meeting a plague of flies descended. At one point Joy counted 40 on me. *Blacktown*: in the afternoon we drove to a reservoir which was a popular swimming resort. We sat and sweltered. *Chatswood*: a sizeable, self-respecting Sydney corps with a fair number of youth and a buoyant timbrel group.

We must have visited just about all of the corps in the city environs. It could be colourful; we once met a young man who assured us he came from Romanov stock (the Russian Tsar). Another man told us he was descended from the composer Brahms. He looked like him too!

We went to one corps to conduct a young people's weekend. We entered the officer's room (vestry) and I was given a printed programme. Between the items was written, in red, the word 'joke'. The character who gave me the programme wore a huge, round badge (the size of a small saucer) on his chest; it read *Stage Manager*. I said: 'What is this "joke" in red every now and again?' 'Ah,' he replied, 'that's where we have to get people on and off or move props; you have to tell a joke!' I told him: 'You should have invited a comedian, not an evangelist!'

It escalated. The 'stage manager' overflowed his role. A Chinese girl had done rather well with a piano solo and as the applause was considerable I invited her to take another bow – which, as chairman/compère I was entitled to do. The 'stage manager' came across very aggrieved; he felt I had imposed on his preserve. I told him: 'You do your job and I'll do mine.' There was, of course, a need to fill in during the pauses for setting up and Joy and I could see that the audience was a difficult cross-section to have to entertain. The back third was mostly senior citizens, the middle third the parents of the kids taking apart (mostly non-Army), while the front block was children, cubs, scouts and guides. We got them on side (we hope) by reading from a 'bumper fun book' we fortunately had in our bags. Encouraging audience repartee, we said: 'Shall we read some more?' They all yelled 'NO!' in good panto fashion. They probably meant it. The corps officer was nearly crying with mirth.

Rockhampton: the train runs down the centre of the main street. *Brisbane*: we accompanied the territorial leaders for our first Australian Easter. The worship and Resurrection celebrations also included a corps picnic. *Wagga Wagga*: we were so familiar with its unusual name that we could hardly wait to visit. *Rockdale*: during our stay, a nearby corps was commanded by very hardworking and caring people, Major and Mrs Karl and Elva Banks, with whom we have maintained contact. Like so many of their countrymen they were direct. Outside their hall a sign hung saying 'We Care'. After they had moved on they received a phone call: 'How do we stop the phone ringing?' Elva's answer was: 'Take down the sign.' *The Riverina*: almost on the Victoria border, this was a wine-growing area. There was a morbid interest in that there had been a fairly recent murder there related to drug trafficking.

Canberra: we liked Canberra, the capital of Australia and a divisional centre. Among events in Canberra we took part in a holiness weekend series of seminars. *Hurstville*: the corps had a competent band and an excellent songster brigade.

The bandmaster was a British expatriate; I had known his wife and her family as a teenager and had stayed with these people in 1970. The songster leader was Dr Ron Smart, with whom I had stayed in Los Angeles when he was at Hollywood Tabernacle where he was the bandmaster. Currently he was on the staff of the Sydney Music Conservatory, where I appreciated the occasional lunch and chat. With his gifted wife Janette, he was pleasantly supportive. He had contemporary ideas (which worked well) on songster programme presentation and brought the Sydney Staff Songsters to Kettering when we had retired there. Occasionally the Smarts had a music evening at home to which we were invariably invited.

Orange: we were treated to monsoon-like weather here, the heaviest rain we have ever known. It sheeted against the windscreen and we had to stop driving. *Dubbo*: the town, far to the west, gave us the most wonderful sunset we ever saw. *Townsville*: this was the place of gorgeous purple jacaranda trees and a lovely, spacious quarters verandah.

One could go on. These were unique opportunities for us to see the territory, meet and encourage the music sections (if any), conduct meetings and talk with the officers in their homes. Australia can be a vast and lonely place for isolated corps officers and a strong, self-interpreted part of our role was to share with and encourage them. We always assured them that we not talking to them with any official brief and we respected confidences. At the end of our appointment, the reception from the officers – gathered with General Jarl Wahlström for a Congress – left no doubt of their regard and even affection for our presence among them.

The Music Camp

The music camp venue was Collaroy, a large area on the north shore. It had been acquired by the Army years before. An estate with retired officers' homes was here and a conference centre, which is where they held adult and youth events. It has since been modernised.

The music camp did not come under the Music Department but, traditionally, the Youth Department. Barrie Gott had been directing the music for some years with Errol Duck Chong doing the vocal side. Barrie was unavailable in 1980 so I was asked to look after the brass; Joy did the vocal. It was a gratifying week with a festival in Sydney Congress Hall. One evening, around suppertime, the youth took it into their heads to react with a 'glory march'. They had flags and plates as pretend tambourines, marching about the dining hall singing Army choruses. That encouraged us.

The Army Spirit

How can one generalise? We found and enjoyed a solid Army, traditionally-rooted but naturally with slight cultural differences, and feeling its way toward more contemporary forms of outreach and expression. Here and there church growth and country-and-western were in fashion. On TV *The Hour of Power* and broadcasts from California's Crystal Cathedral were transmitted weekly.

The soldiery and officers were very dedicated – indeed, impressively so; we warmed to them. When Commissioner Howard Orsborn arrived he brought with him a small flag which he waved vigorously in meetings. In a few weeks hand-held Army flags had taken off.

Personal Composition

Arising from the annual congress was the stimulus of producing and rehearsing music. Additionally there was the occasional request from the UK (which brought forth the choral suite 'My New Day') and the then bandmaster of Camberwell, Brian Davies, requested a piece for a tour. The result was an apocalyptic work, 'At the Edge of Time', which has since gained wide appreciation. I wrote it in our front room with the aid of a two-manual electronic organ. The theme of the last movement occurred to me just as I was parking the car in a busy thoroughfare. Not far away from our home was a small Army hall which was used for home league and community purposes and was quite often empty. In a back room was a good piano where, when time allowed, I could get on with some creative work.

Chapter Twelve

Fairest Isle

We Come Home

THE year 1983 had begun as usual: very hot! January and February are the worst months for heat in Sydney, running into March and then beginning to cool slightly. One of our fixtures was to be a visit to Broken Hill, the furthest corps west in the territory. Our return home to the UK left this regrettably unfulfilled – but the main planning in hand was the May Congress because General and Mrs Jarl Wahlström were coming to conduct it. Our territorial commander, Commissioner Howard Orsborn, had been seen as a possible successor to General Arnold Brown, but it was not to be. Howard had proved to be a vigorous leader as far as we were concerned and we had a balanced, friendly working relationship with him and his wife Amy.

A good deal of Congress planning came into the realm of the Special Efforts Secretary. We continued with our side of the planning: forming a chorus, inviting participants, selecting music together and so on. A nationalistic song, 'I Still Call Australia Home', was in the charts. We decided that we simply must include it. Also, as the General was Finnish, my band arrangement of 'Finlandia' was appropriate.

The Congress preparations did not mean a relaxation in routine – quite the reverse. I was plodding on in the office and Joy was in a gathering discussing women's meetings when we were summoned to the Commissioner's office. We sat in front of his desk and he pushed a letter towards us saying: 'I have been instructed to give you farewell orders.' We were, of course, overjoyed. Home! In Sydney there is a tall, slim structure that has a revolving restaurant; it is a city feature and very plush. Joy had said that when we received farewell orders we would go and have a meal there. She went straight to the telephone and booked for the same evening.

At that stage I was not notified of my new appointment. It should be mentioned here that, quite a time before this, I had heard that the production of the new songbook and tune book had slowed down. Norman Bearcroft, responding to my lobbying, had for some time tried to get the current Secretary to the Chief of the

Staff to bring me back to the UK to help with things. International Headquarters felt this was not a task 'commensurate with my rank'.

When notified that my new appointment was as Editor of *The Musician* I admit that I was shaken. It was hardly the most tailor-made task, as I had no training in weekly deadlines or indeed any experience in newspaper and magazine editorship. As previously mentioned, my conversations with General Brown had indicated a different direction. The 'war' has its exigencies and it can't be easy, I reflected, moving senior and technical people about in a comparatively limited field. So I determined to give it my best shot. We were going home, and that was the important thing at that time. Lieut-Colonel Malcolm Bale – an outstandingly gifted and extensively experienced former London editor – gave me a crash course and a file of guidance which proved to be invaluable.

Much earlier, and of course unaware that we would be returning home, we had accepted an invitation to visit Auckland, in New Zealand, to conduct Easter meetings. It was a wonderful time but there was a bonus in that Joy was reunited with her cousin Ron who took us around on a whistle-stop tour of the area with its hot springs.

Our Farewell

With General Wahlström coming it was decided to book the Sydney Opera House, a prestigious venue for a concert. Normally we used the Town Hall for such occasions; I liked its touch of Edwardian atmosphere. On the night we could tell that the General appreciated 'Finlandia'. Our use of 'I Still Call Australia Home' with massed chorus and band received a tremendous reception. Towards the falling away of the ovation I turned and faced the audience and did something I would never have dared when we first were there. Following the singing about Australia – with all its nostalgia and patriotic fervour – I brought a small Union Jack from behind me and held it up. The crowd just roared and fell apart. Many knew by then that we were homeward bound and we had built up an excellent acceptance and rapport.

A part of the General's visit was meetings with the officers. Our farewell had been announced and my successor was introduced. He spoke graciously and glowingly of us. At this the whole crowd of officers stood and broke into sustained applause. We were stunned, at once thrilled and humbled. It was an overwhelming response to our ministry among them. The General just beamed.

At the airport a friendly group saw us away. Our only problem was that we ended up with extra, unforeseen baggage: last-minute gifts! We were deeply moved by the generous manner of our send-off, reminding us yet again that we were leaving behind many friends and taking with us a strong respect and affection for the vibrant witness of the Army in that part of the world.

Post Australia

Having been wished Godspeed at Sydney airport, we peered down at the diminishing panorama of New South Wales and settled back for the long flight home – unremarkable except for a break at Bangkok. At Heathrow we were met by Lieut-Colonel Eric Northwood. He and his wife were to become close friends. A long-time friend, Lieut-Colonel Norman Bearcroft, also appeared and was most helpful regarding our baggage. Our new quarters was in Beckenham and had been beautifully refurbished. We decided to link up with Croydon Corps as Leslie Condon, a former colleague and front-rank composer, lived nearby and was the bandmaster there. On Sunday mornings we sat in the gallery. South London was largely unfamiliar territory to us; we had no car, so finding public transport routes was urgent.

Editor of *The Musician*

My new appointment as Editor of *The Musician* was also a new challenge, one of techniques and weekly deadlines, but I was well supported by Major Connie Croly and poet Peter Cooke. The Campfield Press at St Albans was still the Army printing works, which necessitated a day a week there putting the paper 'to bed'. Initially, whereas in my previous experience as Editor-in-Chief of the music publication programme I was totally confident, the new demands promised to be the nightmare of my apprehensions. The printers had moved from the old Linotype offset system to computerisation and, after a draining day at St Albans being shown all the new equipment, I recall tottering home and saying to Joy: 'This'll crucify me!' Soon, of course, things fell into place but I never really relished the assignment, though the creative aspect and the opportunity to write editorial comments brought their own sense of worthwhile contribution.

Reporting and reading incoming contributions provided many lighter moments. For instance, as we parked our recently acquired car near Camberwell to report the commissioning of new officers, the car keys fell into a drain, which meant taking a bus home to pick up duplicates. On the first day in the office the phone rang. It was the leader of a youthful pop group complaining that the paper never gave coverage to their style of outreach. So I said: 'Send pictures of your activities accompanied by testimonies and we'll run features.' In this way we gave quite a lot of publicity to a number of groups.

The South London Divisional Chorus was a superb choir made up of local songster brigades, and once I had to report a concert under the direction of Bernard Adams – the former iconic ISB Bandmaster. During Handel's 'Amen' Chorus the organ and voices parted company, with voices popping in with 'Amen' from time to time. The conductor's sheer control righted things, but how could I print an honest description which wouldn't wound? I was writing about volunteer amateurs. In the end I wrote: 'Only those present will fully appreciate the impact of this item.' Incidentally, Bernard put it on again for his retirement concert. It went perfectly.

Returning to the British scene brought me back into the activity of the territory, some specialling, writing music for events and publication and visiting music camps. We were involved with the first two of the Adult Music Schools under the direction of the then Captain Howard Evans. The Bands Department made full use of me in assisting with rehearsals for Royal Albert Hall occasions, which provided some enjoyable trips and the opportunity to meet up with music sections.

To attend once again the annual Music Leaders Councils was of course a treat but, after many years' involvement, the presence of a new Music Editor (my successor Lieut-Colonel Ray Bowes) caught me on the hop more than once. Old habits die hard; on one occasion a question came up and I leapt to my feet to answer it, then realised that this was no longer my role! Another time Ray was holding forth about singing 'O Happy Day' in a march style and acknowledged it as a good suggestion coming from General John Larsson. In fact, I think the General had produced a fine band arrangement, which we were to sing. Having incorporated this idea in a march some twenty years earlier, I could bear it no longer and, rushing to the platform, stopped Ray in his tracks and exclaimed: 'Whatever happened to "The Scarlet Jersey"?' Forgive me, General John!

Soon after we arrived back in England, Peter Wilson, editor of the Rosehill Music Publishing Company, took Joy and me to dinner at London's Swiss Cottage. I was happy to accept his invitation to publish with him, and for starters I wrote 'The Beacons' for the centenary of *The British Bandsman*. This was a fruitful relationship and was followed by such test pieces as 'Stantonbury Festival', 'The Journeymen' and 'Hymn At Sunrise', which was commissioned for the Cambridge Masters Contest. Additionally I had the privilege of scoring for band accompaniments the brass backings of many of Sir David Willcocks's carol arrangements and writing a selection of the songs from Andrew Lloyd Webber's *Joseph and the Amazing Technicolor Dreamcoat*.

Joy's Role
Joy went to work for the IHQ Property Secretary. Former lawyer Shaw Clifton, then a major and the Legal Secretary, found himself temporarily without his office secretary. Aware that, prior to officership, Joy had worked in that capacity for a firm of solicitors, Shaw obtained her assistance, a service he warmly referred to at the time of my public award of the Order of the Founder, by which time Shaw had become General.

Earlier in our service, headquarters officers' wives had no separate official appointment; one of the pleasing aspects of our work in Australia was that Joy received one. This is a suitable point at which to record her work as the Army's representative on the governmental body, the Women's National Commission.

During her time on the Executive, she was on a committee concerning Violence against Women and chaired a committee dealing with Women and Debt together with Child Support. It was quite exciting for her to visit Downing Street to talk with Prime Minister Margaret Thatcher's Financial Adviser. Arising from this, she was interviewed on TV and recommendations were incorporated into the final legislation. This was a very fulfilling time for Joy.

Major Leslie Condon

It was good to catch up again with Leslie Condon, who had been a close colleague and who, following a valuable period as National Secretary for Bands and Songster Brigades, had been reassigned to the IMED. It was a shock on the morning of Christmas Eve 1983 to receive a phone call – I was in the garden – to tell us that Les had been promoted to Glory in the town centre of Croydon while his band carolling group was assembling. Just the evening before we had hosted a few overseas officer friends who were, as we had been recently, away from their families. One or two musician colleagues also joined us: Norman Bearcroft and Leslie Condon, who came a little late from carolling. I recall that Les was the last to leave, having talked 'shop' and invited me to lead a band 'spiritual' sometime during the succeeding few weeks. His last shared thoughts then must have been of his beloved band, which was totally typical of that deeply dedicated and highly gifted man. With the awesome quality of his compositions I am sure that I have not been the only one to speculate about what other gems he might have produced.

His funeral at Fakenham is a matter of official record, but hundreds of bandsmen, songsters and friends marched in procession to his graveside. It was a never-to-be-forgotten event – a cold, dreary day, but a spontaneous tribute of affection and respect which certainly put me in mind of similar occasions found in Army histories. The thanksgiving service packed Croydon Corps hall. The band played the Condon setting 'Gift for His Altar' which, with its basic song 'I have not much to give thee, Lord', proved to be deeply moving. Croydon Citadel Band were due to tour Denmark and, with the bandmastership temporarily vacant, I appreciated their invitation to direct for the visit. However, other commitments prevented this and Roy Burton (a boyhood friend) carried the task through highly successfully.

Almost immediately following our return to England, Lieut-Colonel Norman Bearcroft had given opportunities for involvement with music schools and assisting in writing for and rehearsing Congress choruses around the country. This was generous, although it doubtless helped him as well! I might add that the colonel astutely invited older people such as Eric Ball so that younger groups would have the advantage of first-hand experience. For the 1985 Territorial Music School, the National Youth Secretary suggested that the Bible studies run in parallel with a major work to be featured by the A Band. The result was

'Romans 8' and I had the delightful privilege of providing a score. I learned that the total experience was highly significant and made a profound impact on the week. The work itself has been widely featured, particularly by the ISB who have recorded it.

In 1985, the New York Staff Band (then with Bandmaster Derek Smith) honoured me with one of their annual 'Profile' Festivals. It was during this visit that I met Peter Graham, a young Scotsman who was a member of the music staff and band. Peter was already making a name for himself, his most recent major work being 'The Dawning'. We used the limited available time to have a useful chat, he sharing something of his future hopes in which I was most interested and, I trust, encouraging. It has been good to see his massive and successful creative career.

The 1986 Songbook and Tune Book

The 1986 songbook and tune book were still in preparation. As far back as 1976 my department had produced a substantial book of congregational songs with the title *Keep Singing!* Looking ahead, it was envisaged that most if not all of these songs would very likely be incorporated into the next official songbook. The book was accompanied by band parts, which would also provide for a future collection. By 1979 we knew a new songbook was due and I had secured from various contributors promises to give us a some arranging help when tune choices were eventually firmed up.

Our Australian appointment of course removed me from membership of the Song Book Council or masterminding the subsequent production. I admit I had rather cherished this operation as a kind of 'career swan-song', and more than once I requested to be brought home to assist with what I gathered was a Herculean task. The publishing programme of the Music Department was expected to continue and the pressure on a small staff was immense. Two years after our return I was finally appointed project co-ordinator, as things had come to a standstill. The music origination had been entrusted to an overseas company and it seemed that the only English-speaking contact had gone. I requested the territorial commander of that country to sort it for us and the stream flowed once more. Then some arrangements had to be rewritten – and all the time there was a fearsomely close deadline. We engaged a home-based origination firm. Their man happened to be in our area for Christmas and he brought the final proofs.

What then happened is an intriguing little incident. The conversation went something like this: 'The page layout leaves space for another tune; is there anything you want included?' Well, there isn't much point on being the co-ordinator if one can't exercise a bit of initiative. I'd noticed, and regretted, the dropping of Purcell's magnificent tune 'Westminster Abbey', particularly as it had gained even more popularity since I had arranged and published it some few years previously. So, promptly, I responded: 'We'll put in "Westminster Abbey".'

My colleague Trevor Davis had already wrestled superbly in producing the metrical index needed for the words edition on account of a publication deadline involving the General's foreword. So it was best to leave administrative channels untroubled. The Chief of the Staff, when privately advised, was gracious – which was as well, as I had forgotten to tell Lieut-Colonel Ray Bowes, my illustrious successor and (fortunately) friend!

Retirement fell due in 1987, which event found us already living in Kettering, having received permission to commute. Why Kettering? We had hoped to find a place of our own, and Joy came across a copy of *Exchange and Mart* which indicated that property in the Midlands was reasonably priced. We still had the cottage in Wales. Typically, Joy got on with her sums and we felt able to consider a move. It so happened that Kettering Corps was celebrating its centenary and, as *Musician* Editor, I was able to cover the weekend and we could house-hunt! We liked what we saw and arrived in Northamptonshire in due course. The move meant that we had enjoyed retirement celebration concerts in London (with staff sections) and also a full house at Corby Theatre where Enfield Band and Hendon Songsters provided the programme. Commissioner Denis Hunter presided over the event which went on until 10.30 pm! At its end Mrs Hunter turned to Barbara and whispered: 'The rest of the evening is your own,' a phrase Barbara has repeated in many other circumstances. Our private IHQ retirement was graciously conducted by General Eva Burrows.

Chapter Thirteen

In Quiet Pastures

Retirement

RETIREMENT brings situations of which one may have been aware – but they begin to bite, many of them linked to age or popular concepts of it. Specialling invitations dry up, and people ask: 'Are you still writing?' You discover that charity shops and stores have no seats for the elderly shopper. The world moves on and the Army with it so you don't know the new songs and perhaps you seldom get to sing the old ones. Everything has suddenly speeded up: drivers race and cut in more, just about everything is online; electronic evolution means you can't keep up with the jargon, never mind the spate of the latest must-have products; newsreaders seem to gabble; visits to the local surgery become more frequent; catalogues of medical cure-alls pour through the letterbox. You read the Gazette in *Salvationist* and find that friends and former colleagues with whom, sadly, you've lost touch, pass away or are announcing their golden wedding. And so on and so on. But while that's true, it's negative. There are so many compensations. While health holds out there is more time to share together, more time to pursue interests, places to explore, new friends to enjoy. Perhaps, after many years of being separately siphoned off into a music section, you are able to sit together in a meeting. Another and important point – there are always people to encourage.

After city life, a smaller town had its attractions. We had moved to Kettering, and out and about we met acquaintances more frequently. We joined the library. Kettering Corps absorbed us into its fellowship. I soon found myself the recruiting sergeant, responsible for the teaching and training of new Salvation Army soldiers, plus spiritual counselling. Joy accepted the task of home league secretary – leading a weekly meeting for ladies. As usual she pushed herself to the limit: planning and leading the meetings, plus outings and regularly visiting (which grew the numbers to 120). She would take her ladies each a tiny pot of homemade marmalade. She also returned to primary school teaching, which was helpful towards financing our new home.

Soon after our return to the UK, Joy had a telephone call from her New Zealand cousin, Ron. We had spent time with him during our Easter weekend in Auckland just before coming home. Upon Joy expressing her delight at his call, he admitted that he had been given just a few weeks to live. Had we been near him we could have visited immediately; what could we do? We asked our International Headquarters for the name and address of the local corps officer, appraised him of the situation and requested that he visit. Ron came on the phone again; he had been visited, and, said Ron, 'He did for me what you would have done.' The funeral was conducted by that captain and a continuing contact made with the family. It emphasises what a close-knit and effective spiritual network is our worldwide Army! It also points up the quality of service our officers give. We were happy to write to the then New Zealand Territorial Commander, Commissioner John Larsson, and express our deep gratitude.

We had expected to live fairly quietly – on my part a little writing, some non-stressful DIY if need be, seasonal pottering in the garden and exploring the countryside. It turned out to be much more. For a start, a new Salvationist friend, David Thompson, one-time mayor, invited me to become a Rotarian. I found myself involved with fundraising and community events and a widened circle of friends and families, which was good for Joy and me in a new town. We organised corps charity concerts at which Rotary members turned out in full force. Shortly after our arrival in the division we were asked to head up a reopened divisional music school at Stowe, which we did for two years. Additionally the divisional commander was keen on the songs of Sidney Cox and it was pleasurable once again to organise, rehearse and conduct local songster brigades in a choral evening featuring those songs. Kettering Band (Donald Manning) took me with it on tour to Norway, and Wellingborough School approached me for music, which included writing material for their Centenary Pageant.

Time was at last on my side to complete my doctorate dissertation on the history of Salvation Army music. Over the years I had gained the resource and knowledge, or knew where to look, so that was helpful. That, plus a folio of compositions, secured the degree. Having also laboured towards the Durham M.Mus, with its seeming endless data on the medieval and baroque together with orchestration, writing examination fugues and 16th-century styles, it was a relief to come to the end of that particular concentration. Joy and I have a fondness for the city of Durham, partly because she is from that part of the world and I went to school in the county. The cathedral, burial place of the Venerable Bede, is a marvellous place of history and serenity.

Some Music Commissions
To my gratification, commissions came my way which brought forth 'Hymn At Sunrise' for the Cambridge Masters, 'A Corunna Suite', a soprano cornet solo 'Hymn and Dance for the Creator' (Sodertalje Band), 'The Beacons' (for the *British Bandsman*), 'The Journeymen', 'Amaranth', 'Images' for brass quartet and 'A Conwy Suite' – plus a variety of smaller items. There was also 'The

Spire at Cowholm' (not my choice of title), which illustrates past scenes of Norwich including a reference to Edith Cavell, who was accused of spying for the British in Germany and shot. 'A Wansbeck Suite for Oboe and Trombone' with a brass group, written to order – an unusual (unmarketable?) combination – failed to yield the requested fee. During a working visit to Bergena, connection with the Manger Musikklag produced 'Expressions' and 'Paskemorgen' (based on a bandsman's tune) and, more recently, for the same band 'Magnificent Thunderbird', inspired by some of the pictures of the Norwegian artist Edvard Munch – as yet unperformed.

Music for The Salvation Army continued a priority and I have previously mentioned 'Romans 8'. But I would also name a cornet/trumpet solo featured extensively and brilliantly by Keith Hutchinson of Enfield, 'A Mid-Century Concerto' (unpublished). On the subject of cornet solos, I withdrew 'Love's Vision', which includes an Erik Leidzén melody and which Terry Camsey played once with the ISB; the score and parts disappeared and have never been seen since. Fortunately Terry had a version with piano accompaniment which subsequently he played extensively and also recorded. I have not been able to bring myself to score it again. On the choral side the International Staff Songsters, under their splendid conductor Dorothy Nancekievill, recorded, among other songs of mine, the suite 'My New Day' which I originally wrote for the Bearcroft era. Then the famous King's Singers recorded a 1947 song of mine 'O Lovely Name'. These resurrections gave me quite a lift.

Music Organisations
Becoming President of the National College of Music, at the invitation of the Secretary, Eric Hayward, has proved to be an enjoyably fulfilling role, attending the executive meetings and the centenary celebrations with prize-giving held in London. In the academic realm there was something of a proliferation of music associations and fellowships of three or four of these extended links with other musicians. As a vice-president of the National Association of Brass Band Conductors, and by personal reputation, my links with the brass band movement were strong. I was delighted when the president (and sponsor) of the band at Kettering (which was originally Munn and Felton, then GUS and was now Rigid Containers) opened his factory for an annual meeting. The band played the current test pieces with conductor John Berryman, and the discussion which followed took place in the presence of Dr Roy Newsome and other Association key figures. It became an excellent opportunity for personal contact. Other than a visit or so, and when I had produced some arrangements for the BBC's *Songs of Praise* in which the band was involved, my link with the band was minimal.

Professor David King of the University of Salford invited me to tutor a group of students who were preparing compositions for degree examinations. Peter

Graham was on the staff. This kind of assignment – advising on compositions – had occupied much of my life and I loved it. The only snag was the train and taxi journey to Manchester. It was with regret I later had to decline a further period, as the journey – now from Kent – was not feasible. One of my star students, Chris Davis, later became a Lieut-Colonel and Principal Music Director of the Royal Marines.

Over the years I corresponded with a number of people, including students who wished to use me for their dissertation. Then others shared their interests or research, and all of this was stimulating. I was visited by a gentleman writing a study about Richard Slater who asked to come and see me. My chance mention of Slater diaries just about revolutionised his work – almost uniquely he gained access to the great man's own observations. Bob Getz, the American biographer of Emil Söderström, exchanges emails on musically interesting subjects; a long time ago his Cambridge, Massachusetts, Band recorded my 'Prelude on "Randolph"'. I appreciated that.

Canada beckoned again, this time to London, Ontario, as guests of Bandmaster Bram Gregson and his wife Ann, with band events there. I also participated in a territorial programme in Toronto, which coincided with a visiting band – Enfield (formerly Tottenham where I had been bandmaster from 1955 to the end of 1959). So there was something of a reunion. Following the festival we travelled some 40 miles to a midnight supper and a waterbed. A trip to Niagara was a must. As, during the visit, Bram had invited a number of the old Tottenham émigré crowd, we had a rare evening of fun and 'do you remember?'.

In his term as bandmaster Bram put in some excellent work. One particular inspiration of his was the production of at least three tapes consisting of tunes from the 1928 Salvation Army tune book. For us they create a special nostalgia for what we call 'the old Army'. Many a time we have played them when out and about in the car. They always bless and lift the spirit. Although I have a good deal of arranging under my belt, I am still convinced that the plain and unworked-over originals carry their own special effectiveness.

Meetings at Clearwater, Florida, followed. We went again to London and this time, staying with his brother and enjoying birthday celebrations, was Eddie – Professor Edward Gregson, later Principal of the Royal Northern College of Music. He is a brilliant and internationally recognised composer and he and his wife Sue have been our friends for many years.

I Rejoin the Music Editors

When Norman Bearcroft retired, Robert Redhead headed up a newly combined Bands and Music Editorial Department. Robert invited me to rejoin the editoral team on a part-time basis, an involvement that lasted until 2005. The staff were very nice to me although I was aware of a large disparity of age! Mostly my task lay in the vetting of new compositions and formulating review comments as appropriate. My experience, knowledge of departmental history and ability to locate earlier music was, I believe, helpful. Robert moved on and I had the pleasure of working under new 'bosses' who had formerly been colleagues. There was a brief time of being without an official head of department and I was glad to be able to provide a helping hand. I look back on this fulfilling period with a great deal of affection, not least the lunch breaks with their animated conversations. Certainly Dr Stephen Cobb, then the Territorial Music Director, did not want me to leave his team and a warm relationship has continued.

Travels And Events

The year 1990 saw the Centenary of the Melbourne Staff Band (Colin Woods); we were excited to be invited to conduct it. Being stationed in Sydney in 1980 we had led the 90th celebration too. That was the occasion on which, there being an air strike, we motored down and were booked for speeding. Just for the record I'd also led the 80th anniversary when I was in that country on a six-week tour. The ISB Centenary took place in 1991, when Colonel Robert Redhead was the bandmaster. He invited me to write something for it, which became 'Spearhead' – a tribute to the band's pioneering role. I haven't cherished this among my better pieces. It is rather long-winded, what with working in solo bits for the 'corner men' based on quotations from pieces in which they had 'starred'. I'm currently revising and slimming it down. On the same occasion it was fun to be a part of a large group of former ISB trombonists in a series of published trombone features which Robert had brilliantly put together. A vivid memory is the Composers Festival, with 86-year-old Colonel Albert Jakeway sensibly forsaking the very high rostrum to lead the massed bands in his march 'Rosehill'. Like many others, I have conducted on some precarious elevations and on this occasion I balanced to conduct 'Logos I' – I hope with sufficient concentration.

Our ruby wedding in 1991 was celebrated by an open house with refreshments, with an evening concert by the family for a few close friends and relatives. Ten years later, for the golden wedding, we renewed our vows in our home. Then in 1992 another link with the past snapped as my old boss Colonel Albert Jakeway was promoted to Glory. A sturdy, outspoken man, he could sometimes be misunderstood but I found him fair and prepared to do battle for his team. He had recommended me to succeed to the editorial chair. After I had conducted his funeral, Mrs Jakeway wrote to my wife and me: 'Dear Joy and Ray... One could feel the warmth and affection which was expressed by all who took part... I knew that the service would be safe in your hands.'

Mid-decade I conducted the retirement weekend of famed Bandmaster James Williams MBE of Enfield. He had been my deputy bandmaster at Tottenham and I valued his support then and his superb cornet playing.

During the Second World War, Bedford (home of John Bunyan) was close enough for me to visit when on leave, my parents being the corps officers.

Around 1944 the Glenn Miller Band was stationed in Bedford and it is a historical mystery that Glenn took off from nearby Twinwood Airfield and was never seen again. I have since been a little surprised that the presence of the Miller Band in Bedford was never mentioned at home as, at that time, my parents were there.

In 1994 a re-enactment Miller tribute show was staged at Twinwood, complete with a uniformed band on a wagon and many folk dressed in Second World War uniforms. It was a special moment when we heard from a former WAAF, who had actually been working in the control tower on the fateful night. We went again the next year when a guest of honour was Beryl Davis who had been Miller's singer during those days of the mid-1940s. Despite her advanced age she delighted the crowd with more than a half hour's stunning solo act. She signed our programme. The event was still being staged annually when we came south.

Life continued busily. I developed an interest in computers, beginning with a Sinclair and booklet picked up at a local boot sale. Then a visit to the Cambridge premises of Jonathan and Daniel Finn, who were producing the Sibelius music programme, set me afire. To press a few keys and hear what one had written, with tone colours, was a dream! In those days the programme was for Acorn computers. Though having now moved on, I still have one – on its last legs! In 1995, Joy became President of the Kettering Huxloe Inner Wheel, the ladies' counterpart to the Rotary Club. She arranged a visit from Richard Yorke, who played a variety of medieval instruments, including Northumbrian bagpipes which were new to me. Unfortunately, that same year Joy was diagnosed with Parkinson's Disease about which, at that time, we had known almost nothing.

The Second World War came into the picture again for the VE Day anniversary celebrations. Kettering had an enormous street party in the town centre to which, as senior citizens, we were invited. There was entertainment by the local operatic society, arrayed in 1940s gear and singing wartime songs in which we all joined. The nearby village of Burton Latimer really went to town. Streets were ablaze with flags and bunting. We watched the local organisations in a grand parade from the Parish Church and felt thoroughly sentimental, whereas the history they were honouring was in fact far from sentimental.

It was a refreshing privilege for we two 'veterans' to conduct the Sunday's meetings at Regent Hall (affectionately known as the Rink) in connection with the same national event. Over the years we have served there many times and have an affection for the corps. After all, we were married there! It is appropriate to stay with the Rink, as in 1997 and 2007 reunions of former delegates to the 1947 Territorial Music Camp took place there. Yes, it *was* a camp, sited on the old Hadleigh Colony Farm and taking its pattern from the United States. By those dates I had the sobering honour of being the only surviving member of the camp staff, but it was a shot in the arm once again to conduct 'Hadleigh Camp' – albeit with an understandably smaller band.

Over the years we have had strong links with the Swedish band of Tranäs which, under Gunnar Borg, made an impression in the UK in 1947 – particularly by their tremendously drilled performance of 'Moments with Tchaikovsky'. So it was a pleasure, again in 1995, for us both to lead the band's centenary celebrations.

Young Salvationist musicians from France, Belgium and Switzerland came to a music camp in Chambon-sur-Lignon, in which we were involved. The programme was on traditional lines, plus drama and musicals. Joy was in her element with the stagecraft, and someone had translated into French a catchy song from my 'Inspirations from the Bramwell Booth Memorial Hall'. It was most interesting to learn that the village – in the non-occupied zone – had aided and hidden many Jewish refugees during the Second World War.

I had long wanted to see Vienna, home of famous composers and the venue of the annual Strauss New Year Concert, so we signed up for a Danube river cruise. Sadly we couldn't get into the concert hall by reason of refurbishment, but an encounter in the horrific Malthausen concentration camp is worth a mention. We had wandered around the place with its cruel associations, and then, in an out-of-the-way spot, I caught sight of a small patch of ground with a young man kneeling. I avoided disturbing him but knelt quietly alongside. When he spoke to me it was to share the fact that his Jewish grandfather had been a prisoner and died there. He had come to pay his respects. We talked a little and then he gripped me in a bear hug. It was a solemn and never-to-be-forgotten moment.

In 2002 Kettering Corps kindly arranged an 80th birthday concert for me and a special birthday spot was also laid on during that year's musicians councils festival in the Royal Albert Hall. This time the Rotary Club chartered a bus, which I felt was good PR for the Army. A half hour was given over to my music, for which Dudley Bright – Principal Trombone of the London Symphony Orchestra – had organised 40 trombonists. A wonderful sound! It was also a thrill to be able to conduct the ISB in my arrangement of 'St Clements'.

To be nearer family we decided to move south to Rainham in Kent. At my last Rotary meeting in Kettering, on the eve of us moving to Kent, Joy came and, to our surprised pleasure, Norman Bearcroft was also there. I was presented with a Paul Harris Award, a recognition of service.

Wilfred Heaton

It is impossible to look back on 2002 without a reference to Wilfred Heaton, a consummate composer whose life and creativity had begun a little earlier than mine and whom I have held in exceptionally high regard, almost in awe. As is unfortunately the way in our filled-up lives we had little contact with one another and, though our far-too-rare and brief communications were cordial in tone, neither of us moved in the direction of anything approaching a communion of mind and spirit. The fact that we lived so far apart was no help! Nevertheless, I have always thought of him as a friend and studied his scores in depth. In this life I shall never find out how he arrived at the amazing intertwining opening bars of 'Contest Music'.

We met briefly in Leeds when I was there to honour the 80th birthday of Bandmaster Harry Kirk. Wilfred was standing at the rear of the hall as I arrived and we said 'hello' and not much more before I was caught up in official duties. Later in 1993 Joy and I were in Harrogate for a weekend break. We had arranged to call on Wilfred and I was looking forward to a good chat at last. At the eleventh hour the visit had to be postponed as he was unwell – a touch of flu I think. We never did get together for that good chat.

A few years back I was disturbed by a review of *The Heaton Collection* (a double CD album by the ISB and Black Dyke Band) which struck a rather sour note about alleged 'rejections' of Heaton's music by the Army's Music Editorial Department; some comments struck me as unjust or negative interpretations. As I had worked in the department for much of that period I wrote an appreciation of Heaton's music (a regard shared by my predecessors) and a refutation from the Army viewpoint – which I then did not publish. Let me give just one instance: there was no adverse word about 'Contest Music' waiting ten years before its use, yet there was a complaint that the festival march 'Praise', submitted prior to the war, was 'delayed'. The *Festival Series* band journal for which 'Praise' was intended was not issued throughout the war and republishing began only in 1947. Issues of four items a half-year need balancing; the processes of approval and printing take time, and other music has its claims, so that a 1949 release date was not unreasonable. Other items were mentioned which were unfamiliar to me, but I take the opportunity here to defend the editor at that time, Colonel Bramwell Coles, who carried out his responsibilities to produce what the Army needed in a most conscientious and thorough manner. Incidentally his score comments of 'Praise' are complimentary to the composer.

The story of 'Celestial Prospect' is intriguing. As some of it is in my direct experience it may fill out an otherwise slightly sketchy account. When in 1967 I was appointed Head of the Music Editorial Department I inherited a set of parts for 'Celestial Prospect' – one of each, minus any solo cornet copy. Manifestly there was no basis for publication. The work had originally come in before 1951 as it was rehearsed and perhaps played by Rosehill Band, which was disbanded that year. At that time it had not been passed by the Music Board (the approving authority) for publication as the solo cornet part was felt to be too difficult for general release.

It was my thought that, considering the technical levels now being reached by our bands, it was timely to publish this obviously fine work. In the hope that it might be possible to retrieve or reconstitute the score, I wrote to Wilfred asking if he could help. I did not know whether the score had been returned to him, though that was standard practice. Wilfred replied that he was unable to assist and did not wish to pursue the matter, and that we should in effect 'forget it'. Presumably there was nothing to be done along those lines, so regretfully I abandoned the project.

In 1985 I visited New York where New York Staff Bandmaster Derek Smith, who had been in Rosehill Band, mentioned that he still had a solo cornet copy of 'Celestial Prospect'. Back in 1951 Derek had come back from a military band tour, an away Rosehill Band weekend, his wedding and honeymoon, to find the Rosehill Band about to be closed down. 'The rest of the parts are back in London,' I told him and explained that the whole thing could perhaps now come together – except that the composer himself had vetoed it. Imagine my surprise when, some time later, I learned that the New York Staff Band had eventually acquired it and featured it and that it was now in print.

In reply to a recent email, Derek told me that Lieut-Colonel Ray Bowes had visited Star Lake and mentioned the work and the missing cornet part. Derek responded as he had to me and produced the part, and Ray took the copy back to London. Then it appears that the NYSB had a centenary coming up and various composers, Wilfred Heaton among them, had been approached for music. In response to the invitation, 'Celestial Prospect' arrived from the composer. By that time Brian Bowen – a valued ex-member of our department – was the New York Staff Bandmaster and he informed me that he wrote out some parts and had the remainder copied by someone else. We can now only speculate how Wilfred was able to come up with what I had unsuccessfully requested. He had either reconstituted it from sketches or discovered the original. Just for interest I would like to have seen the old 'office set' for comparison, though Derek said that 'it didn't seem much different'. I had a helpful chat to Peter Graham, who was then in New York and who refers to this incident in the published score notes. It seems almost certain that it was not the old original that Wilfred sent.

I asked Ray Bowes about it, but it was quite a long time after his retirement. As Ray is no longer in our midst, we can only speculate that Wilfred changed his mind as to a future for the piece. Writing to me at an earlier date and perhaps not wishing to put the department to inconvenience, Wilfred might naturally have been delighted that at last the work was now surfacing. Whatever happened in this little intriguing mystery, although I was not able to see this fine work into print myself, I'm glad it was ultimately published.

Sadly, also in 2002, my brother died. David was my younger sister Vida's twin and a keen bandsman; he had played baritone in Harrow Band when I was bandmaster. Latterly he had been compelled to set aside his assistant band sergeantship due to work commitments which, together with moving to a village some distance away, prevented the full service which was his ideal. We appreciated that members of his former band of Reading Central travelled to play for his funeral in the Wiltshire village church.

Medway Badge of Courage

In the meantime, Joy had determined not to succumb to Parkinson's; it can be depressive. Instead, she was strongly convicted that she should find one or two fellow Christians to form a prayer and support group. The kindness of the *Salvationist* editor allowed her to invite other sufferers to contact her. The group has expanded – some have died of course – but at the time of writing there are some 50 couples, a few overseas, who receive a monthly newsletter. Thus far, by faith, she has never been out of pocket on costs and postage. In 2009 she received a Medway Towns Badge of Courage award.

Eventually they had to say goodbye to me in the Music Ministries Unit. My basic continuing role had been the evaluation of compositions which had been submitted for publication. It was the kind of work I had done for many years and I was well aware of the sensitivity of that situation. Nearly everyone who sends in music or verse does so hopefully, and one bears in mind that these submissions are virtual gifts. There are huge differences of capacity, and even when pieces are well written they may not be suitable for the Army's ministry. I had also sought to continue a working lifetime of offering suggestions where appropriate. This is a subject about which I have already expressed some thoughts. Now the time had come, at the age of 83, for me to leave. Naturally, I missed being at the centre of what was going on, but I have maintained a warm relationship, as have many former staff members. Sadly I no longer see new scores and am now out of touch with developments and emerging composers, as I realised recently when called upon for an article.

Order of the Founder

The UK Territory really laid it on for me! During the 2005 Musician Leaders Councils Festival, 'Sounds of Praise', I received the Order of the Founder, a great honour and wholly unexpected. For a year or two the attendance at both the Sunday councils and its preceding evening festival had been proving a little overtaxing for us, and on this occasion we had not planned to go on the Saturday. However, there was family pressure and, indeed, Joy said: 'Wear a clean shirt!' 'Do you know something I don't?' I demanded, and suspected something was afoot. Then I found out. We arrived early with Rosemary, who had an ISS rehearsal, so we co-ordinated for some tea. They had given me a box seat to which I was led in real VIP style, and I had my instructions as to where and when in the programme I should make my way to the platform. Even after many years backstage I have always felt the RAH corridors a bit of a maze, so I was relieved when my guide came back to collect me.

We stayed in the wings until the moment Joy and the girls appeared on stage, together with the Army flag, Dr Stephen Cobb and General Shaw Clifton. The General made some generous remarks and presented me with the Order. The citation reads: *Lieut-Colonel Ray Steadman-Allen both in active service and in retirement has exemplified the highest possible standards of Salvationist spirituality expressed through creative musicianship, constant encouragement to others, both inside and beyond the Army, and through his preaching and teaching ministry.* It is dated 11 June 2005, and signed by General John Larsson. Joy received a spectacular bouquet of flowers, and then to our delighted surprise the whole audience gave a standing ovation, which seemed to go on and on. A real thrill! I was so glad that Joy and the girls were in it all – they have each, in their own way, been so supportive and inspirational to me. I would be failing if I did not add that each, in their own way, has made – and still makes – a rich contribution to the work of the Kingdom.

Orders of the Founder have not been plentiful, especially for musicians, and I am aware only of Colonel George Fuller, Colonel Bernard Adams, Bandmaster William F. Himes (Chicago), Major Joy Webb (UKT) and my illustrious Music Editorial predecessor Lieut-Colonel Richard Slater who has been termed 'The Father of Salvation Army Music' (he was still alive in 1939 and I wish I'd known). The territory didn't just present the OF – it also organised a concert of RSA music in Croydon's Fairfield Halls on 22 September 2007. All-star participants were the ISB (Stephen Cobb), the ISS (Dorothy Nancekievill), Songster Leader Derick Kane (euphonium) and Songster Leader Susan Turner who sang 'Serenity', which I had written for her many years earlier. Bramwell Tovey, renowned orchestral conductor and composer (and former Army deputy bandmaster at Lewisham), played my 'Fantasia for Piano and Band – Christ is the Answer'. On screen were video tributes from Professor David King (Australia), General Shaw Clifton and Dudley Bright, who, since being in my North London Youth Band, has developed into a gifted composer, conductor, principal orchestral trombonist and conservatory professor.

Even though I was in my 80s invitations still arrived. It was exciting for Joy and me to conduct the 2006 Annual New York Staff Band Retreat. That privilege had been ours in 1998 and we looked forward to the opportunities for sharing. Following the 1998 weekend Jeff Schulz, Music Director in New Jersey, had whisked us to Washington for a whistle-stop visit. We saw the sights, visited the White House – with the rare treat of seeing the band room in company with a Salvationist State Trumpeter – and met former friends including Presidential Staff Arranger Steve Bulla with whom we had enjoyed a connection since Star Lake in 1972 – when student beards were in fashion. We visited Colonel Ernest Miller, an old friend who had been a top PR man for The Salvation Army in the capital city and was due to retire. On his desk lay a pile of beautifully printed, gold-edged cards for his retirement celebrations. From a safe Ernie produced a can of ice-cold soft drink. Our talk became animated and Joy, making a sweeping gesture, knocked her can over. As the sticky liquid began to run perilously close to the pile of expensive-looking cards, I joked: 'We can't take you anywhere!' – and then knocked my can over! In panic, we hastily mopped up. Ernie said:

'You've trashed my office!' and the last picture we have is our host, duster in hand, polishing his very imposing desk. We're still good friends, dating back to associations which included my writing for his band a set of variations, 'Now God be Praised', when the Chicago Band visited the UK in 1968.

To return to the New York Staff Band Retreat of 2006. Ron Waiksnoris and the Staff Band gave us the warm, enfolding welcome which has always been their way in our various encounters with them over the years. Description of a detailed programme would take too much space. It is an occasion when former members come, food is wonderful, the guests share experiences, there is a music reading session –featuring the guest's compositions – with a hugely hilarious evening when previous tours are recalled together with film on screen. Following the banquet I was 'interviewed' by our old friend Lieut-Colonel Norman Bearcroft. This has happened on a few occasions and is now almost a two-man act! The worship service was most intense and inspiring. I had chosen the subject of 'Grace' with some reference to Herbert Booth and the spiritual needs evident in his songs such as 'Grace there is my every Debt to Pay'. It was a bonus to meet the band's Executive Officer Major Richard Munn. His father, Ray, and I were great buddies in our training days; Ray had been the brilliant top cornet in our cadets' band. Serving later in what was then the Congo, he brought his Leopoldville Central Band to Britain for the 1965 Centenary celebrations, making a big hit.

I linked the two previous New York occasions, but in between them the Chicago Staff Band invited me for a weekend. Due to geographical distance the USA Central Territory combined various events into a weekend. During the Commissioning weekend, there were concerts on the Saturday and the commissioning and ordination meetings were held on the Sunday. Many corps and social centres provided items for the morning and afternoon concert programmes, which included brass and vocal groups, dance and gymnastics, drama and comedy. The evening was also musical and more traditional with the Staff Band (William Himes) as the anchor.

A goodly number of my pieces were featured, and I had written 'Noah's Carnival', a piece for piano and band, specially. Deriving inspiration from Saint-Saëns's 'Carnival of the Animals', it is quite light with humorous touches, having a few movements such as 'Camels' and 'Monkeys'. Noah's family has a movement containing the idea that living at close quarters must have been a strain, so the music gets testy, melting into 'There's No Place like Home'. The music is drawn together by the theme 'The Animals went in Two by Two' and in the finale there is a reference to 'Who Built the Ark? Noah Built the Ark'. It was a thrill, after a long time, to play piano with a band once again, and it was well received, especially as humour in music is always a bit risky! As an encore I improvised on my tune 'Blacklands'. Bill Himes and I did a double act, and they were gracious enough to invite me to give my testimony during the commissioning meeting where I used the theme of covenant. The evening prayer meeting was powerfully intense with many commitments. A tender memory is that of the large number of men from various institutions who sang 'Jesus is All I Need'. The whole weekend was recorded on DVD.

Back home I'd had a little annual task as one of the three selection judges for the local schools Young Musician competition. I've never really warmed to the judging business, but it was a useful community contribution and one could be encouraging. I demurred when offered a judging place in the finals but it was flattering to be asked.

Paul Hindmarsh transcribed, for a performance at the Royal Northern College of Music, my 'Chorales and Tangents for Band, Organ and Fanfare Trumpets' which had been written in the 1970s or 80s, and played by the ISB under Bernard Adams with Michael Clack at the great organ of the Royal Albert Hall. I say 'transcribed' but in reality he produced a beautifully computerised printout from my possibly hastily handwritten manuscript. I do recall that the chorale group (fanfare trumpets) scores were in green. Paul was well versed in this kind of exercise, having spent much time reconstituting and finalising the scores left unfinished by Wilfred Heaton. 'Chorales and Tangents' is in the catalogue of Studio Music.

In his 'Baroque Variations', Edward Gregson dedicated each variation to people he held in special regard or who had been influential to him. I am very proud to have been included; he has linked me to 'The Sicilian'. A significant part of 2009 was occupied with writing a series of movements – stimulated by the pictures of Edvard Munch, famous Norwegian artist – for the Manger Band (Norway), with the title 'Magnificent Thunderbird', an appellation once given to Munch by a poet.

Then Lieut-Colonel Ray Bowes had a fall at home. He did not survive the subsequent operation. His funeral and thanksgiving meeting was at Harlesden, north London, where he had been the bandmaster for 60 years. I had been a young bandsman at Harlesden and it was a strange feeling entering that hall again after some 60 years – dating back to the early months of the Second World War. It was my privilege to pay a tribute, and as Ray and I had been friends since we had been billeting partners in the ISB, I was able to speak from the heart. We had been colleagues in the IMED and then he had followed me as Head.

I should also refer to the passing of Colonel Brindley Boon, historian, songwriter and raconteur par excellence. He was older than I and had been a celebrity on the Army scene for some years. We'd known each other well, but he used to tell how, when he and his wife entered the training college as mature cadets, he found it a test of grace to have to clean my sergeant-major office as his work section. When we were both appointed to nearby corps in Kent we were amazed to meet in Maidstone Zoo where we had both brought our Sunday school children. Subsequently, our paths crossed frequently in London where he had editorial responsibilities and then organised the complex 1978 International Congress Celebrations.

Joy and I attended the retirement meetings of General John Gowans and his wife Commissioner Gisèle. I had known of John through the Gowans-Larsson musicals, the majority of which had been published through the Music Editorial processes. I had seen him from afar and then got to know him better in the mid-1970s, when we both served on a songbook council committee convened to choose the interim congregational song book *Keep Singing!* – a 100-song paperback which we published together with band arrangements. John and I became friends and on occasion he could give one a bear hug.

We found ourselves among the invited guests for the finger buffet which followed the retirement meeting. As we were leaving, John shook my hand and said: 'We're coming to live down your way so we'll invite ourselves for a coffee.' We felt it was a gentle way of offering future friendship, and so it turned out. Quite frequently we would share a meal in their Rochester home and in turn they would come to us. Those afternoons were wonderful times for us all, I believe, as with experience of the international Army and common interests freed of official restraints, our times of sharing were a rich meeting of minds and hearts together with much laughter. Additionally, of course, there was the creative aspect of John's gift of poetry and my music.

This was a refreshing period which included such diverse events as supermarket Christmas dinners and, on one occasion, picking blackberries nearby. Then John's memory began to falter. In a meeting we would be singing one of his own incomparable songs and he would be looking searchingly at his songbook. Eventually, nature tragically took its course and we had to say goodbye as John went into care. We hold both John and Gisèle in high regard.

At Chatham Corps our bandmaster was Ray Maycock who, before his retirement as Major Maycock, had held a highly responsible position on the staff of the famous military music establishment Kneller Hall. Ray's story was a fascinating one, from an orphan childhood to his later achievements in military banding. Our then commanding officer was Major Malcolm Westwood, a gifted preacher and poet. He wrote up Ray Maycock's life story, complete with new and appropriate songs for which I supplied the music. Featuring a group of corps vocalists the production was a well-attended presentation. While still in office, Ray had invited me to write a concert march for Kneller Hall and Joy and I had the extreme pleasure of being present to hear it during one of the Hall's famous evening outdoor concerts.

Staff Bandmaster Dr Stephen Cobb has begun a *Heritage* series of CDs in which the ISB is set to record pieces from each decade, starting with the 1930s. Stephen, knowing I had been a staff bandsman in the later 1940s and that I am well acquainted with Army music, invited me to come in on the project, and so I have written the CD notes and we have added to the discs recorded conversational discussions so far for the 1930s, 40s and 50s. Recently 'On Ratcliff Highway' has again been used as a test piece, this time in North America. The latest news to hand is my being in the 2011 radio Classic FM Hall of Fame for 'The Lord is King'. Someone had put the piece forward and, according to the blurb, people 'voted in droves'. Apparently, it was a 'breakthrough' for the brass band and of course, by association, the work's publisher – The Salvation Army – and recording 'artist' – Yorkshire Building Society Band conducted by Dr David King.

An important and stimulating event took place in London early in June 2011. It was the International Staff Band's celebration of its 120th anniversary. Seven other Staff Bands were invited: Amsterdam, Canadian, Chicago, Melbourne, New York, German and Japan. The Royal Albert Hall was full. During the Saturday afternoon each band played for 20 minutes, the evening culminating in the united bands. Looking upon the representatives of nations which, but a few decades earlier, had been locked in a ferocious global war made a deep impact on me. I had the privilege of writing a piece for the band's centenary and this time, of course, made way for newer composers. It was, however, a special moment for me when the bands played my 'In Quiet Pastures', sensitively led by Canadian Staff Bandmaster John Lam – but, oh how I wished I could have had the thrill of conducting it myself with that great band! Barbara was with me and Rosemary was with the Staff Songsters.

With Joy I was among the large group of former staff bandsmen, many of whom had travelled from overseas. So we enjoyed General Linda Bond's powerful Sunday morning meeting for the bands. The singing was just fantastic. It was like old times to share with a fine young man when he came forward during the prayer period. Later, the eight bands marched down the Mall and played in the forecourt of Buckingham Palace. I was on a 'high' when the sounds of 'Crown of Conquest' and 'Silver Star' were heard. The crowd was immense and I hadn't reckoned on hearing so many voices singing along with the trio of 'Silver Star'!

A young uniformed couple graciously helped us to be near the railings, as Joy was finding it tiring. The husband asked Joy: 'Does your husband like bands?' She replied: 'If there's a band, he's there!' It was evident that we were unknown to them, but there must have been a growing suspicion and eventually Joy was asked our names, which of course she gave. Subsequently, we wrote to them appreciatively. The rain held off until the bands marched away, but we were grateful then to our friends the Bearcrofts who secured a taxi and shared it with us back to the Westminster Central Hall.

It is fulfilling to look back on such a variety of experiences, including wartime naval service, Salvation Army officership and work as an editor of music and text. The experiences are wide-ranging: public evangelism and conducting in the Royal Albert Hall and Sydney Opera House are just two very different scenarios. There have been extremes – for example, from contributing to the prestigious

Groves Dictionary of Music, to taking into a hostel an alcoholic lifted from a city gutter, to being humbled and moved to learn that a Belfast family was spiritually supported by the message of my music following the sectarian murder of the father. Some might say: 'Then why didn't you make more money?' to which I can only answer: 'A calling is just that – a calling.'

I conclude with a reference to our Diamond Wedding. We planned a renewal of vows and an 'open day' for visitors. Many expressions of goodwill arrived, including a card from the Queen. I thank God for my wife, Joy, who has always been there with a positive, loving influence; for my daughters Barbara and Rosemary, who shine as lights in a dark place and have done their best to prevent me from turning into a fossil. And I praise an almighty God who has guided me through an occasionally convoluted path of service, often had to overrule my wilfulness and mop up my mistakes, and has entrusted me with a creative gift that it has been a joy to share and which I believe may have helped to make just a little difference.

(Right) With Albert Jakeway in the International Music Editorial Department at Judd Street, 1956. On the wall is the citation for Richard Slater's Order of the Founder.

(Below) Ralph Vaughan Williams with General Wilfred Kitching, Bernard Adams and Albert Jakeway, when the ISB presented his Prelude on Three Welsh Hymn Tunes to the Music Board, 1958. Sadly, by some oversight Ray was not present.

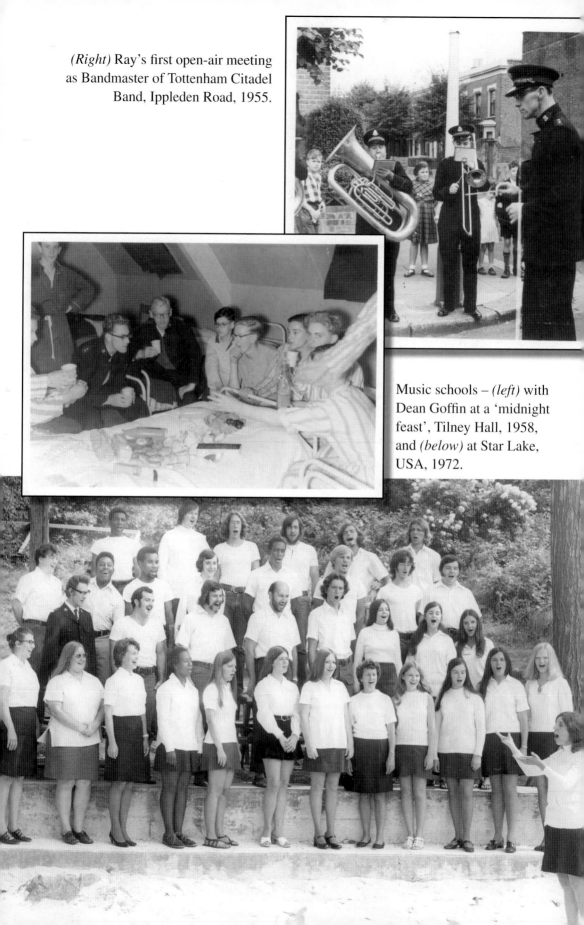

(Right) Ray's first open-air meeting as Bandmaster of Tottenham Citadel Band, Ippleden Road, 1955.

Music schools – *(left)* with Dean Goffin at a 'midnight feast', Tilney Hall, 1958, and *(below)* at Star Lake, USA, 1972.

(Right) Rehearsing for the recording of *Jesus Folk*, Barnet, 1972, including singers Janine Prince, Ruth Pender, Enid Weaver and Rosemary Steadman-Allen.

(Below) A rare photo of the family in uniform – Ray, Rosemary, Joy and Barbara – in the garden at Barnet, 1973.

(Above) The working editor at the International Music Editorial Department, 1974.

(Below) Conducting the ISB in carols for television at the Commonwealth Institute, 1973.

Chapter Fourteen

Daystar

Three of the significant influences in Ray's life – officership, marriage and family life.

Officership

We asked Joy to write about the significance of officership for herself and Ray and how it has made a difference to their lives.

RAY and I first met when we both entered the Peacemakers Session at the Salvation Army International Training College at Denmark Hill, Camberwell (1948/49). Ray's parents had gone through training at the Clapton International Training Garrison, his father (Fred Allen) in 1910 (Conquerors Ever) and his mother (Daisy Gladys Hext) in 1918. Ray's mother and my mother (Elizabeth Sharp) had both been in the 1918 Peace Session, an excuse that was readily up both our sleeves if questioned why we were talking to each other!

I was commissioned as a probationary lieutenant and sent to Thorne in Yorkshire. Ray was Cadet Sergeant-Major of the Standard Bearers Session (1949/50). The Training Principal was Commissioner John Bladin. Commissioning was at 2.30 in the afternoon and the Dedication Service at 7 pm, conducted by the Chief of the Staff, Commissioner John Allan.

One of the responsibilities Ray readily accepted as Cadet Sergeant-Major was that of the Special Service Brigade. This involved witnessing on the streets of London's West End, specifically in and around Hyde Park and Soho, which, in spite of the throng of tourists, was never the easiest part of town. He also made regular visits to some of the Army's social institutions for those with alcohol dependency and developed an interest in the work of Major Alice Sigsworth, who had dedicated her life to the deaf people of Bethnal Green.

Ray had entered the ITC at the suggestion of Colonel Bramwell Coles because it was seen as a demonstration of commitment to the Movement and a way of furthering a 'career' within the organisation. However, by the time it came to Covenant Day on 10 May (the Tuesday before Commissioning on the Friday) – a day on which prospective officers make their final commitment – Ray had developed a much deeper and broader view of officership. Being the son of officers, he was fully aware of the attitude and expectations of an officer. The concept of being in command wasn't new to him either, since he had been in charge of a section in the Royal Navy. Being a Cadet Sergeant-Major was a different matter. This involved caring for the spiritual welfare as well as the physical welfare of his charges.

The Commissioning souvenir programme comments that: 'The training authorities are constantly aware of the challenging fact that the cadet's nine months' training is "training for life". Consequently, it is the aim of all who influence cadets that, during their days in the college, they may above everything else become firmly established in their own personal convictions about God, his provision for their soul's development and his purpose for their lives.' It was a high ideal. This grounding still forms the basis of Ray's approach to all that he does. First and foremost is the sense that his music has meant something in eternal Kingdom-terms, and this has been an important balancing factor in the awareness that other, non-Army, composers receive greater public acclamation.

Ray bound himself to Salvation Army regulations which, in those days, prevented interaction either creatively or financially with the wider world. However, that commitment to the Army world had given him a platform and freedom in a different way.

Ray came out of the ITC as a full lieutenant and was sent to Sheerness as its commanding officer with a probationary lieutenant, Frank Wingfield, as his assistant. It was a long year of separation for us but he took his duties seriously. I was the commanding officer at Forest Hill from March 1951 and we were married four months later in June, after which Ray was appointed back to the International Music Editorial Department. So we never shared a corps together. I would have enjoyed corps work with Ray if only for the year he was at Sheerness. Instead, I had to adjust to being a housewife until I also became a mother when Barbara was born in 1953 and Rosemary in 1955. Headquarters wives were not allowed to work unless for the Army, and there were no posts of any consequence. But I was glad to be Ray's wife and that made up for all that might have been.

I had wanted to be an officer since the age of five, so much so that I had asked my mother to make me a captain's uniform to wear on Sundays. I officially offered for officership when I was 15, but I wanted to be a unit with Ray and give him the support he needed. I entered into what I could do wholeheartedly, and the local neighbourhood in which we lived became my sphere of pastoral ministry. People would knock on the door for help and support. Neither of us lost sight of our separate calling as officers. We shared 'specialling' engagements. Invitations usually included me. Ray has always expected others to recognise me and my ministry. I always had a job at the local corps – assistant young people's sergeant-major at Tottenham Citadel, corps cadet guardian at Wood Green, songster sergeant at Hendon and songster leader at New Barnet.

As Ray was at his desk in the IMED during the day and went to the piano in the evening, we lived what must have seemed apparently separate lives; but it did not affect our marriage, because we shared a belief in the purpose of God for our lives. We always had something to talk about when we met on his return home from work and we always began the day with a Bible reading and prayer, into which we brought Barbara and Rosemary. Our Christian faith and identity as officers were mutually helpful components. When it was hard for him I would encourage him, and when it was hard for me he would encourage me.

When Ray became head of the IMED he again regarded the position as his ministry. Although the responsibilities had all the facets of music production – evaluation of manuscripts, copyright, deadlines and so on – in corresponding with contributors he sought not only to advise and encourage on matters musical but also, where appropriate, to touch on spiritual issues. He maintained strong convictions about the use of music in the Army's ministry; it had to lead people to Jesus. He found tremendous fulfilment in steering the publications. General Arnold Brown told him: 'You keep the Army's musical resource in balance.'

There were occasions when, like some of his predecessors, he prayed with office visitors. He has needed to make plenty of opportunity for personal creativity. In 1979 he got very tired and was in danger of suffering from burnout so he let it be known that, while he was not asking for a move, he would be willing to accept a change of appointment, something other than music.

The administration was not really desirous of change but a new appointment came, to Australia East (Sydney) as Secretary for Evangelism plus Secretary for Music (Music Personnel and Congress Festivals). This was a blessed time for both of us, as never before had we been able to share our ministry in quite the same way. Additional to the demands of the appointment, we were able to visit and pray with officers and they soon learned that we didn't break confidences. Quite frequently we were on our knees and took 'More Than Conquerors' as our motto. At no time did Ray allow people to refer to his officership lightly and he knew that he had the support of fellow Salvationists in that territory. Ray especially loved the William Booth Institute (AA) and conducting meetings at the Sydney Congress Hall, as there was always a large squad of people from the institute who, in sharing their experience, had a refreshing language all of their own.

Occasionally he has been called upon to counsel people in difficult situations where there is a need for Christian wisdom. He is living out the song to which he wrote the tune 'Blacklands': 'He giveth more grace as our burdens grow greater.'

Ray wrote our sessional song, which ends with the quotation from Isaiah: 'And my people shall dwell in a peaceable habitation and in sure dwellings and in quiet resting places.' Our officership hasn't always been peaceable or quiet, but we have come to retirement as officers and 60 years of marriage with the calm security that trusting God brings. I thank God that he brought us together and that we have had a happy home.

JSA

Marriage
A reprint from the Southern Star *(a USA Salvation Army newspaper)* 1988

SHE noticed him as he played the organ. Then and there she knew that this was the man with whom she wanted to share the rest of her life.

The problem was that his glasses were broken at the time so he didn't really see her at all! Once the glasses were repaired their love story unfolded and they lived happily ever after. Forty years later the joy they find in each other is readily apparent. They hold hands as if they were married only yesterday.

She was Cadet Joyce Foster and he was Cadet Ray Allen. It was 1948 and they had recently arrived at the International Training College in London. They were married in 1951 as soon as regulation would allow. As Ray Steadman-Allen he has become a legend among Salvation Army composers for the innovative music that seems to flow from his pen. But it is impossible to understand the man behind the legend unless you understand his relationship with his wife. They are much more together than they could be apart.

While Mrs Steadman-Allen has been supportive of Ray's musical gifts and has encouraged him to develop them to the fullest, that is only one of her contributions to his life. Ray has always appreciated Joy as a person with her own identity and capacity. Anything she wanted to do that would give her fulfilment has always been fine for him. Those are not just words. When they were first married Ray was appointed to the Music Editorial Department at International Headquarters and Joy had no appointment of her own. Ray encouraged her to find a teacher for speech training and drama. She worked at it until she got her licentiate from Trinity College in London.

He revealed his commitment to her development in practical ways as he cared for their daughters Rosemary and Barbara or washed up when she was away from home. Today, Joy serves as home league secretary at Kettering Corps. On home league day Ray does the cooking and washing up so that Joy has the day free to concentrate on her ministry with women.

However, Joy realised that Ray needed time for his music after he came home from a day's work at the office. 'His music,' she says, 'is part of him. There is no way he could breathe and be alive without creating music.' So she did not expect him to do an equal share of home chores. Instead she gave him freedom to get on with his writing.

They have never had appointments that were closely linked. The ministry which they have shared has therefore been the result of their own desires, not of any official decision. They have always been actively involved in their local corps and often conduct meetings.

They prefer 'specialling' together and one of their chief regrets is that they never had the opportunity to serve as corps officers together.

The ministry they share has a great deal to do with the kind of people they are. Both Lieut-Colonel and Mrs Steadman-Allen reveal a concern for individuals that is genuine. People feel safe in sharing personal problems and frustrations with them.

By anyone's standards the Steadman-Allens' marriage is successful. When Ray and Joy are asked to explain why this is so they acknowledge that there has always been a certain magic between them. A love that defies analysis. At times that magic may have worn thin as the pressures of life intensified but always they have managed to recapture it. Even so, as they speak of their marriage it becomes clear that they have worked hard to maintain that magic. Joy points out that they have always tried to be honest with each other and to talk things through.

They have always remained sensitive to each other's moods too. 'If I opened the door for Ray when he came home from work,' Joy said, 'and if something had bothered me he would say right away, "What's the matter?" And I have done the same for him. We have sensed something and we have talked about it. We've never gone silent on each other.'

All four Steadman-Allens have very strong personalities. It would have been impossible for them to live together under one roof without someone cutting across someone else from time to time. Conflicts arose then and continue to arise even now that only the two of them remain at home.

Ray describes some of these differences as head-on collisions but neither Joy nor Ray can go to sleep until they have cleared up any problems. 'We couldn't survive knowing the other was unhappy,' Joy declared. 'If we are not friends the whole world is cloudy for both of us.'

With all that honesty there has also been a respect for each other's privacy and space. Joy stressed the importance of such respect. 'When Ray was at the office I would never go into his briefcase and there is a drawer that I would never go into at home because that's his,' she stated.

Has either felt the need for space or time to be alone? Ray was quick to respond: 'No. I've never felt crowded. We tend to fend off the world rather than each other. We are so grateful because we can be comfortable with each other. We don't have to keep up any forced conversation, we are relaxed with each other and are able to communicate with each other how we are and where we are.'

Ray spoke of something else that has helped keep them close: 'I think touch is terribly important – the physical presence.' This aspect of their relationship is easily visible as they walk hand in hand or stand with their arms around each other. They remind one another often that they are there and that they care.

They have helped each other grow in many ways. Each supported the other's intellectual pursuits over the years. Also, they have differing personalities that have proved complementary. These differences have enriched them during their years together.

'I could have been frivolous and light,' Joy said. 'I have a very positive attitude to life and Ray has steadied me a bit. I haven't always seen problems attached to anything, but Ray has pointed out things I should think about. He has also made me more intellectual. Before Ray I thoroughly enjoyed light classical music – but now I enjoy heavier classics much more than I ever imagined I would.'

'I'm more cautious,' Ray pointed out. 'She will take a plunge before me. She has helped me take risks.' He also describes Joy as bubbly. Her lightness has been a relief during moments of darkness that have occasionally gripped him.

Over a year ago the Steadman-Allens added an 'R' to their names. They are enjoying retirement thoroughly. He has more time to devote to composition. She serves as The Salvation Army's official representative on the government-sponsored Women's National Commission – as she has done since 1984.

What they love most about retirement is the time they have to be together. Joy singled out one moment in particular. 'Now we can loll over a second cup of coffee in the morning. We have always prayed together, but now we have time to discuss what we've read.'

For the Steadman-Allens André Maurois's words are true: 'A happy marriage is a long conversation that seems too short.'

(This article is based on an interview conducted by The Musician *at the USA Southern Territory's Music Institute in Camp Grandview, Jasper, GA, on 12 August 1988. Lieut-Colonel and Mrs Steadman-Allen (R) were the special guests of the 1988 institute.)*

Family Life
Dad has always taken pride in calling himself 'pater familias'. *Rosemary and I have compiled some of our memories of family life. R indicates Rosemary speaking and B indicates Barbara!*

B/R We had a happy childhood. Mum and Dad lived out their Christian faith honestly in all areas of life, and this gave us great security. They were a strong unit operating within the same value structures, so we knew that whether we went to one or the other, the answer would be the same! They were fair, reasonable, consistent and always loving. On the whole it was Mum who disciplined us, but we knew better than to try and play Dad off against Mum! We were never 'in the way' but we seemed to know when to make ourselves scarce. They always made sure that they had a catch-up time every day before dinner when Dad got in from a day at his desk in the IMED.

Mum would compile a timetable of jobs on the back of an envelope for the day, and at the end of the list would be 'get washed and changed' ready for Dad coming home. After dinner, Dad would say (in what became a family motto): 'I just want to catch the daylight hours,' which got him entirely out of doing the washing up as he disappeared into the garden. He has always enjoyed gardening. (He also likes painting and does it rather well.) A further disappearance was into the room where the piano was. We remember, as children, lying in bed listening to him playing over fragments of pieces under construction. This was a natural part of our lives. At his 85th birthday celebration in the Fairfield Halls, Croydon, Dad said that he hadn't been there for us because of writing music. We don't remember that at all. Our experience was that he *was* there for us whenever we wanted him to be. Dad always supported us in whatever we did and was committed to our best. He has always adored us. So when Barbara was at Wycombe Abbey and travelled to London for trombone lessons with Sid Langston at the Royal College of Music, he went across London every week to have coffee with her. He played for her ARCM exam. That was a team effort!

Saturday afternoons had a regular routine when we lived in New Southgate – mooching round Wood Green shops, then coming home for tea and watching programmes on the television together – *Dixon of Dock Green, Take your Pick, Dr Who* and *The Avengers*. Mum and Dad have always enjoyed our company and we have enjoyed theirs. Grandma (Mum's side) commented that if we were staying at her house in Hastings (in Blacklands Drive, which is how the hymn tune came to be named), and one of us went into another room, quite unconsciously the other three would migrate there too. That may be from a shared dislike of the possibility of missing out on something!

Mum and Dad had an honest relationship which was sometimes fiery but quickly resolved and that was the way it was for us too. 'Atmospheres' were never a feature; quarrels were never carried over into the next day on the basis of 'don't let the sun go down on your anger'. Saying sorry and being forgiven were praised, so apologies were not a 'climb-down'. Irritations were quickly forgotten, and as a consequence we can't remember any! Dad would sometimes get stressed and express his frustration but we don't remember him getting angry with us.

Our parents have always had a strong sense of commitment and would honour prior commitments even at their own expense. Once they were offered a free holiday with friends in the Holy Land, but because they had agreed to conduct meetings at a Salvation Army corps during the holiday, they turned the holiday down without question.

We remember Dad and Mum's last meeting at Tottenham Citadel Corps. We were just about to move to Cheltenham in January 1960. Dad was bandmaster. I (Barbara) was somehow aware of the highly charged emotional atmosphere, as children are, and can picture the event in my mind even though I was so young.

Tottenham was the place where we changed our name from Allen to Steadman-Allen. Dad came in and asked us to try to spell our 'new name' (27 August 1959). Not a difficult task for a four- and a six-year-old....

We remember the 'Trade' Christmas parties ('Trade' is Army-speak for Salvationist Publishing & Supplies – SP&S): British Rail films and the special meal in the canteen next to the furnishing department smelling of new carpet in the basement of Judd Street. We remember the times spent at SP&S officers councils at Sunbury Court and the smell of perishing rubber in the annexe and the table tennis. A highlight of our year was going to the Christmas carol concert at the Westminster Central Hall, which was followed by a ride on the top of a bus along Oxford Street and Regent Street to see the Christmas lights, and then home in the dark on the train. It was a great childhood.

Dad was always keen to learn about technical aspects of life such as car mechanics. On one occasion he had attended a few night-school sessions for car maintenance. We were on the North Circular Road and, stopping at traffic lights, he noticed the car alongside had seized up. He got out and asked if he could be of assistance. The owner gratefully agreed to his opening the bonnet and peering into the engine. Observing a hanging wire, he joined the wire up in faith and suggested that the driver started the engine. To our (and his) immense surprise, the car started. He got back into the car feeling ten feet tall! We would tease him by knocking on the side of the car door while he was driving, always successfully provoking his panicky voice: 'What's that?' It is a sign of his exceptional patience with us that he never got cross with our teasing.

R I enjoyed being at home. Dad and I would travel up to London together as I went to the City of London School for Girls. Apart from a six-month adolescent phase when my irritability resulted in us getting into different compartments in the train, we had six and a half years travelling companionably together. Those journeys were memorable, as we were on the same wavelength and enjoyed each other's company.

B I was at boarding school, so didn't have anything like the practical interaction with Dad that Rosemary had, because they shared that time in a special way. I came home for holidays, so the dynamic was different. My sharing with Dad has been more through common interests so no anecdotes come to mind. I had worked as a proofreader in the IMED during one of the holidays; then it was a matter of comparing the handwritten manuscripts with the printed version and correcting it with red pen, white notes on a green background (rather than black), more restful on the eyes. Dad did come with me to buy my first car, an Austin A40 held together with haematite and string and mostly Plastic Padding, bought on a dark and rainy night in Finsbury Park for £40. Not much knowledge between the two of us, despite the night school, but a lot of fun.

R I remember Dad getting me a Saturday morning job at Judd Street (SP&S) in the millinery department. I would also work during the school holidays there and loved being at work with Dad; even more so when he got me work in the IMED for a couple of summer holidays. I can remember the smell of the place, and the great atmosphere in the department. It was a really happy time and I enjoyed going down to the restaurant for the meal breaks, and sometimes going out for a walk with Dad round the area close to Judd Street towards Bloomsbury. Dad has a real interest in the historic parts of London.

B We both love stories of a non-line-toe-ing father as he stood in the corridor and answered a loudspeaker making a silly announcement in SP&S or, on one occasion, bent cutlery in protest at a less than acceptable lunch.

R Dad has a great sense of humour and we laughed a lot as children and still do. He isn't a joke teller, but comes out with some great one-liners. He is witty, quick and lively minded. The main thing is that he and Mum have always been best friends. They are a loving couple who cherish each other and cherished us as children and still do. Once, despite it being snowy, pitch black and sub-zero temperatures, Dad put up an iron double swing in the garden in the middle of the night when we had gone to bed one Christmas Eve. The next-door neighbour came out to give him a torch! He did it so we could get up on Christmas morning and be able to play on the swing, which we did at 6 am (poor neighbours).

R I remember camping holidays when the inevitable rain meant we had to entertain ourselves or, when it wasn't raining, the evening country walks, often marching to our own singing of Army tunes. Often we would have a family concert when everyone did an item. Of course, we were very proud of hearing Dad's music at Army events. We grew up always aware that he was someone special and extraordinary and that somehow it was a privilege to belong to him and Mum. That kind of awareness continues to have an impact on us. We are aware that our identity is inextricably linked with being Steadman-Allens.

B We have both inherited an analytical mind which can sometimes appear to others as being critical (and if we were honest, sometimes is) but it is an acumen that genuinely seeks to know and improve something. Something of the perfectionist has rubbed off on us, but it is more a deep desire for and appreciation of excellence rather than the punishing demands of perfectionism. Dad has a thirst for knowledge and a curiosity about the world. He always looks at the books on our respective shelves and finds something that will engage his attention.

B/R We grew up with the language of music as naturally as the spoken word. He taught Rosemary to play the cornet (the usual 1960s type of cornet, with string holding some bits on!) and insisted Barbara call keys by their proper names rather than as a number of sharps or flats. He also encouraged us hugely in our various attempts at composition and he always took us both seriously, enjoying our efforts and engaging with them, suggesting how they might be improved or where we could go with them.

R I remember him asking me whether I meant two written parts to be independent of each other, and feeling very proud when he saw this intention as positively creative. He was also keen to include us in what he was writing and would often call us into the front room to ask us what we thought of a bar or phrase, even listening to suggestions we made. We both felt (and still do) like a million dollars when a suggestion set him thinking.

B Not surprisingly, we all share musical interests. I enjoy the technical language of music and engaging with Dad in conversation about his current piece or the compositional challenges I seem to set myself.

R I never studied music academically but I am fascinated by the mathematical side of it, which is why I share with Dad and Barbara a passion for Bach. Surprisingly, for a set of confirmed brass players, we all picked up string instruments: Dad plays the viola, Barbara plays the violin and I play a cello. It was an annual Christmas treat for us to play together, with Mum on the piano. Definitely not for an audience! Dad wrote us a 'Family Suite' one Christmas, when Mum, Dad and Barbara had all clubbed together to buy me a cello, and every year Dad or Barbara would add a movement. We love to play music when we get together.

B/R We absorbed a sense of musical discernment from an early age, and learned to assess what was technically good through comments Dad made and through compositional advice he gave us. Our early days were mainly spent hearing a wide range of classical music, and of course we were exposed to what he was writing all the time. Dad sometimes played (and still does) blues and jazz and boogie because he loves those styles, and we would stop whatever we were doing and go and listen. He would just have such a great time, and it was brilliant to listen to him. He has a very wide-ranging taste and we have been encouraged to be the same. His acute analysis of music (he analyses all the time while listening) did mean that his negative view of contemporary pop music in general filtered through to us. Barbara analysed *Abbey Road*, her first album, as consonant with sonata form – not a mindset normally found in a 16-year-old.

R Dad was very interested in The Who. He said that the middle movement of 'The Lord is King' started off with 'Who' chords! Much later he got the job of revising the *Tommy* book.

B Mum's father's trombone was there to be played when Wood Green YP Band needed a trombone player (an old Army peashooter that I still have as a family heirloom), so I inevitably drifted towards the trombone. But it does seem as if trombone chose me rather than vice versa. I think there have been nine trombone players in the family, one of which was Dad in the ISB at some stage in his life. Dudley Bright was my motivation for improving when we played together in the North London Youth Band under Dad as the bandmaster.

B/R Dad has no hidden agendas; but there are many facets to his personality. He is prepared to weep at beautiful experiences that take him by surprise, like a sunset, and is touched deeply by spiritual things, whether music or words or seeing someone at the mercy seat. He is also quietly and practically responsive to the vulnerability of individuals he encounters and we have seen him communicate with alcoholics at the London train stations with care and personal interest.

B He does like to be in control (imagine four people who are strong-minded and share this characteristic!) but Rosemary says that she and Dad only get into conflict these days over map reading. Any irritation I experience is generally because I want him to see things my way or do things as quickly as me, so it's not really deserved by him at all, and is usually short-lived. He doesn't like change but that doesn't mean that he holds out unreasonably if it's important or if he sees the point of making the difference.

R Dad's DIY skills were good but it was more productive if we kept out of the way. He cooks an OK curry and his spag bol isn't bad. We were once on holiday in a caravan as a family. We had been put to bed and Dad had the temerity (and lack of wisdom) to say: 'You know, Joy, I've never been what you might call full on this holiday.' Characteristically dramatic, Mum made him a whole packet of instant mashed potato and two fried eggs and set the food mountain in front of him. Barbara and I were giggling because we could hear all this going on.

B Our parents were prepared to sacrifice personally for us, because they believed God had a purpose for us too. It was a sacrifice they never referred to and of which we were largely unaware. I needed the discipline of boarding school and went to Wycombe Abbey, which I loved. Rosemary went to the City, which suited her down to the ground too. That we didn't go to the same school (which would have actually been financially easier for them) was a measure of how they treated us as individuals and in terms of what suited us best. It's characteristic of how they treat everyone, which is why they make everyone they meet feel so special.

B Dad gave both of us great advice which we both ignored and then regretted. He said that I should do music but I trained as a science teacher. I finished the three-year teaching course, but within my first year at teacher training college I had applied to do a BMus at Birmingham University. Dad supported me greatly in this venture. Never 'I told you so'!

R We share a love of books; Dad is an avid reader. I certainly share with Dad a fascination for the morbid. I did a psychology degree and worked at Broadmoor Hospital as a psychologist for a year, then went to Cambridge University to do a Master's degree in criminology. I got a place and a research grant to do a PhD at Cardiff University to conduct research into police carrying weapons. When I decided to forego this so that I could enter The Salvation Army's training college, believing that the course would not help me as an officer, he advised me to do the PhD first. Stupidly I ignored that advice. He has always been really interested in what we have done and encouraged us.

121

R   Dad is a wonderful grandpa and both my children, now adults, love him dearly. They appreciate his humour and his intelligent interest in what they are doing and are very proud of him – and he of them.

B   Underpinning everything has been our parents' strong, unwavering commitment to us and to each other. Our childhood was like a secure rock which has proved a solid basis for us to be able to survive the knocks of life. It has to be said that our strong sense of identity as a family makes us fearful of the day when one of us isn't there any more, even though we all share a strong belief in actual life after death. We are all the stronger for knowing that in the new Jerusalem there will be new bodies for us all, but in a very real way now we are incomplete without each other. We don't live in each other's pockets, but we are close. We don't seem to ask each other questions much when we get together, we just glide into parallel living alongside each other.

R   Barbara and I share characteristics which relate to having been brought up seeing Dad's work acknowledged in a public arena.

R/B   In the privacy of the home environment we have known without doubt that we have always been loved unconditionally. Mum and Dad have provided a Christian home in its very best sense for us, not burdensomely religious but deeply spiritual. The family prayers that continue to be at the start of each day and which include us when we are with them at breakfast time are symbolic of the glue that has held us together. We have laughed and cried together. It is a real home created by them and characterised by love, care for others, loyalty, fun, and above all, faith and commitment to God.

B/R   As we look back, we both believe that we have enjoyed the kind of family life that fulfils the purpose of the family unit, where parents reflect God and his loving ways to their children for a while till they get on the road for themselves. This doesn't mean our parents never made mistakes, but we have been modelled the truth of a Christian life lived out for real. We were brought into the world by our parents, and into the world of our parents, and we have wanted to share it.

Chorus of 'Peacemakers' Sessional Song (1948)

Will J.Brand

Ray Allen

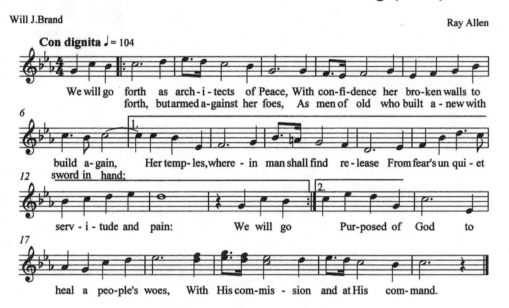

Con dignita ♩ = 104

We will go forth as arch-i-tects of Peace, With con-fi-dence her bro-ken walls to
forth, but armed a-gainst her foes, As men of old who built a-new with

build a-gain, Her temp-les,where-in man shall find re-lease From fear's un qui-et
sword in hand;

serv-i-tude and pain: We will go Pur-posed of God to

heal a peo-ple's woes, With His com-mis-sion and at His com-mand.

Evangelism Department
Music Ministries Unit
Tel: 020 7367 4960   e.mail: *stephen.cobb@salvationarmy.org.uk*

The
Salvation
Army

United Kingdom
Territory
with the Republic
of Ireland

SC/bc

13 April 2011

Lieut-Colonels Ray & Joy Steadman-Allen
8 Chalky Bank Road
Rainham
Kent
ME8 7NN

Dear Ray and Joy

What a real privilege it is to send greetings to you at this time!

It seems that you have been part of my life in some way for so many years.   During
my teenage years we were at Hendon Corps together and our two families enjoyed
many Sunday night suppers together.

Since those days at Hendon our paths have crossed on many occasions from being
at college at the same time as Joy to a meaningful period in my life as Territorial
Music Director when we were colleagues together in the Music Department.   I think it
was during this time I truly understood what a giant Ray is; not just as a musician but
also as a man.   It was at a very low point in my time here when Ray was the first to
offer support and counsel.   I also learned just how much Joy's 'behind the scenes'
care and concern for others was happening in a very discreet manner.

It has been very clear to me just how much you love one another and how you have
truly modelled a strong and secure Christian marriage to people such as myself.   It
was so good to see you both recently at Chatham where again Ray's expression of
love and care to Joy was so clearly evident.   Thank you for the many lessons you
have taught me and continue to teach me.   Your influence is still significant and I
thank you both for that.

I would love to say that on the occasion of your 60th Anniversary we have invited the
eight staff bands from around the world to meet in your honour – but, of course, we
haven't.   However, it does mean that people like me will not forget your anniversary
on 2 June.   I hope it is a beautiful occasion for you and your family.

Elaine joins me in sending our love to you both.

Yours sincerely

Dr Stephen Cobb
Territorial Music Director

Territorial Headquarters:
101 Newington Causeway
London SE1 6BN
Tel: (020) 7367 4500
thq@salvationarmy.org.uk
www.salvationarmy.org.uk

a Christian church and registered charity
No 214779   and in Scotland SC009359
Founder: William Booth

with heart to God and hand to man

PART TWO

Harmony

Chapter Fifteen

'Patriarch of Salvation Army Music'

Andrew Blyth

THOSE who are familiar with or connected to The Salvation Army's rich musical heritage will be aware that the title 'Father of Salvation Army Music' has been given to Lieut-Colonel Richard Slater OF (1854-1939). Slater was the first Head (Editor-in-Chief) of The Salvation Army's Music Editorial Department (MED) which commenced its work in 1883. It was his duty to meet the needs of the fledgling Army musical activities and then to resource the groups with a regular handful of religious songs and ballads, together with band arrangements in monthly issues. His energy, spirit and commitment to the cause were exceptional and the foundation he set still has an influence and impact today. Slater's ideal was that 'the Army should be strong, always able and powerful enough to meet its own musical requirements without being indebted to anybody'[1].

This ideal was to turn into the ongoing mission of the MED which has continued to develop the following facets of Salvation Army music, these being principally:

1 The editing and arranging of music for publication.
2 Meeting the needs for music groups within The Salvation Army to minister on a week-to-week basis.
3 The development of music composition and style.
4 The development and encouragement of composers within the Movement.

In essence the International MED has become a 'parental' figure since its inception. It has nurtured many Salvationist composers and provided music for bands and songsters to prepare and produce on a weekly basis. Richard Slater's title of 'Father of Salvation Army Music' is a worthy title but it may be a little misleading in the sense that it is the Head's role to help and encourage those who pursue this musical service. The subsequent occupants of the chair have had basically the same remit as Slater and so my preference for his title would have been 'Founding Father of Salvation Army Music'.

It was in 1946 that RSA became a member of the IMED under the leadership of Colonel Bramwell Coles. His duties would have included proofreading scores of both brass and vocal music and any compositional tasks given to him by the Head. The department has historically included writers who are able to provide, on a regular basis, compositions which would feed into the published journals. The new recruit had already had music published before his appointment to the MED, with the march 'Gladsome Morn' (*General Series* 1257) published in 1945.

His first term with the department was brief, as he entered The Salvation Army's International Training College in 1948, but he returned after a year as Cadet Sergeant-Major and a period as corps officer at Sheerness.

His appointment as Head of the Department in 1967 was greeted with an enthusiastic response. The departing Head, Lieut-Colonel Charles Skinner, commented: 'I commend to you my successor who brings to his task outstanding ability and wide experience.'[2] Will Burrows lyrically quipped: 'Major Ray Steadman-Allen comes to the office of Head of the Music Editorial Department well-known for his outstanding compositions which have delighted the aesthetic, tested the executant and teased the musical plebeian. But he comes also as a long-standing member of the Music Editorial Department, as one willing, unknown, unsung, to submerge his own talent to the needs of the Department. For both of these qualities we welcome his appointment.'[2a] He succeeded a long line of distinguished Salvationist musicians with a rich heritage of music publishing and innovation behind them. *The Musician*, then The Salvation Army's periodical for music groups, reported the appointment of its new Head: '[RSA] brings to his new task wide public experience and his musical ability has been widely acclaimed.'[3]

It is to be noted that at the time of RSA's appointment, The Salvation Army had experienced more than five generations of music-making. This had resulted in the development of composers who had a greater opportunity for academic training, the ongoing progress of many 'amateur' Salvationist musicians who had learnt their craft looking, hearing and gleaning their musical knowledge from Salvation Army published works, and a greater need for Army music to reflect the different styles and genres of the time. The emergence of what was then called the 'rhythm group' was gaining pace with Major Joy Webb's leadership of the Joystrings pioneering the way for a different style of music within the Movement, and this needed catering for. Of course, this was allied to the constant demands of an Editor-in-Chief to provide resource material for the ongoing brass and vocal publications on a regular basis. RSA was an established and leading composer among the ranks and this needed maintaining – the editor needed to be seen to lead from the front! The difference of qualities of a composer and those of an editor is important to note, and not all brilliant composers make good editors; this was not the case with RSA who would effectively run the two disciplines side by side during his leadership.

One of the main responsibilities of the editor (as already outlined above) is to maintain and develop a relationship with the composers who offer their work. In his first year as Head, RSA had a chance to reflect on this relationship when challenged about the need for new composers within Salvation Army journals. In a letter to *The Musician* he wrote: 'My responsibility is to cater for the requirements of Salvationist musicians and maintain as high a degree of excellence as is compatible with practicality. If received contributions are unsuitable there is no alternative but rejection. No Salvationist editor relishes doing this; he is only too well aware that the majority of these creations cost a great deal of thought and endeavour, with no expectation of reward but a desire that the God-glorifying ends of the Movement shall be served.'[4] The sentiment is honest; the editor is always seen as the villain as many compositions often are just not good enough to merit publication; for many this can be a painful process – rejection is never easy! RSA continues in his assessment of introducing new composers in the same article with the following: 'New names mean encouraged writers for the future, and we are not so short-sighted as to discourage those whom we hope will give us more and more suitable works.'[4a] Numerous new writers emerged during his leadership. His encouragement was a key factor in their development. An article, which was written by a student of the National School of Music at Tylney Hall and published in *The Musician*, recalls the following:

> 'It is good to feel that people are interested in us. Today we were surprised, as into our band rehearsal walked Major Ray Steadman-Allen, Head of the Music Editorial Department. He had heard that some budding composers are to present their efforts later in the day, and out of sheer interest had come to hear them.'[5]

The relationships forged with these writers were the inspiration for many to pursue the art of composition not only as a 'hobby' but as their profession. I know from personal experience the time, patience and care he has shown me in my own humble pursuit of musical composition. I, along with countless other students, have benefited from personal and written instruction often followed up by an encouraging phone call to see how the work is coming along. It was not just that RSA recognised the need for future composers within the Movement; it was far more than that. It was a genuine pastoral approach in aiding and developing a practical subject. His criticism was concise but always followed up with a positive way forward. This has not stopped since his retirement and he is frequently called on by music students and composers for practical and pastoral help.

Of course, there are times when the composer will not agree with the editor's review of their work and diplomacy is needed! Some people will just not believe that their work is not good enough, maintaining that 'it has come from God';

others believe they are doing the Movement a favour by sharing their music, when actually the favour would be to have forgotten it and moved into something else other than music! At all times Ray's handling of rejection letters was to the point but never discouraging, always recognising talent. In an article entitled 'Passing Notes', he comments about this predicament of rejection: 'The difficulty is to convey something adequate to the disappointed author or composer in a few lines of a letter.' He continues by describing the music he received: 'What I dislike is the watery collection of clichés, the threadbare sequences and ageing cadential formulae; the feeling that it had been said before, often much better.'[6]

What makes the Salvation Army publishing process unique is that most of the contributors are members of the Movement. The main difference between publishing music for The Salvation Army and that of any other publishing house is that many of the contributors would have known RSA personally. This personal acquaintance was either through weekend campaigns, family connections, corps service, etc. It was important then for him to dispense disappointment appropriately and with a firm but fair approach.

Regular Journals

One of the regular tasks of the MED Head is to select music for the ongoing journals, which are primarily brass and vocal. The music published is not bought by the Army from composers. It is freely offered as a contribution to the Army for its work. Before publication is possible, the works are considered by a board which, although it includes practising musicians, is non-technical. It decides as to the suitability of the work for Salvation Army purposes. Once it is approved, it is the Head's role to decide when and where to place the work into the journal. This has been an established model for most of the existence of the department. The volume of musical output has been and continues to be sizeable, with more than 50 brass titles and 25 vocal titles per year. During the leadership of RSA this was between 25 brass titles and around 80 vocal titles. This does not include the 'extra' publications that are included and worked on during the year. At present (2012) there are more than 800 manuscripts awaiting publication and I would imagine that, at the time of RSA's leadership, this number would have been far greater. His stewardship of these journals was carefully and sensitively handled, even though there were a number of challenges to be considered. The brass journal was graded in terms of size and difficulty, from the small band edition of the *Unity Series* through to the full band and technically challenging *Festival Series*. This system seemed to be established and needed little tinkering with – people knew what they were subscribing to and there was a quality of composition coming through that helped in choosing a balanced musical programme for each issue.

The mixed vocal journal entitled *The Musical Salvationist* catered for songster brigades. This quarterly edition had a page restriction and required selecting music which suited the varying degrees of capability within each group. This 'all ability selection' is not an easy task, and when asked about producing a journal that catered for all abilities RSA said: 'By grading a magazine publication, the sale of each individual grade is reduced. This leads to increased costs; it deprives the better group of easy material unless they make additional purchases. This increased cost probably leads to "playing safe" with a negative result of stifling experiment and progress. This, in turn, produces a level of conformity and in due course the better groups lose interest and no one buys anything.'[7]

The argument for a graded series was growing apace as there was a widening gap between brigades with little or no musical resource and those more adept in their music-making. Ray's strength of argument held out, with a continued selection of music in each quarter, which always catered for all groups to feature in at least half of each issue.

The Challenges

There have been those who challenged the way The Salvation Army published music. This included the thorny subject of Salvation Army brass music being restricted to Army use only (a restriction which is now lifted). It is my opinion that RSA struggled with this issue personally. His compositional craft was at its height, and the opportunities that could have been afforded him with a new open ruling would surely have benefited him greatly. The 'establishment' thought differently, however, and in a letter published in *The Musician* the question about this subject, entitled 'Army Published Music', was tackled with due consideration and care. But the personal torment could be seen by the Head as he responded: 'The view is that music written for Salvation Army bands should be retained for the purposes of its creation. Anything the writer might comment beyond this would be purely his personal opinion which is out of place in an official statement.'[8]

Throughout his life Ray has seen himself as an officer first and a composer second. For this reason he submitted to the Army's embargo on composition for outside bands in particular. However, it was never a policy with which he agreed. It was never a matter of who got the money – he would have been happy for the Army to have benefited – it just seemed to be fundamentally unfair that some were allowed to compose for non-Army contexts, but commissioned officers like himself were not. He still feels that The Salvation Army's compositional ethos of preaching the gospel and a commercial ethos seem to be incompatible.

It seems a little ironic that since this regulation was lifted in 1992 by the then Territorial Music Secretary Major Robert Redhead, the music of Ray Steadman-Allen has been featured heavily by contesting bands, and this has included a number of CDs dedicated to his music. There are very few composers that have the standing and reverence that RSA has today among the brass-banding fraternity both within and outside the Army musical circle.

There was also the problem of supporting the future and moving on from the past. For many years tonic sol-fa was included in all songster journals, but this was to be dropped in 1975 for a clearer and cleaner typeset. This was a move that caused a fair share of reaction among some older Salvationists at the time but paved the way for the formula that we still use within our vocal journals to this present day. When challenged about the dropping of tonic sol-fa and subsequent feeling that the department was 'losing touch with the musical sections within the territory', RSA responded: 'I am sure, not before time, the editor of any Army paper dwells in no remote ivory tower. He may himself soldier at and doubtless "specials" at corps where all is not big and bright. If his productions are out of touch, his family, or his colleagues, will soon tell him!'[9] This was a statement borne out of experience! The Steadman-Allen family were all active Salvationists serving and leading music sections. RSA had held various songster leader and bandmaster appointments along with his wife, Joy, who also was a participant and leader within the songsters. Both his daughters, Barbara and Rosemary, had compositions published by The Salvation Army and took an active role. In an article written in *The Musician*, Joy commented: 'For the past two years I have been songster leader at New Barnet Corps and this is a privilege. Needless to say, my husband fulfils his marriage vows in being a tremendous support in all these activities.'[10] Experience of 'the front line' was crucial in the support and knowledge of what was needed. The many weekends spent ministering the gospel were also times when the editor could hear and determine what was good (and bad) among the music forces and how to act appropriately.

There was also a growing need to provide music for rhythm groups. This was catered for with a monthly series of songs appearing in *Vanguard*, a magazine catering for the younger Salvationist.

The late 1960s and early 1970s also saw the emergence of the The Salvation Army's stage musicals, employing the talents of Captains John Gowans and John Larsson. These were hugely popular among Salvationists around the world and music was duly edited and collated in quick time for publication. Not only did RSA support this venture, but his brass band arrangements of the musicals also employed a clever move to make this music mainstream among the Army banding fraternity. Pieces such as the selections 'Hosea' (*General Series* 1654) and 'Jesus Folk' (*Festival Series* 362) became standard fare for most bands to play. His recognition of Larsson's ability to write a beautiful melody became evident, with many of the melodies arranged or transcribed for band by him. This was popular music within the Army being played and sung regularly and it was music literally on demand.

Leading the way
Historically, every Head of the Music Editorial Department has been a composer of note. This includes the Salvation Army 'March King' Colonel Bramwell Coles

through to the tunesmiths such as Colonel Richard Slater and Colonel Charles Skinner. It was vital that the Editor lead the way. This had its advantages on two points – in ensuring that there was sufficient material for the journals and in providing suitable music for the size and style needed. Pieces such as 'Sparkling Slides' or hymn tune arrangements such as 'Bethany' were a direct result of the department needing something 'quick' to fill a publication deadline.

The second point was that many composers would follow the compositional style and lead of the Editor, particularly RSA. It must be stated again that there were many within the era of RSA's leadership who were 'amateur' composers, although there was a growing number of those academically trained. For many it was what they heard within The Salvation Army which affected their compositional direction. This was a concern for RSA and he was always keen to show composers within the Movement that there was a whole expanse of music awaiting them outside of their corps (church). In an interview in *The Musician* he noted: 'The men who have done the most vital work for the Army in expanding its musical horizons have been fully aware of music outside the Movement. Our early composers obviously knew the classics but it was Eric Ball who brought, as one of his valuable contributions to his generation, much more of form – beyond the selection, beyond the march, beyond the variation, to the suite and sonata form. Men like that help to expand thought.'[11] The reality for many, though, was that established composers within the Movement were seen as people whom they would try and emulate in style and direction. It is to be remembered that the corps was the heart of community activities and that people spent most evenings within the walls of The Salvation Army, either rehearsing or in weekly meetings. This meant being surrounded by a musical world which revolved around the music of Eric Ball, Wilfred Heaton, Dean Goffin and Ray Steadman-Allen; these in essence were educated composers educating the aspiring composers!

For many, the strength of RSA was his ability to bring different musical genres to the attention of the Movement. This was done with due care, for there was always a minefield of opinion within The Salvation Army of what music style was 'suitable' for presentation of the gospel. It is important to remember that it was not only larger-scale works such as 'The Holy War', 'Christ is the Answer' and 'On Ratcliff Highway' for the brass band and vocal works such as 'My New Day' that became pieces of huge significance in terms of widening the Army's musical horizons. Pieces such as 'Wonders Begin' and 'Sparkling Slides', which featured the trombones and employed a 'big band' approach, were innovative and daring but were hugely successful with many bands. Among vocal music, his extended setting of verses from Psalm 144 entitled 'Blessed Be The Lord My Strength' became a favourite 'anthem' among many songster brigades and his strong rhythmic setting entitled 'Why I Love Jesus', which was adapted for publication, became popular among varying abilities and size of groups.

He was instrumental in introducing new hymn tunes to the congregation's attention with the publishing of band arrangements. This was formed as part of a series of hymns found in the *General Series* under the occasional title 'Congregational Tunes'. These tunes had become part of mainstream church hymn singing and would transfer well into an Army setting. This idea developed and ultimately gave rise to a supplement, published in 1976, entitled *Keep Singing!*. This included 102 tunes with both piano and brass band accompaniment, and many of these were to be featured in the next edition of the songbook published in 1986.

Ray's ability to produce music at an enviable speed and quality helped greatly in supplementing the constant publishing demands. This is shown in many of the journals he selected during his tenure as Head. For example, the *General Series Band Journal* (1597-1600) for August 1969 contained the following titles:

1597	Meditation	While my Heart is Tender	Ray Steadman-Allen
1598	Trombone Ensemble	Wonders Begin when the Lord Comes In	John Larsson Arr Ray Steadman-Allen
1599	March	To the Front	Brian Bowen
1600		Congregational Tunes No 6	

Here we have the programmatic, light and up-tempo 'Wonders Begin' supplemented by a beautiful and meditative setting of George Marshall's tune 'South Shields' entitled 'While my Heart is Tender'. This is a fine but not unusual example of a balanced approach to publishing music within a journal while still providing high-quality music fare.

Ray's selection of music was usually met with positive responses; of course, there is never going to be universal approval – what is good for one is not necessarily good for another – but his planning was always meticulous and thoughtful. An analysis of the *Triumph Series Band Journal* for September 1969 was greeted with the following comment: 'Once again Major Ray Steadman-Allen is to be congratulated on his practical approach to the planning of this journal. It is no easy matter to care adequately for the variety of bands for which the journal provides, yet this collection of four pieces is attractive and of good quality.'[12] It is interesting to note that contained within this issue was a functional and attractive selection entitled 'The Unfurled Banner' from his own compositional pen.

Another affirmation of the work put into a journal was found in a review by Bandmaster Roland Cobb of Hendon. He commented: 'On studying the latest *Festival Series Journal* I am once again overwhelmed with gratitude, privilege and pride that such fine standards have been maintained by our Music Editorial Department over so many years. I have often thought that the department has been wrongly maligned on occasions; but when one pauses to think of the tremendous responsibility its members carry in directing our musical thinking, we as Army musicians have a great deal to thank our colleagues in the department for, and long may they continue!'[13]

Conclusion

RSA's tenure as Head of Music Editorial ended in 1980. He had served in this appointment for 13 years but his association had lasted for well over 30 years. During the intervening time no fewer than 180 of his own compositions for bands and 150 compositions for vocal groups had been published by The Salvation Army, to say nothing of the many works that were still awaiting publication and those that were prepared for Royal Albert Hall events and numerous other special occasions. The sheer intensity of responsibility, musical output and day-to-day office procedure for such a sustained time was perhaps a catalyst in which to seek different avenues of service within The Salvation Army.

He was leaving The Salvation Army's music publishing in rude health with all the brass and vocal journals maintaining good sales. His final comments written in *The Musical Salvationist* vocal journal for January 1980 state: 'Vocal standards have perhaps never been higher; this is a constant challenge in the direction of the widening of the range so that the technically advanced may be catered for, while there must be no overlooking of the needs of those with more modest attainments. In the 12 years during which I have been responsible for the production of this and other of our publications it has been my aim to provide music that will best serve the Army's ministry, to have a positive approach to new trends and to encourage new writers. This maintains a tradition of close on a hundred years for we look forward to 1986 when *The Musical Salvationist* celebrates its centenary. Relinquishing editorship at a time when circulation is at a peak 26,000 copies per quarter, I seize the opportunity to record my appreciation of an editorial team that, although changing in personnel over the years, has given such fine and helpful support in so many ways.'[14]

His new appointment took him to Australia as Director of Evangelism for the Australia Eastern Territory. He had been the father figure to many Salvationist musicians for many years and thankfully that was not to discontinue. After his tenure in Australia and his final appointment working on the 1986 edition of the Salvation Army tune book he continued to be instrumental in helping and offering advice to composers and arrangers. An invitation to join the newly merged Music Department (incorporating the Bands Department and Music

Editorial Department) as a reviewer of new manuscripts brought with it a chance for my own generation to experience his enthusiasm and energy for the day-to-day work that had been so integral to most of his professional life. This has continued and I, as the present incumbent involved in heading up the Editorial Section of the Music Ministries Unit, have benefited from his vast knowledge, his warm friendship and his caring ministry. This working relationship has showed me more of the man, not just as someone whose talent I admire greatly but whose leadership of the department was, and continues to be, a blueprint for my direction and leadership. His pastoral concern for Salvation Army music and its musicians was of prime importance to him and that alone should be placed amongst anything he has achieved musically. His role as editor was intertwined with his ministry as an officer of The Salvation Army, and his approach to dealing with office personnel, composers and countless Salvation Army bandsmen and songsters was of the highest integrity and standing. I have felt it a huge privilege to say that I know him and have gained so much from him.

Lieut-Colonel Norman Bearcroft, in paying tribute to RSA before his departure to Australia, commented: 'I heard someone say to RSA, "I'm glad you are now going into evangelism" – I thought that he had always been in evangelism! There is rarely a meeting held during which RSA is not heard at some time, either in the praise, prayer or sharing part of that meeting. To name "In Quiet Pastures", "By Love Compelled" or "His Guardian Care" will prove the point. To be more correct, it is not RSA who is heard but the Lord Jesus speaking through one of his very dedicated messengers.'[15]

Lieut-Colonel Bearcroft's statement is still true today; RSA's influence compositionally on The Salvation Army will never be matched. I would note, though, that his achievements within the Music Editorial Department should also be recognised in the same breath as his compositions. This association with Army music publishing, which commenced more than 65 years ago, has helped nurture and develop the future of The Salvation Army's musical work and will never be fully appreciated. He has dedicated his life to this avenue of ministry and has justifiably become the 'Patriarch of Salvation Army Music'. He is not just a 'father figure' but someone whose musical and editorial output has touched every Salvationist musician that has ever played or sung within the Movement. That influence continues to this day. Ray regularly submits compositions and supports the ongoing work to a large extent.

In a further quote from his final comments in *The Musical Salvationist* 1980 he said: 'The musicians of The Salvation Army are constantly in our prayers and, as far as my wife and I are concerned, the change from the position of international music editor will make no difference to our belief that God will continue to use the great potential of music and song, and our concern that – in Army music-making – there will always be a clear sense of the right priorities.'[14a]

His priorities and influence continue and he is the inspiration and benchmark that we within the Salvation Army music fraternity strive to emulate.

References

1   Music Commission   27 January 1916
2   *The Musician*   29 April 1967
3   *The Musician*   22 April 1967
4   *The Musician*   25 November 1967
5   *The Musician*   29 August 1970
6   *The Musician*   9 December 1967
7   *The Musician*   30 January 1971
8   *The Musician*   9 August 1969
9   *The Musician*   30 January 1971
10   *The Musician*   4 February 1978
11   *The Musician*   23 June 1973
12   *The Musician*   31 January 1970
13   *The Musician*   27 September 1980
14   *The Musical Salvationist*   January 1980 Volume 94 Part 1
15   *The Musician*   12 January 1980

(a)   JOURNALS PRODUCED BY MUSIC EDITORIAL DEPARTMENT 1967-1980

BRASS	VOCAL
Unity Series	*The Musical Salvationist*
Triumph Series	*New Songs for Male Voices*
General Series	*New Songs for Children's Voices*
Festival Series	*New Songs for Women's Voices*
	Songs for Home League Singers

EXTRA EDITIONS	CONGREGATIONAL SONG BOOK
The Festival Soloist	*Keep Singing!* (1976)
Youthful Praise (1969)	
Harvest Praise (1974)	
Youth Songs (1979)	

Andrew Blyth is a composer and Assistant Territorial Music Director for the UK, and is responsible for publications for the Salvation Army Music Ministries Unit. He is also currently serving as a Salvation Army bandmaster at Gainsborough.

Chapter Sixteen

The Vocal Work of RSA

Cliff Matthews and Dorothy Nancekievill

WHENEVER the name of RSA emerges in a conversation it is very likely that the discussion will revolve around many of his major brass works such as 'The Holy War' or 'The Lord is King', with perhaps some reference to smaller works such as 'In Quiet Pastures'. There may perhaps be mention of 'Blessed be the Lord my Strength', but this is likely to be a simple, passing comment before moving on to further exploration of 'Lord of the Sea'. In many ways this is natural, as brass music tends to be more complex and offers a composer wider opportunities to explore form and technique than much vocal music – though try explaining that to lovers of 16th-century counterpoint or analysts of the vocal fugues of Bach! This is particularly true within The Salvation Army, where functionality and communication is hugely important for the singing groups within the organisation and where over-complication can cloud that purpose of expressing spiritual truths through the combination of music and words. The tendency to elevate instrumental music above vocal composition is a situation that exists throughout the world of music, where symphonies are more likely the topic of technical musical debate among the wider listening public than perhaps oratorio.

In the work of RSA, the situation is compounded by the very range of styles and techniques adopted, as well as the often imaginative and personal ideas used in the construction of that music. This variety can be heard from the perfectly formed four-part hymn tune of 'Blacklands' through to the more significant demands on his compositional skill when he was asked to set the doctrines of The Salvation Army to music for the International Congress in 1978, the more contemporary (for its time) arrangements for the *Trumpet of the Lord* record or the more instrumental style of 'Blessed be the Lord my Strength'. This range of style and technique is remarkable and unique within the Army.

It is no surprise that vocal music has played such a large part in RSA's output. From a young age he grew up involved with singing. He joined the singing company at the Army and, while at school with an encouraging and good music master, he was able to participate in such classics as Vaughan Williams's 'Let us now Praise Famous Men' and Sullivan's 'Orpheus and his Lute'. He was also a vocal soloist at this time.

He was, therefore, surrounded by music and much of this was to have a great influence on his creative impulses. He recognised, in contributions of George Marshall, how his music communicated within the context of The Salvation Army. The music of Erik Leidzén and Eric Ball was suffused with great craftsmanship. Ray was also becoming a pianist of quality which added a further range of influences, giving him different ideas of musical line, rhythm and harmony. There are some pieces where the piano is used more predominantly than in a simple accompaniment role. One example of this is 'Vespers', a seemingly straightforward piece but where the piano is integral to the conception. To describe and analyse RSA's contribution to the vocal repertoire of The Salvation Army is therefore no easy task.

Perhaps the place to start should be in his melody writing. The hymn tune 'Blacklands' has already been mentioned. This straightforward, four-part melody demonstrates a very simple idea of melodic structure so often found in his work. Rhythmically it is repetitive, each line having a very similar rhythmic shape. The first two lines complement each other, each having a slightly different ending and cadence. The third phrase has a rising sequence leading to the highest note at the very beginning of the final line whence it descends to its rest. With such classic and beautiful shaping, it explains why it has remained a popular and frequently sung congregational song.

Blacklands (SATB 591)

Where the music and words are wedded together in quality and import of meaning, then great songs emerge, such as in the songs of Schubert, Schumann or Fauré. Clearly the sentiment and depth of liturgical works also have this effect on composers, where belief acts as a mortar for the two elements. Bach's *B Minor Mass* would act as a prime example of this fusion.

RSA has confessed that the quality of the words plays a large part in his inspiration and it is difficult to find many works where the words are not at least significant. Where the poetry carries a simple but effective meaning this will often be reflected in simple and effective settings. One example of this is 'Lead Me, Saviour'. Even here, despite its immediate impact of being the straightforward strophic setting, the need to emphasise elements of the text musically is apparent in the downward melody at the words 'Gently down the stream of time'.

Lead me, Saviour.

Gen - tly   down the stream of   time,   Sa - viour   lead   me   all   the   way

Word-painting occurs with some regularity throughout RSA's output. Sometimes this is very subtle, such as in 'Love's Baptising' – one of those delightful songs which has dropped out of regular use. This starts as many ordinary songs of its time did – a strong melody with the basic harmonic outline of many other contemporary pieces – until the words 'Jesus, how lonely is thy dying' when, through a small chromatic change in the harmony, it augments the interval of the fifth (very James Bond theme-like). The inference, through this small change, is suddenly of a darker mood, until it moves back to a more traditional lightening of atmosphere and into its straightforward chorus. Just this minor change lifts the song above the ordinary.

Many more examples of the use of word-painting can be found throughout his output. These include passages such as the chromatic melismatic writing in the chorus of 'Humbly I Wait', emphasising the sometimes restless nature of the soul's inability to relax and wait for the leading of God.

Humbly I Wait

SOPRANO ALTO

Hum - bly   I   wait_   Hum - bly   I   wait_   Wait_____
I
wait

TENOR BASS

Incidentally, the way in which the words 'What would'st thou have me to do, dear Lord' are repeated with greater intensity also underlines the importance of the music reflecting the emotion rather than just being a melody on which words are hung.

Another celebrated example is in 'Blessed be the Lord my Strength', where the text relating to the lute is conveyed in vocal interpretation of the characteristics of a lute – if possible! There is a link with the brass world where 'The King's Minstrel' evokes James Bateman's use of the banjo.

'Blessed be the Lord my Strength' was one of the more challenging pieces for the aspiring songster brigade and fitted well into the now defunct idea of

'The Songsters' Section' within *Sing to the Lord*, which succeeded *The Musical Salvationist*. Each edition included pieces which were more involved than might normally be expected. This allowed composers to flex their musical muscles a little while not being way above the abilities, with some work, of most corps groups. Here is an area where RSA may be considered to be a little under-represented. 'Blessed be the Lord my Strength', though, was an unusual piece which set itself apart from many others by its sheer instrumental context. The opening vocal unison melody is melismatic in a way not generally employed by Army composers. Later in the piece, as the music returns to the opening theme, this musical device is extended further, so emphasising the instrumental quality of the voice.

Blessed Be The Lord My Strength

Imitation is also employed in two short passages. The musical phrases are short and often angular. These themes are not isolated from the accompaniment which regularly continues either the rhythmic shape or melodic line of the vocal part, thus integrating the piano and voice as one unit rather than just melody and accompaniment. The shifting focus is clearly heard in the section with the words 'I will sing a new song'. Yet in the moments where the piano is (ideally) removed, the writing becomes identifiably vocal in concept. This is particularly true of the ending where the expanded texture releases the full impact of the voices on to the listener. In short, this piece includes many compositional skills and requires a great deal of care and preparation to sing, yet is composed of very small segments of different ideas.

Returning to the importance of words, it has to be remembered that the creative life of a Salvation Army composer is not always governed by individual choice and that requests, or even demands, are made on the composer that might not have been his or her first choice.

When General Arnold Brown, in preparation for the 1978 International Congress, had the idea that the doctrines of The Salvation Army should be enshrined in a musical setting, there could be little doubt as who could rise to the task and so RSA was approached. Just one glance at the prose and its already old-fashioned, Victorian language will show just what a difficult undertaking this would be. Normally the large-scale canvas was always something that RSA enjoyed, but on this occasion his heart sank; however, being the ideal 'court composer' he put his mind fully to the task. To underline his consideration of text, he quickly realised that some changes were needed and so John Gowans was asked to look at doctrines 5 and 11 which were 'versified' for the setting.

In addition, the ending needed something a little more uplifting and affirming for such an occasion as the Congress. The final words should have been 'the endless punishment of the wicked' but the work ends instead with a recapitulation of doctrine 6, 'Whosoever will, may be saved'. Clearly this is the positive note of faith and creed that the very title of 'The Salvation Army' encapsulates. It even allows for the congregation to join with this rallying call.

This is a major work, with 22 pages of short score alone. A great deal of space could be devoted to an analysis of this work and that would be a rewarding study. That luxury is not available at this time. However, it is worth noting some of its characteristics. Of necessity it is an episodic work reflecting the nature and mood of each doctrine. It starts with a clear rhythmic reference to the words 'We Believe' and this brief rhythm is used at various points in order to give some unity to what could become just a series of unrelated expressions.

The challenge of setting such prose is evident throughout, with phrases of differing lengths, and of unsettling melodic fragments that often remind us of the

Anglican service settings (Doctrine 3) and the hint of that tradition is evident at various points throughout.

Doctrine 8 provides a very different musical landscape and takes us into a traditional 'chorus' type of setting, joyfully expressing the fact that we are justified by faith.

SOPRANO ALTO

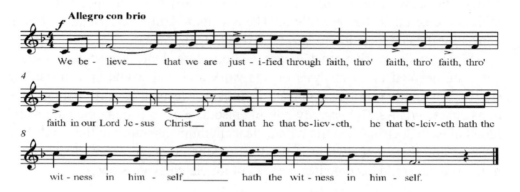

There can be no doubt that the volume of work required for such a composition was immense, even for a composer with tremendous facility and imagination. It must have been a frustration to have spent considerable time and energy composing, only to find that a last-minute decision meant that the piece was not performed in its entirety on one of the occasions for which it was planned.

Of course, this would not be the only piece of music to have either not been performed or only performed rarely. Large-scale choral works tend to be the preserve of the Festival Chorus, Staff Songsters or some more able songster brigades. A piece such as 'Battle Honours', for example, is unlikely to have many, if any, subsequent performances. Nonetheless, these more demanding pieces were given the same attention to compositional detail by RSA as any other composition, once again demonstrating the unselfish nature of this composer.

'My New Day' is a complex composition that includes wit, humour, innocent awareness of a new world and reflective vocal writing. From the very start the jagged, syncopated rhythms from the piano set the scene for the first movement and beautifully capture the excitement of the new day. It is also another example of piano and vocal collaboration as the piano swirls around the excited voices, giving a sense of running around with its rapid scales and rhythmic pounding. A time for breath, and then rich chords emphasise a warmth of feeling in a waltz-like section which restates the excitement of the opening. These ideas are explored further leading to an exciting ending with a held discord, after which the piano concludes in a rhythmic exhaustion.

The second movement, a setting of 'St Patrick's Breastplate', is vocal writing at its purest demonstrating a compositional understanding of sound, scoring and texture while providing a reflective counterpart to the outer movements. Of all the movements this could stand alone.

The final movement begins again with a rhythmic piano start but with a chromaticism and sense of tonality not unlike Shostakovitch or Martinu. It also contains a variety of ideas with another Viennese-like section with a fugue-inspired episode all expressing the joy that 'This is the day that the Lord has made'. The result is a finely crafted and balanced work that should command the same respect as quality brass compositions.

It is difficult to escape the role of accompaniment and this has been reflected in comments so far. One piece where this was taken to a much more integrated level – indeed it could be argued that the piano is often more important than the vocal music – is the 'Childhood Suite'. It also exemplifies RSA's classical influences and his clear affection for past styles, particularly in the first movement where there is a modern take on classical style. Indeed, the first movement contains a very simple vocal arrangement of 'Yes, Jesus Loves Me', while the Haydnesque piano part (assisted by flute) takes a prominent part around which the choir sings in mock-oratorio style. The concept even includes timpani to give even greater credence to the stylistic idea (despite its chromatic use).

'A Little Ship' is the featured song in the second movement. This section moves away from the classical style into another waltz. Again the vocal writing is in many ways subservient to the accompaniment. The theme is scored simply against the accompaniment with block chords against a soloist in one verse. The drum kit is added for rhythmic variety. The music is allowed to flow with little stylistic deviation.

There then follows a setting of 'Now the Day is Over', which ranks as one of RSA's favourite vocal compositions. It begins with an ethereal opening and choral writing that has a simple clarity which communicates the meaning of the words in a pure and straightforward manner. The simplicity and beauty of the piano part evokes this song's use often as a childhood prayer, and the sparse texture creates a reflective canvas that makes the message accessible for all.

The classical mood is revisited through an instrumental interlude which moves through different styles until it becomes a 'cakewalk' for the final movement. A further interlude interjects and leads to a chorale prelude section with a similar structure to works such as 'Jesu, Joy of Man's Desiring'. The music then concludes with a flourish from the instrumentalists into a grand and exciting finish.

In smaller pieces, further examples of the elevation in status of the accompaniment can be seen, as for example in 'Remember Me', with its piano solo as an integral part of the whole conception. In 'Vesper' there is a very clear sense that the accompaniment and the vocal interchange in importance. The 'classical' influence in its broadest sense also occurs through arrangements such as Fibich's 'Poem' and 'The Source of Peace'.

Anyone asked to survey RSA's vocal output will always struggle with deciding what to include, whether this be from a stylistic or compositional standpoint, and if ten different people were asked so to do, it would most likely result in ten very different responses, such is the range and volume of work available.

There is music specifically composed for bands and then adapted for vocal arrangements such as 'Christ Brings Peace' and the solo 'Water's Edge', both from 'Lord of the Sea'. Miniatures also exist for female voices, such as 'Gone My Care'.

Many would class 'O Lovely Name' as their favourite because of the beauty of its melodic line, highly skilled and effective harmony and the outstanding way that Will Brand's words and RSA's music complement each other. All singers have crucial and demanding parts to sing, the poetry demands depth of interpretation, while the suspensions, chromaticism and flowing bass line make this a very special, and unique, song in Salvation Army repertoire.

The theme of 'Love Divine' seems to investigate the idea of short episodic and rhythmic shape and is unmistakeably a conventional strophic piece for choir.

It seems that no area of vocal music has been untouched; it even includes a medley of Christmas carols.

There is one area of RSA's vocal influence that is in danger of being overlooked as the realm of his compositions is investigated. That is the breadth of vocal music published during his time as Editor-in-Chief in the Music Department. A glance through issues of *The Musical Salvationist* at this time reveals a diversity of style from 'Psalm 121' by Bruce Broughton to other more popular styles of the day. He may have been fortunate in having this diversity available for him to consider but it is hard to see quite such a wide range evident in periods since then.

What a journey – and what a legacy – from those musical beginnings and influences! Learning the vocal trade through time, and with access to opportunities such as his experimental vocal soundscape using only vowels, written when 22 years of age, and then moving through all the various styles, complexities and commissions, one thing shines through.

Unfailingly through RSA's Army output there was always the desire to push forward a message, a belief that inspired and compelled him to balance a love of evangelism through both his music and the various ministries of his officership. It offered the opportunity to use the spoken as well as the sung word to further extend the Kingdom of God, or encourage and uplift both listeners and performers. This occurs now on a daily basis through rehearsal time, in corps of all sizes, in festivals, church halls, vast concert halls and numerous recordings. That was why the words set were so important – there is no substitute for depth of meaning allied to a real depth of spiritual experience.

Across the world congregations will be challenged about their own Christian experience as they sing the familiar words to the tune of 'Blacklands' that remind us that:

His love has no limits, his grace has no measure,
His power no boundary known unto men;
For out of his infinite riches in Jesus
He giveth, and giveth, and giveth again.

Cliff Matthews is a currently serving Salvation Army bandmaster at Gloucester and is a member of the Salvation Army International Staff Songsters. Dorothy Nancekievill is Director of Music at Wells Cathedral School and conductor of the International Staff Songsters.

Personal Observations

Norman Bearcroft

WELL over two hundred songs from the pen of Ray Steadman-Allen appear in the music publications of The Salvation Army, with titles ranging from 'O Lovely Name' for mixed voices, published in 1948, to 'We'll Take some Eggs to Mrs Brown who's Poorly with the Flu', written for the Home League in 1966, thus proving how varied are the compositions from this very remarkable man.

'So this is it, my day for living, hurrah, hurrah!' were the opening words in a startling new work in the form of a suite of three parts, written by Ray at my request for the newly formed International Staff Songsters back in 1980. The first movement opens with a setting of a poem from Albert Mingay entitled 'I've Got a Lot of Living to Do'.

The second movement is a setting of a verse from 'St Patrick's Breastplate':

> Christ be with me, Christ within me,
> Christ behind me, Christ before me,
> Christ beside me, Christ to win me,
> Christ to comfort and restore me,
> Christ beneath me, Christ above me,
> Christ in quiet, Christ in danger,
> Christ in hearts of all that love me,
> Christ in mouth of friend and stranger.

The third movement is a setting of Psalm 118:24: 'This is the day that the Lord hath made; we will rejoice and be glad in it.'

This is truly a great work, and also one which needs a very gifted pianist! The International Staff Songsters recorded the music and it appears as 'My New Day' on a recording aptly named *So This is It... My Day for Living!*

The first composition that Ray wrote for the International Staff Songsters, which is found on their first recording, is 'Praise the Lord, O Heavens!', a setting of Psalm 148 as found in *The Living Bible*. The psalm is calling for all living creatures and creations to 'praise the Lord' – the angels, the sun and the moon, dragons, fire, hail, snow, mountains, kings, young men and maidens, old men and children, beasts, cattle and all creeping things! Ray's composition, truly a great and glorious work, caused much merriment in our rehearsals, and a need for the audience to have a couple of minutes' rest following its performance. This setting was sung in every programme given by the Staff Songsters during their first two or three years of service.

I am unable to say which of his vocal works is my favourite, but I do remember the incredible feeling I had when I first heard his original music to the words of Isaac Watts, entitled 'Remember Me', which was published in 1973:

> Alas! And did my Saviour bleed,
> And did my Sovereign die?
> Did he devote that sacred head
> For such a worm as I?
> Remember me, Remember me,
> O Lord, remember me;
> Remember, Lord, thy dying groans,
> And then remember me.

The verses are set in the form of a duet for women's voices with men's voices in a different rhythm which, along with the pianoforte accompaniment, gives a feeling of urgency to its message.

The second verse has these heart-rending words:

> Was it for sins that I have done
> He suffered on the tree?
> Amazing pity, grace unknown,
> And love beyond degree!

The last verse must be our response to his gift of salvation:

> Dear Saviour, I can ne'er repay
> The debt of love I owe!
> Here, Lord, I give myself away;
> 'Tis all that I can do.

Following this verse there is a solo for the pianist based on the chorus of the song, 'Remember me, remember me', with some very moving echoing parts, following which the men take up the chorus, which is then echoed by the women. The song ends with a repeat of the final line, 'And then remember me.'

The words of Isaac Watts must have dug deeply into Ray's heart, as he was inspired to write very challenging music with which to clothe them. The song takes time to sing and needs a time of quietness following its final chorus, while listeners ask themselves: 'Was it for me that Jesus died?'

Will J. Brand, a Salvationist who has written the words to 15 songs in the present (1986) Salvation Army songbook, collaborated with Ray in the writing of a song entitled 'O Lovely Name'. Published in 1948, it commences with this verse:

> O Lovely Name! Calling to sweet remembrance Galilee,
> With lowly men who toiled upon the sea;
> A Kingdom published, and a hunger born,
> Exceeding theirs who plucked the ripened corn.
> Yet rich beyond their need was One who said,
> 'Come unto me, I am the Living Bread.'
> And they who came to thee, O Jesu, Living Bread to claim,
> Learned then the wonder of thy lovely Name.

These words call for music of real weight of character – music with depth and emotion. The song ends with these lines:

> This is their glory, that on earth they came
> To know the meaning of thy lovely name.

In complete contrast, Ray came up with a new setting of the much-loved words 'What a Friend we have in Jesus'. It became very popular and I always had the feeling that the audience wanted to join in the singing, so much so that, when conducting this song, I would turn around and signal the listeners to join in singing the final verse, the words of which most people listening would know. The response was usually so good that I would suggest that this would be a good time to pass the offering plates around because the music has just the right feeling to make the listeners glad they came!

Words selected from Psalm 144 were the inspiration for an anthem type of setting commencing with the opening words of the psalm, and which Ray wanted sung loudly and jubilantly: 'Blessed be the Lord my strength, my hope and my fortress, my defender in whom I trust.' The men's voices in unison then declare: 'I will sing a new song unto thee, O God.' This then develops in a most convincing way with all voices taking up this same statement, leading to the declaration: 'Blessed are the people who have the Lord for their God.' The work concludes with a restatement of 'Blessed be the Lord our God'. This is marked to be sung very slowly and with all the sound the singers can make! Following the presentation of this work, I always felt that a few moments of quietness were needed before any further music or speech.

151

Ray has great ability in arranging existing melodies for singers. A good example is found in his arrangement of a song written in 1878 for The Christian Mission called 'Marching Along'. Commencing with a trumpet-like call, the words 'marching along' are repeated three more times in a style that makes the listeners feel they are actually marching. This leads to the first verse:

> The mission is gathering from near and from far,
> The trumpet is sounding the call for the way,
> The conflict is raging, 'twill be fearful and long,
> We'll gird on the armour and be marching along.

In the many years I was responsible for the yearly festivals at the Royal Albert Hall in London and for two international congresses, Ray, at my request, wrote new music for those occasions. The events called for music for a vocal group comprised of anything between 800 to 1,000 voices, accompanied by the International Staff Band or a smaller ensemble. The recordings made at these events give witness to the quality and variety of music from his pen. Many of the recordings were released on those big vinyl records and some of these have been remastered for the compact disc.

Here is a list of some of the music he wrote for these events.

'Battle Honours' – containing new arrangements of the following five songs used in Christian warfare: 'The Son of God Goes Forth to War', 'Ever is the War Cry, Victory!', 'I'll Stand for Christ Alone', 'Strong in the Lord of Hosts' and 'Forward, ever Forward!'

'A Childhood Suite' – children's songs set in four movements; the first, 'Yes, Jesus Loves Me', written in classical sonata form; the second, 'A Little Ship was On the Sea' set in a Victorian waltz style; the third, 'Now the Day is Over', in the style of a child saying an evening prayer; and 'Father, Lead Me Day by Day' in a baroque choral prelude style, featuring piano, flute and percussion.

'Songs of the Sea' – having been in the Royal Navy, Ray has a love for the sea and its songs; this fact becomes obvious in a work he wrote for 700 male voices, which included 'We are Out On The Ocean Sailing', 'We are Sailing', 'Let the Lower Lights be Burning', 'For Those in Peril on the Sea' and 'Over and Over like a Mighty Sea', the chorus of which appears in several different keys and different timings. Where else would you find so many men in one place singing God's praises to such exciting music as this?

'One in the Spirit' – this work contained choral speech in groups as if speaking in tongues, as referred to in chapter eleven of St Paul's letter to the Corinthians, and two further songs, 'We are One in the Spirit' and 'Our Blest Redeemer'.

'Sounds of Glory' – original settings of 'To God be the Glory', 'The Glory Song', 'Ring the Bells of Heaven' and 'The Lord's Prayer'.

'Battle Call' – written for one of the Congress gatherings, this opens with Ray's own song 'March to the Battlefield', followed by 'To Feel Thy Power' and ending with the question: 'Who is on the Lord's Side?'

'Songs on the Golden Road' – the applicable songs contained in this selection are: 'Through the Night of Doubt and Sorrow', 'We shall Walk through the Valley', 'How Wonderful it is to Walk with God' and 'Welcome Home'.

'1865' – the title recalls the date of the end of the Civil War in the United States of America and the commencement of The Christian Mission (later to become The Salvation Army). It is interesting to note that a song used in the USA Civil War, 'Marching through Georgia', was given new words by George Scott Railton and became a song used in The Salvation Army and its war against sin and the Devil: 'Shout Aloud Salvation, and we'll Have Another Song'. Two songs written by the American songwriter Stephen Foster, 'Way Down upon the Swanee River' and 'Beautiful Dreamer', became respectively 'Joy, Freedom, Peace and Ceaseless Blessing' (at the hands of Herbert Booth) and 'Blessed Assurance, Jesus is Mine' (Fanny Crosby). Ray took all these songs and made a complete and very exciting work of them under the title '1865'.

'Trumpets of the Dawn' – this was a suite of three songs: 'Glory to Thee, my God', 'Morning has Broken' and 'When the Roll is Called up Yonder'.

'The Giver' – here is another suite of three songs, this time with organ accompaniment. The first of these is Ray's own beautiful melody entitled 'Blacklands' for the song beginning with 'He giveth more grace as our burdens grow greater', words by Annie Johnson Flint. This is followed by 'My Maker and my King', words by Anne Steele, and 'All Good Gifts Around Us', words by Matthias Claudius.

'Inspirations from the Bramwell Booth Memorial Hall' – the Bramwell Booth Memorial Hall was the name of the assembly hall in International Headquarters, situated in 101 Queen Victoria Street, London. The walls were decorated with portraits of the Generals, and Ray, seeing them there, realised that four of them had written songs for the Army. He then decided that my request for a piece that year would include these songs. The order in which he used the songs were not the order in which their writers adorned the walls but were in the order that best suited his offering for that year's Royal Albert Hall festival: 'I Know Thee who thou Art' (Albert Orsborn), 'He Remembers Sin No More' (Wilfred Kitching), 'O When shall my Soul Find her Rest' (Bramwell Booth) and 'The Wounds of Christ are Open' (Evangeline Booth). Ray ended his selection by borrowing a part of a song from Charles Wesley (whose portrait was not on the wall, but whose song has been on the lips of Salvationists since the Army began), 'His Blood can Make the Vilest Clean'. William Booth's song 'O Boundless Salvation' would have been included but his portrait was absent from the Bramwell Booth Memorial Hall. The

Founder's portrait instead graces one of the walls of William Booth College in London.

'My Journey Home' – songs included were 'Amazing Grace' (to a different melody) and 'They'll Sing a Welcome Home to Me', words by Robert Lowry.

'We Believe' – at the request of Arnold Brown, then the General of The Salvation Army, Ray wrote a setting for each of the 11 doctrines of The Salvation Army. This was an enormous task! If each doctrine were given three minutes to sing, with a short break between each, the item would have lasted for 40 minutes! (I think General Brown was thinking more of 10 to 15 minutes to complete.) Ray gave me the finished music and we made enough copies for the 1,000-voice chorus that was to sing it at the opening festival of the Congress in the Wembley Arena. As the conductor, I found the music to be an amazing collection of melodies. Some were very sombre and others, particularly doctrine number eight, leapt from the pages! 'We believe that we are justified by grace through faith in our Lord Jesus Christ and that he that believeth hath the witness in himself.'

The recordings made at these events give witness to the quality and variety of music from the pen of Ray Steadman-Allen.

From the many, many requests for music for special occasions, Ray never once said it that it could not be done or that it was too much bother. Even during the time he was stationed in Australia he responded to my request for a song for the Royal Albert Hall festival and, forgetting the time difference between Australia and England, he rang me at about three o'clock in the morning (British time) and sang the opening bars of his new work to see if it was what I wanted! It really was what I wanted and excelled my expectations, even though his singing at three o'clock in the morning was not the best I have heard!

Lieut-Colonel Norman Bearcroft is a composer, a past Music Secretary of The Salvation Army in the UK and Canada, a past conductor of the Canadian Salvation Army Staff Band and founder conductor of the International Staff Songsters.

Chapter Seventeen

Ray Steadman-Allen:
Salvation Army brass band music –
an appreciation

Dudley Bright

MUSIC by its very nature proclaims its message through sound, such that its appreciation in words can at best only be approximate. If a song tune aims to illuminate its lyrics, then instrumental music, if it is to have meaning, speaks to the emotions. Salvation Army brass band music exists uniquely to communicate through the unsung lyrics of its associated song material. The development of that music can be said to be paralleled by that of Ray Steadman-Allen for more than 60 years and, during that time, his works have been labelled trendsetting, groundbreaking and even avant-garde. Yet behind that façade is a man of great vision, humility and dedication: a man for whom any music is God's gift, endlessly fascinating and stimulating.

As a young man growing up in the narrow environment of Salvation Army music, Ray set about expanding his world through a self-imposed programme of study, beginning from the Army's own bandmaster's training course, through diplomas to degree and doctorate, considering inspiration no substitute for thorough technical competence. His view that it is important to look outside to avoid stagnation and derivatives of earlier times has seen him lead growth and expansion of musical creativity in The Salvation Army.

Even before his formal training began, almost by chance he taught himself brass band scoring but in reverse. As a young piano soloist on Army programmes he provided himself with material by arranging band music. Subsequently the thorough and disciplined form of the bandmaster's correspondence course gave him the taste for self-improvement leading him to seek professional training, initially while abroad with the Royal Navy in South Africa and latterly through Trinity College of Music and Durham University.

The fading years of peace had seen Ray at an impressionable age, often sitting on the stairs outside the band room of the International Staff Band[1] listening to lunchtime rehearsals. These were halcyon days for Salvation Army banding with a feverish level of activity, never quite regained in the postwar world. Even so, postwar, when the latest young employee of the International Music Editorial Department found his desk, the publishers were still supplying music for a dizzying range of Salvationist musical requirements.

This was a time when most towns and many villages had at least one and often more Salvation Army corps (churches) with rarely less than a full-sized or even larger band. Television was in its infancy, the electronic age was still some way off and cinema and football were very much frowned on. Army bands provided, in addition to its core Sunday worship and evangelistic functions, what, in essence, was wholesome recreation for its players. In addition to two or three Sunday meetings and a similar number of open-air services and marches, special events abounded that always demanded band participation. Weekend 'campaign' visits to other centres were a regular activity of most reasonably competent sections, and star ensembles also featured at regional and national events.

To serve all these requirements, the Music Department provided three subscription series: *Festival*, *General* and *Triumph*, each catering, with a full range of marches, selections, air variés and solos, for slightly differing markets – *Triumph Series* for bands of slightly less than full size and ability; *General Series* and *Festival Series* as their titles suggest, but with the latter being prohibited from use in worship meetings. Army bands were required to play only music published by Salvationist Publishing and Supplies and, in turn, secular bands were prevented from buying it. In the department, Ray's colleagues busied themselves preparing music for publication, ensuring that every piece contained at least one full statement of a hymn or song and the strict rules of the austere Victorian professor of music Ebenezer Prout were faithfully observed.

The allowable song material was a mixture of Methodist hymnody and Victorian ballad style, with the band music of Coles, Marshall and Jakeway owing a certain amount to composers such as Liszt, Wagner and Mendelssohn with their mild diatonic chromaticism. On the other hand, Eric Ball had looked towards the Englishness of Elgar and Parry but, in general, the style reflected the quasi militaristic ethos of the church. Dotted and triplet rhythms abounded while diminished fifths and augmented sixths were about the limit of harmonic development. The task for a Salvationist composer was to write music acceptable not only to congregations but also to largely self-taught and enthusiastic bandsmen, as a vehicle for their many and varied talents. If all this tended to restrict artistic freedom, on the positive side the subscription scheme allowed for less commercial but more demanding pieces to find their way into print.

Not that Ray's earliest pieces immediately broke the mould, but they do exhibit a lively, inventive mind underpinned with solid craftsmanship. His first published work, a march entitled 'Gladsome Morn' (1945)[2], was full of good interesting ideas and mild chromaticism, whereas 'Bethlehem Story' (1947) was only the third suite to be published in that form. Featured widely by the ISB in its first postwar programmes, this new promising composer's first pieces made an immediate impact. Now sounding somewhat dated, they bore few hallmarks of his forthcoming mature works. But before long, Albert Jakeway in his score notes[3] for 'Blessed Sunshine' (1946) signalled controversy: 'The modernistic flavour may not be accepted by all.' In fact, Ray remembers Bram Coles looking over his shoulder, interested in some of his boundary-pushing. In no way was there composing by committee but inevitably there would be a certain degree of cross-fertilisation, particularly as other forward-looking young bloods joined the office. Ray quickly became established as his initial creations found approval with the ISB (of which he was now a member), its audiences and wider Army banding fraternity.

The oft quoted comment – 'A new era of Salvation Army brass band music has begun' – was made in 1965 in the columns of the Army's *Musician*[4] magazine, but 18 years earlier, in 1947, another reporter had detected 'the dawning of a new day in Army music'. Commenting on the ISB annual weekend at the Regent Hall in London, he found two new pieces by Ray Allen to be 'unusually exacting, extremely interesting, new in idiom, unique in conception'. Going on, he expected that 'discerning musicians will wait for further contributions with keen anticipation'. Thus Ray Allen became the darling of the *cognoscenti* and the dread of the more conservative. The music in question was the tone poem 'When they Crucified my Lord' and a novelty, 'The Three Gardens', a miniature piano concerto with a septet of brass. In Staff Bandmaster Bernard Adams, Ray found a worthy champion who 'was willing to do anything' and with his ISB he was to be entrusted with the first presentations of much of Ray's music.

Without pigeon-holing any particular piece, a clear dichotomy begins to emerge between what might be classed as Ray's functional music and his creative output. 'When they Crucified my Lord' was definitely an artistic expression born of a very personal consideration of passiontide and is, in the truest sense of the form, a tone poem, only the fifth published in that form[5]. As will be seen, listeners tend to find more adventurous music acceptable if it is linked to a strong extra-musical narrative. At the time Ray Allen was particularly interested in the music of William Walton, the composer of the stunning choral work *Belshazzar's Feast*. Since Ray's boyhood, English composers, in particular Ralph Vaughan Williams, had provided a stimulus, but the extended tonality and dramatic intensity of Walton is evident in this work. Drawing, not for the last time, on the treasury of Negro spirituals, the melody is introduced in fragments throughout the work, sometimes the initial three notes being enough to suggest the question: 'Were you there?'

The opening pentatonic[6] fanfare, derived from the musical phrase 'sometimes it causes me to tremble' in reverse, is intended to portray the secular Roman power.

Appearing in various forms throughout the work, this kind of thematic transformation[7] became a feature of many of Ray Allen's works. It is a subtle technique, which maintains contrast and variety but supplies an element of cohesion and unity, sometimes quite imperceptibly. This contrasts with motivic development, where a fragment or motif is quite clearly related to its original material, maintaining its identity throughout its development.

Although Ray has been sometimes painted as the Army's *enfant terrible*, accused of perpetrating lengthy, dissonant pieces, the truth goes well beyond that to Ray's genuine desire to expand the formal and stylistic scope of Army music, thus increasing its expression and relevance. Taking his example from Eric Ball he was keen to introduce forms besides the ubiquitous march, selection, air varié or hymn tune arrangement in both his functional and creative output. His critics cared little or didn't even notice his name on the programme or on the top right-hand corner of popular band items such as 'In Quiet Pastures', ''Neath Italian Skies', 'The Veterans' and 'Crown of Conquest' or cut their playing teeth in junior bands on 'Nicely Saved', 'The Great Crusade' or 'Exultation'. Not someone to take this too much to heart, Ray did betray a little good-natured frustration in an interview at Bandmasters Councils (1962) reported in *The Musician*: 'Captain Ray Steadman-Allen expressed gratitude for the opportunity to speak about his latest work[8]... modestly likening it to the chance of opening a window into what some might consider a very mixed-up mind. Commenting on the General's earlier reference to cake he said: "I admit this piece is in the nature of a cake but I have got quite a lot of bread and butter in the journals."'

At the expense of pushing the analogy it should be acknowledged this was not soggy supermarket white bread but wholesome, crusty, wholemeal fare, such as 'Wells of Gladness' (1947) which, years later, he did admit was produced to counter the perennial famine of bright, happy music. Should that idea offend those who consider Army bands to have a higher purpose, he offered these comments:

> 'I suppose if "entertaining" is taking someone along with you and making them feel happier and more cheerful, "taking them out of themselves", I think it is quite legitimate. After all, nobody gets upset because we break for a cup of tea in the Home League[9], that doesn't seem to have any spiritual significance... purely to make people happy is a function of Christian service although we must not let the main object become obscured.'[10]

A traditional selection with little or no thematic development, 'Wells of Gladness' is a model of interesting scoring and finely judged modulating transitions, engaging to play without presenting excessive challenges, but above all attractive and enjoyable to listen to. One of his emerging hallmarks, having as it were done his duty, is Ray's tendency to allow himself an exciting, extended coda in which to gently push harmonic and rhythmic boundaries. There is indeed good precedent for this kind of afterthought from, among others, Beethoven, who having fulfilled the structural demands of sonata form often embarked on a kind of second development section before his final cadence[11].

Not averse to taking his cue from secular popular arrangers, Ray Allen modelled 'Walk in the Light' (1956) on the kind of light music popularised by Debroy Somers. Although classed as an air varié, it is quite unlike any other of the time. With only one small hesitation, the music runs continuously in a rhythmic 2/4 tempo. It is a brilliant showpiece for band, tossing the theme and its fragments between one section and another through abrupt key changes, episodes and a fugato. Seeing the light of day with the ISB at Regent Hall in 1949 it was eventually published in 1956.

A long list of pieces written in response to special requests, many remaining unpublished due to their particular format, difficulty or length, began with 'The Ransomed Host'. Written for a bandmasters councils festival, it was published after revision in 1954 and has been a mainstay of the solo euphonium repertoire ever since. Nominally it is a traditional set of variations where the soloist weaves showy decorations, designed to test technique, around a given theme or its phrase and harmonic structure. But two of the variations have a rhapsodic outlook: the first, a restrained waltz, is built on a four-bar modal progression, the soloist entering with a derivation of the third phrase of the theme. The third variation, a slow movement, only vaguely suggests the theme before the fourth 'running' variation. One might then expect to hear a brilliant coda. But, almost true to form now, the composer chooses to return to some earlier material first before a cadenza and the obligatory 'gallery ending'.

Ray's training for Salvation Army officership began in 1948, which fortunately didn't entirely stem the flow of new compositions. Desmond Rix, who was a fellow cadet with Ray and Joy in the Peacemakers Session, remembers that on Thursday afternoons the cadets were subjected to PT sessions, the men's dining hall being cleared for these classes. One week the instructor, who came from another college in central London, had the men cadets lying on the floor moving their legs as if riding a bicycle. RSA couldn't have been doing it right because the instructor pointed to him saying: 'You there, with the glazed eyes, watch me.' Afterwards at the tea table, going over the event, RSA admitted that he was rather uninterested in the PT session, his mind being preoccupied with a new selection that he was then composing. He was later given leave to try it with the cadets' band before publication. Two of the three songs included were quite new at the time. The first, a Swedish tune, Ray had first heard played at the piano by Gunnar Blomberg during the 1947 visit of the famous Tranås Band to the UK. It seems, though, that Colonel Ernest Rance was not entirely flattered by the treatment of his song 'Shepherd, Hear my Prayer'. However, not only was Ray's setting of his song and its following episode beautifully done, in fact inclusion in a popular band selection would also tend to increase its circulation. With subtle but interesting scoring, smooth transitional modulations and contextually relevant episodes, well within reach of any average band, 'In Quiet Pastures' has remained a devotional classic for over 60 years.

A year or so after completing training, Ray and Joy married and it was presumed in some quarters that Ray would resume his position in the trombone section of the ISB. There followed some difficult times until the matter was resolved. It was perhaps then an acknowledgement of Ray's true worth that he was approached to write a trombone solo for Maisie Wiggins (née Ringham), at the time principal trombonist of Barbirolli's famous Hallé Orchestra, to be played at the festival celebrating the ISB's Golden Jubilee (1951) at the newly opened Royal Festival Hall. Brindley Boon described the event for *Musician* readers:

'2nd Lieutenant Ray Allen's new selection, "Young In Heart" (1952), incorporating sophisticated versions of well-known children's songs, followed the sequence of a child's day from morning to night and made pleasant listening, demonstrating the lighter qualities of the band. From the same composer came a virtuoso trombone solo, "The Eternal Quest" (1952), played with artistry and unerring technique by Sister Maisie

Wiggins. Some of this music was quite moving and with something of an intriguing cadenza. A masterpiece.'

'Young In Heart' was an example of the kind of versatility and facility that could weld together references to 16 different songs in one piece, while 'The Eternal Quest' was an eloquent response to the challenge of writing for such a fine soloist and band at an auspicious venue for a discerning audience. Its form was a complete departure from the traditional theme and variation solo. Following what is in essence a classical sonata form movement, the music's descriptive and dramatic style might have challenged some of its first listeners. After the dark, brooding introduction (with just a tinge of George Marshall) the solo trombone (destined to carry some of Ray's most profound expressions), at first alone, embarks on a troubled narrative intended to depict the spiritual struggles of a biblical prodigal but, on his own admission, giving some expression to the composer's recent troubles. Only briefly does the chorus melody, associated with the words 'Jesus is looking for thee', interrupt the restless atmosphere. Reaching a climax, moments of reflection follow asking, in the words of the associated melody: 'Is there a heart that is waiting, longing for pardon today?'

But the plea goes unheeded and after a reprise of the opening material the soloist embarks on a cadenza, not of virtuosic display but for a time of soul searching and reflection. Interestingly, there appears little thematic development of the one chosen melody, but with closer inspection the composer has included a small fragment as a unifying element throughout the music. Similarly, Johannes Brahms begins his second symphony quite simply with three notes, one step down and one step back. Providing as it were a binding agent, this tiny gesture, at times upside down, crops up throughout the whole symphony. Is it mere coincidence that the same three notes, garnered from the beginning of the song, bind together the entire 'The Eternal Quest'?

For years Ray Allen had admired the music of Ralph Vaughan Williams for its spaciousness and flow, but when Vaughan Williams attended Judd Street to hear his 'Prelude on Three Welsh Hymn Tunes' which he had written especially for the Army, an oversight meant that Ray wasn't present. Sadly, Ray was never to meet his hero, but the great composer did encounter 'The Eternal Quest', which he praised highly, although he felt it was somewhat spoilt by that 'so and so' hymn tune in the middle. But for Salvationists that is the very point of this moving trombone solo, still chosen by soloists nearly 60 years later.

Ray was now established and increasingly prolific and his name was appearing in virtually every issue of the band journals. This creative flow was due in some part to his substantial improvising skills and prodigious memory. Those spontaneous musings at the piano during collection time in whatever corps he worshipped at might have been, in embryo, a new masterpiece!

Occasionally, the discerning might spot the style of another composer, a talent he used both for his own amusement and edification. Enjoying this ability to get under another composer's skin, he wrote items he would have liked them to have written. As a tribute to Arthur Gullidge, the Australian composer of fine, distinctive marches, who lost his life on board a troop ship while being transported as a prisoner during the Second World War, Ray wrote the march 'Crown Of Conquest' (1954). Similarly, Ray took the design of the late George Marshall's 'Army of the Brave' and paid him homage by creating 'On Active Service' (1958) – a popular work that the much revered northern bandmaster himself could no longer provide. However, as we can come to expect, in the final bars Ray gives himself space for his own distinctive creativity. In reality, he considers that there is always something of this process operating even in original works. In June 1973, in an interview with Anthony Leggett for *The Musician*, Ray expressed the view: 'Inspiration does seem to come in a sense of digested thoughts within your mind and yourself. I don't think that much comes brand new, it is a resurgence of absorbed elements which are reborn through your own thinking and consciousness.'

He goes on to express his fondness for another of his 'essays in style', 'Prelude on Randolph' (1960). Based on the melody of the same name it was written while under the spell of Ralph Vaughan Williams who wrote the hymn tune. As with 'Crown Of Conquest' and 'On Active Service', Ray was satisfying his wish for more music in the style of the great man. What an achievement! In many ways it sounds more typical of Vaughan Williams than VW's own 'Prelude on Three Welsh Hymn Tunes' with Ray achieving that seamlessly integrated musical flow that he admired so much. Such is the lot of a composer that one's most cherished works sometimes fail to achieve the recognition he would like. Regretfully, Ray feels that perhaps it was the lack of a 'gallery ending' that let the 'Prelude' down, but listening to this piece one can hardly fail to be moved, after a glorious final verse of the hymn, by a beautiful extended coda gradually fading with some sublimely ethereal sounds. More likely it was its publication in the *Festival Series*, with its restrictions on performance, that has obscured its true worth; a most moving meditation, whether it is associated with the words 'God be with you till we meet again' or 'Take my life and let it be' matters little.

Happily, composer, performers and listeners do sometimes agree. With the air varié 'Go Down, Moses' (1954) the composer felt that he had broken into something bigger and it soon became a hit. Taking his cue from Eric Ball's 'The Old Wells' he gently pushed at the boundaries of Salvationist musical forms. Returning once again to the treasury of Negro spirituals he takes a slave's plea for freedom and turns it into a set of variations, relying less on melodic and harmonic shape and more on the theme as 'a storehouse of musical material, small portions of which might become the basis of whole variations'. Thus the first variation, a restrained waltz, uses a counterpoint to the theme (a) balanced with the distinctive falling minor third. Although in the major key there is still an incipient sadness.

The same short motif heralds a capriccio 2/4 variation, with soloists showing their dexterity before embarking on a total flight of fantasy building to a climax before the theme is heard in counterpoint to the main theme.

A beautiful Berceuse, the next variation offers but a memory of the theme as a solo cornet weaves an elegant counterpoint above it.

Not content to leave it there, the composer extends the variation, adding yet more thoughts on the theme before a lonely flugel horn laments over pizzicato-like bass. Using a motif associated with the words 'Let my people go', one can picture the Hebrews' flight from Egypt in the last variation.

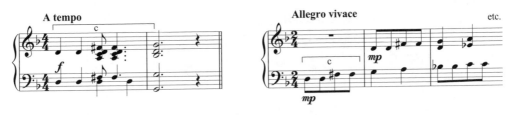

Yet again we find the composer is ready to throw in some new or startling feature for the closing bars. In 'Go Down, Moses' it is the cross rhythms of the final bars that caused a certain amount of consternation among some bandsmen and bandmasters, with solutions being proposed through the letters page of *The Musician*.

In many ways it was a perfect festival number for its time – challenging, but not too difficult for an average band, full of strong, easily recognisable motifs with programmatic associations but unusual and innovative enough to please the connoisseurs.

Serving Salvation Army officers are expected to submit their writings to the Movement's own publishers. That Captain R. V. Allen (as he was then titled) entered a piece called 'Neptune's Diadem' in a BBC competition for an original brass band work might have raised official eyebrows, and one can only guess at the situation had it actually won instead of being placed second. Revised and renamed 'Lord of the Sea' (1957), it was premiered at Regent Hall in 1956 by the ISB, eliciting a favourable reaction from the Chairman, Dr W. Greenhouse Allt, the Principal of Trinity College of Music, who commented: 'It deserves special mention as it exhibits a restrained and pleasing modernity which elevates it and gives it the hallmark as the work of an outstanding composer.'

Yet for all its restrained modernity it is not easy to appreciate why, at the time, this piece was considered so controversial. With the poetic talents of Miriam Richards wedded to the themes of the first and second movements it was published by the Army. Little in the first two movements might have been considered particularly challenging, though there are features that show how the harmonic palette is developing. Although chromatic, this is a perfectly logical progression – passing quickly through several keys with all the discords prepared and resolved smoothly.

Dissatisfied with the original 6/8 third movement of 'Neptune's Diadem', feeling it fell away at the end, Ray wrote an entirely new third movement. Here in the introduction we are in an unaccustomed sound world for 1950s listeners. With just two notes widely spaced, a flourish of horns and baritones calls forth a phrase from the sea. Although in itself not highly dissonant, this flourish is made up of two fourths, one on top of another – unprepared and unresolved discords.

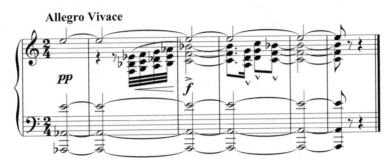

Gestures of this kind would have been quite an unfamiliar sound in those days. The movement's energetic hornpipe-like theme has a refrain which must also have been a thrilling new sound for the time – wild high trills over a sound like sea spray shooting up into the air. If some of this was going too far for conservative Salvationists, others found it thrilling and beautiful. In a letter to Ray, Swedish/American composer Erik Leidzén tells how students at the famous Star Lake music camp, many having heard it on a recent ISB tour, begged to be allowed to play 'Lord of the Sea'. After some intensive rehearsals, at the climax of the school:

> 'An unusual hush of expectation fell over the audience. And into that hush the young players poured out your lovely music. When the last whirlwind of the finale had suddenly stopped and the last glorious bars thundered through the summer night, the crowd was on their feet in an ovation that would have melted you entirely. I just waved the young musicians to their feet and left them standing... the tears blinding me.'

Ray Allen himself wrote in *The Musician*, reporting on the 1957 Bandmasters Councils festival when the ISB performed the work: 'We have seen the word controversial occasionally applied to this piece but the appreciation of the crowd of the presentation was not in doubt.'

For the sake of conformity, 'Lord of the Sea' might be regarded as coming at the end of R. V. Allen's first period of development as a composer. If 'Prelude on Randolph' won few fans then 'Via Dolorosa' (1957)[12] was even more of a disappointment. Although *Musician* correspondent Brindley Boon described it as 'an important new work' after the ever-faithful International Staff Bandmaster

Bernard Adams had conducted its first performance in Hereford Cathedral, it failed to find common acceptance. Perhaps it was the strange Latin title, the flowing counterpoint, or its publication in the *Festival Series*, but this deeply spiritual work, pointing in a new direction, failed to engage.

Another piece which suffered a strange fate at about the same time was another 'Via', two composers apparently receiving inspiration for a similar title and similar music incorporating the same song. Dean Goffin's lovely 'Road To Emmaus' (1953) was published in the *General Series* and used extensively whereas Ray's 'Emmaus Journey' (1953), published about the same time in the *Festival Series*, was relatively neglected. Needless to say, some of the composer's personal favourites, including 'Christmas in Europe', 'By Love Compelled' (1953) and ''Neath Italian Skies' (1956), were featured widely and his popular 'Go Down, Moses' was the subject of a short film made by the International Staff Band.

In 1955 Ray Allen became bandmaster of the famous Tottenham Citadel Band, proving himself a fine conductor and band trainer as evidenced by recordings and broadcasts. It was an experience he found both rewarding and stimulating and, with the opportunity to experiment, new ideas were germinating. While his contributions to the *General, Triumph* and newly inaugurated *Unity Series*[13] continued with attractive, immediate and well-crafted pieces, his thoughts were pointing in a new direction. It was, therefore, a shock in 1960 when yet another of the Army's outstanding composers[14] suddenly found it necessary to relinquish his officership and seek work in the secular brass band world. So it was that the Allen family found themselves living in a cramped upstairs flat on a farm near Cheltenham with Ray finding employment as Managing Editor of Wright and Round Publishers.

It was a difficult time and therefore a real pleasure to have Leslie Condon, a friend from the Music Editorial Department, come and stay for a weekend while his band from Woolwich visited a nearby corps. During the weekend the band played one of Ray's *Triumph Series* compositions, 'The Great Crusade', which Les invited him to conduct. As Ray stood in front of the band he looked round to see Les grinning his head off. Realising he'd been 'had' he muttered under his breath: 'You dirty dog' – the tune running through the piece was the old song 'Never Quit The Field'.

Thankfully, the break was not permanent and Ray Steadman-Allen[15] resumed duties at the Judd Street office. With his new name, his music might seem to have a new identity: producing works with a fresh approach and greater freedom, or so it seemed. But the truth is that what might be thought of as his second period had already begun in the Tottenham days. Although no original works were published in the *Festival Series* until 1965, among ground-breaking pieces already taking shape was 'Rhapsody on Negro Spirituals' (1967), inspired by Tottenham's terrific cornet soloist and deputy bandmaster, the legendary James

Williams. Indeed, some new pieces were in development during the time in Cheltenham. 'The Immortal Theme', a new suite for trombone nearly twice the length of 'The Eternal Quest' and first performed in 1962 by Maisie Wiggins at the Bandmasters Councils Festival, originated during 1959. From the outset the toccata-like first movement is written in a demanding, uncompromising language, with the soloist alone declaiming a pure 12-note row[16] which Ray, ever the craftsman, organised with increasing intervals for the first six notes and the remainder decreasing.

Skilfully woven into this short, energetic movement, with remarkable stylistic consistency, is an old Salvationist chorus, 'Oh the Lamb'. The second movement contrasts a sad yearning cantilever with the song 'Some Day I shall be Like Him'. If the first movement is harmonically and tonally challenging, then the second has a new lyrical depth and spirituality, a quality often ignored by critics of his increasingly chromatic and dissonant voice. The third movement, beginning with a long pensive introduction, ponders fragments of the chorus 'This is Why I Love my Jesus' and then gives way to an energetic and joyous allegro built around the words:

> I do believe, I will believe,
> That Jesus died for me;
> That on the cross he shed his blood,
> And now he sets me free.

This is the longest movement with much interplay between soloist and band. When the opening pensive material returns it culminates in the soloist's high-register portrayal of the chorus 'Calling, Calling, Jesus is Calling'. After an emphatic pronouncement, 'This is why I love my Jesus', the suite ends with a short brilliant coda.

Maybe he was still haunted by the memory of his recent brush with authority, for the composer became apprehensive at the first performance of 'The Immortal Theme'. He shared his fears with Norman Bearcroft who, as National Bandmaster at the time, was responsible for the festival. In his book *In Good Company*, Norman writes that Ray had dreamt that, in the middle of the playing of this solo, General Kitching had stood up and said: 'It is too long and not suitable for an Army programme.' He worried that this might actually happen. At the end of the programme, General Kitching signalled to Ray that he wanted to speak with him. Fearing the worst, Ray came face to face with the General who said to him: 'Ray, I was deeply moved during the playing of your new solo, so much so that I want to have it played again tomorrow afternoon at the Councils and I want you to talk about the piece before it is played.' The programme had to be rearranged – but Maisie was not free, and Arthur Rolls[17] had to play it. Norman writes: 'It was one of those unforgettable moments.'

In his comments for *The Musician*, Bandmaster Michael Kenyon wrote of 'The Immortal Theme': 'It was an example of music which fulfils the purpose of declaring the Christian message through the medium of contemporary musical art at the highest order.' Being too long for normal use and publication, it has continued as a kind of 'special occasion' piece. Arthur Rolls featured it on the ensuing ISB tour of USA and Ian Hankey also featured it later in the decade.

Although no original RSA works appeared in the *Festival Series* at that time, mention should be made of his many classical transcriptions for the medium. It has to be said that the success of a brass band transcription is dependent on the skill of the arranger to choose the right music. Ray seems to have an instinct for music that will transfer convincingly. Originally planned as one piece, a selection from the music of Dvořák included extracts from his *New World Symphony*, but realising it would be too long it was split into 'Melodies Of Dvořák' (1964) and 'Themes from the *New World Symphony*' (1963); both became immediate favourites.

With the Centenary celebrations of The Salvation Army fast approaching (1965), it was expected that new music would feature at the big festivals in London. With the main focus on the Royal Albert Hall, Dean Goffin, himself a fine composer, then National Secretary for Bands and Songsters, modestly ensured that Steadman-Allen compositions would be the highlight of the musical celebrations. In 1964, Ray had been invited to the USA for a festival of recognition by the New York Staff Band. It included the first performance of the cornet solo 'Rhapsody on Negro Spirituals' played by Derek Smith, and a new, highly innovative piece for solo piano and band with the composer as soloist. Based on the song 'Christ is the Answer' by the then executive officer of the NYSB, Colonel W. Maltby, the central section also featured the band's fine male-voice chorus, sensitive comments coming from piano and euphonium soloists. 'Fantasia for Piano and Band on Christ is the Answer' was an ingenious working out of Maltby's song and in particular the simple rising phrase of the chorus. Immediately attractive, modern but undemanding in idiom, the work had its British premiere in the Royal Albert Hall at the Centenary of Salvation Song to a standing ovation[18]. But another new work was to provoke a strong negative reaction among some listeners.

The story of the 'The Holy War' (1966) really deserves a separate chapter of its own. Originating in 1958, an earlier version of this major work was tried out with the assistance of the bandsmen at Tottenham Citadel. Ray was conscious of the step he was taking with this momentous music and it was to go through a second version before its final form emerged. Comparing the first and final version gives a fascinating insight into the mind of a composer and his compositional processes. Unmistakably the same music, some parts of the music appear at a completely different time in the musical structure while some parts stylistically hark back to an earlier era. It might be instructional here to make a brief digression into a series of articles by RSA published in *The Musician* during 1965/6 under the title 'The Evolution of Salvation Army Music'. In part 14, entitled 'Programme Music', he gives a unique insight into his own thought processes:

'Suppose a composer has the "inspiration", perhaps only a phrase or a rhythmic shape. His musical intuition, backed by experience and training, suggests to him a succeeding phrase and he continues to develop his stretch of music, choosing and balancing his patterns, organising his harmonies, shaping melody and counterpoint until his judgment is satisfied. He will then proceed to a new section, which may spring from what he has already written, expand it or contrast with it. He may not necessarily begin at the beginning and work through to the end (and certainly not with anything more complex), but he will ensure that his final draft has coherence, orderly and inevitable progression. He will do his best to attain a finished product that satisfyingly fulfils the promise of the original idea.'

Without doubt the many steps Ray went through in composing 'The Holy War' were in order to attain the promise of his original idea: a concept quite unparalleled in Army music. And so during his time in Cheltenham the process continued on the top floor of the farmhouse in Golden Valley. Bandsman Gordon Hill, long-time solo trombonist of the International Staff Band, recalls that a version of the piece appeared in the ISB rehearsal room sometime in 1962/3, to disappear and then reappear a couple of years later, a fact attested to in the Anthony Leggett interview. To study the final version of this epic music it is hard to understand how its logic and flow, its strength of structure and controlled thematic development could ever have been any different. Taking John Bunyan's weighty tome of the same name, RSA's new tone poem appropriately was built on Luther's Reformation Hymn 'Ein Feste Burg', at the time not in the Army's tune and song books. Gordon Hill remembers the intense rehearsals as Bernard Adams drilled the band in the new work, pointing out that at the time it was a true staff band, its numbers including various International Headquarters staff who were not all star instrumentalists. The music contained intervals and harmonies which were quite new to many of the players, and the percussionists, accustomed to providing a rhythmic colour, were thrust unwittingly into a pivotal starring roll. Although it is often thought that it received its premiere at the Centenary Congress in London, realising that such an important and significant piece must be given every opportunity to make a convincing impact, Adams inserted 'The Holy War' into an ISB programme in May 1965 at Edinburgh's imposing Usher Hall.

In London the piece was actually performed at the Royal Albert Hall, afternoon and evening in both Centenary Festivals of Praise, on Monday 28 June 1965. Bernard Adams, not satisfied with the momentous afternoon premiere, recalled the men of the ISB for an unscheduled tea-time rehearsal. The evening performance was a triumph, immortalised on LP and reissued more recently on CD. As the huge congregation rose to its feet to salute composer and performers it was as if the celebration of 100 years of salvation war was focused at that one point. The controversy surrounding the music could also be said to focus on one point. To describe the music as 'horribly discordant' is to give one moment of the piece undue prominence. At the climax of the battle there is a chord built, top down, until all but two degrees of the chromatic scale sound together, a massive crescendo which indeed leaves the ears ringing. Breaking the pregnant pause, 'Mansoul' is resurrected! Yet little of this epic music has undue dissonance. As one would expect, the battle music is violent, gritty and angular, but elsewhere, although stylistically contemporary, discord is little more than might be expected in the 1950s.

Called upon to describe the events of that evening in *The Musician* himself, Major Ray Steadman-Allen modestly deferred assessment of his own music to others but confessed to being overwhelmed by the superb rendition of the ISB and thanked General Frederick Coutts for his erudite introduction outlining the spiritual meaning behind the music. It was left to Kenneth Rawlins (Canadian National Music Secretary) to assess the afternoon performance:

> 'RSA has given us a startlingly different and magnificent musical portrait in his tone poem "The Holy War". It was met with a splendid ovation from bandsmen and congregation alike. The new era of Salvation Army brass band music has begun. Featured throughout the composition is one of the hymns of the Reformation, "A Sure Stronghold Our God Is Still". Forces of evil engage the soul in fierce and deadly combat. The portrayal is artistically convincing. The battle for "Mansoul" is preceded by dark and sinister tonal colouring which breaks suddenly into conflict. The band, revealing the sustained, tonal breadth and absolute precision which we are accustomed to hearing, built clearly the colours which flashed before us as the work moved through its varied score. Particularly moving was the climax with its jarring harmonies and its subsequent subsiding as the music moved to its final conclusion.'

However, the demanding music did not meet with universal approval; one critic wrote to say the music made him physically sick; and 'Alpha', an anonymous feature writer in *The Musician*, complained in an article called 'Three Musical Memories of the London Centenary Celebrations – the Music I Liked Least': 'It is a painful memory, one of mental and then nervous protest at this assailment of ears which seemed to become less resistant to loud and unpleasant noises.'

He went on to complain that, on its publication, less able players who traditionally take refuge in secondary parts might become dismayed and begin leaving bands and the Army in droves. Strangely enough he went on to appreciate the music in quite a literal way: 'the realisation that the Holy War in which we are engaged in is as grim and horrible and torturing as the musical interpretation of the conflict was to me'.

Leaping to the defence, Brian Bowen (later Bandmaster of the NYSB) wrote:

> 'There does appear to be a failure on the part of many people to accept the musical offerings of composers, songwriters and performers as dedicated acts of worship representing much time and preparation, whereas the validity of a sermon or testimony is not questioned.... While new music is at times the subject of forceful criticism, I would like to quote Hubert Parry: "Musical works of an elevated kind require frequent hearing to be appreciated and understood, but the things that get most frequently heard are those that please at the first hearing, while the work that requires frequent hearing seems to be in imminent danger of never getting a second because it does not please at the first."'

Whatever the viewpoint, in future new RSA compositions were awaited with a keen sense of anticipation. However, like 'The Immortal Theme', there was a feeling that 'The Holy War' was unlikely ever to be published and achieve general use. Surprisingly, it was indeed published in 1966 in the *Festival Series*, being reviewed for *The Musician* by composer and bandmaster Kenneth Cook:

> 'A lot of ill-considered comment has been passed already on this splendid composition. I would ask the critics to answer one question to their own satisfaction. How can you convey the idea of war in music? Certainly not by pretty tunes and hymn tune harmony. RSA's music is never as difficult to play as it sounds. A great virtue. This time there are two obstacles to overcome: the sustaining power for a composition of this length and the advanced melodic and harmonic idiom.'

During the ISB's 75th anniversary celebrations in 1966 Bernard Adams chose to conduct 'The Holy War', referring to the work's 'almost excessive demands', while Ian Hankey played 'The Immortal Theme' and Terry Camsey played RSA's 'Showers of Blessing', a variation-type cornet solo now thought to be lost.

If major works in the first half of the 1960s grabbed all the attention, there continued to be a steady stream of Ray's 'bread and butter' music into the *General Series* including the marches 'Silver Star' (1962) and 'The Scarlet Jersey' (1965), an air varié 'The Praising Heart' (1963), the selection 'His Guardian Care' (1963) and a meditation, 'In Me, Lord' (1966). The latter is regarded by the composer as one of his best pieces, but perhaps due to the control needed to make it convincing, it has never gained a wide acceptance[19].

According to the composer, composition of 'The Scarlet Jersey', a fine festival march written for the Centenary, flowed easily and this can be heard in the way the tune 'O Happy Day' is totally integrated into its derivative material. This brilliant march was getting away from the traditional Coles/Gullidge type, with more thematic development, increased syncopation and a certain amount of bluesy harmony.

While the cornet solo 'Showers of Blessing' was lost, another one was published in the shape of 'Rhapsody on Negro Spirituals' (1967). It was immortalised in the fine recording by Derek Smith of the New York Staff Band. It is essentially lyrical in character, the considerable virtuosity required growing out of the music itself, as do elements of rhythm and harmony. In true RSA style the extended and spectacular ending is well considered, concluding with a bluesy added note chord[20] that would certainly have made quite an impact in those days.

With his natural and fluent technique, Ray Steadman-Allen might always be relied upon to meet any requirement for a special occasion. One such item was 'Good Companions', a caprice for cornet and trombone played at the Bandmasters Councils Festival in 1966 by Ove Ericson and Brian Midgley. It delighted *Musician* reviewer Tom Rive from New Zealand, himself a fine composer, who described it as extrovert, intricate, unexpected and entirely captivating, despite complaining that the song on which it was based sounded like bits of 'Polly Wolly Doodle', 'Camptown Races' and 'Little Brown Jug'. Composers are human after all and some even have a sense of humour. ('When they Crucified my Lord' appears to contain a passing resemblance to 'Way Down upon the Swanee River'). Fascinating as the duet may have been, it joined the increasing list of works from RSA's prolific pen which have never been published.

In the following decade, the ISB was called upon to present the following new RSA pieces at major events normally held in the Royal Albert Hall: 1967 – 'The King's Minstrel' (1968); 1969 – 'Take-over Bid' (1967) and 'Songs of Peace and War' (1972); 1970 – 'Logos I' (1979) and 'Chorales and Tangents'; 1972 British Congress – 'The Warrior's Psalm' (1974); 1973 – 'Beyond the Sunset'; 1975 – 'The Lord is King'; 1978 International Congress – 'On Ratcliff Highway' and 'Daystar'. The last mentioned was a busy year that also required a massed vocal and brass item of 'Battle Honours', in addition to a song setting of all The Salvation Army's doctrines. The ISB also resurrected 'The Holy War', Portsmouth Citadel Band played 'When they Crucified my Lord', for which Ray composed a new and dramatic ending, and massed cornets played 'The Veterans'.

The appearance of the overture 'Take-over Bid' in the above list shows a continuing commitment to serve the 'bread and butter' requirements of Salvationist bandsmen. In all, RSA provided five overture/selections for various Gowans/Larsson musicals and a whole host of individual song arrangements. For the most part he matched his style to the popular show idioms of the musicals themselves, only allowing himself some flights of fancy after the job was done. The popular, jaunty trombone ensemble from *Take-over Bid* – 'Wonders Begin when the Lord Comes In' – is totally in keeping with John Larsson's style until the coda, when the arranger adds jazzy syncopations and bluesy chords, concluding with a Technicolor ninth chord.

The old Army idea that jazz is 'of the Devil' was now fading fast, aided by input from a new generation of exceptional American Salvationist composers. Yet Ray has always had a broad perspective on musical styles, turning his hand to whatever is required. At about the same time, his links with Hendon Corps inspired yet another trombone feature. Quite a number of the bandsmen had professional and military experience and were capable of quite an effective jazz style. 'Sparkling Slides' (1975) was based on the song 'If Jesus keeps me Polished I will Outshine the Sun', confirming that RSA was equally fluent in popular and modern brass band idioms. As few bands could make such a convincing job as Hendon, it waited a considerable time to be published, until more bands could boast a reasonably competent kit drummer. Thirty years on we hear how well this number stands comparison with the latest crop of contemporary light music.

In the lovely lyrical cornet solo 'Someone Cares', Ray gives himself the freedom to substitute Larsson's simple harmonies for a rich, big-band style accompaniment. In fact, the origin of this arrangement was one of the many tracks he scored for two LPs entitled *Trumpet of the Lord* and *Sound the Battle Cry*. Using trumpets, french horns, trombones, tuba and rhythm section to back a small vocal group, the aim was to present light popular swing-style music. Another track that escaped from those vinyls was 'Bound for the Promised Land', which found its way into 'Beyond the Sunset'. Built around Eric Ball's lovely song 'In that Beautiful Land' and 'Beyond the Sunset', it is an expression of the Christian's yearning for the world to come and was Ray's idea to provide the ISB with something less epic for the occasion of the Bandmasters Councils Festival in 1973. There is some lovely music with a sublime, drawn-out ending as life fades into eternal peace. Harold Nobes of Portsmouth Citadel wrote: 'It caused us again to think hard while revelling in the full spectrum of sound and effect. A rewarding experience.' Unfortunately, Ray felt the music did not meet with general approval and withdrew it.

If, in broad terms, experiments to integrate atonal aspects were characteristic of his second period, then perhaps the last of these is 'The King's Minstrel'. Portraying an early-day Army character, James Bateman, the first movement is the most interesting. Energetic and brilliant, it begins with an almost complete 12-note row in unison (compare it with 'The Immortal Theme' and Leslie Condon's 'Festivity'), then tosses fragments around with remote keys and bitonality. Always fascinated with sound, RSA once rehearsed Regent Hall Band in this piece. Coming to the colourful penultimate chord of the first movement he held the band on a pause, cocked his head on one side, knit his brow and said: 'Hmmm... interesting!' This detached view of his own music can sometimes baffle those who treasure it. But for him, his is merely a small part in a fascinating sound world that he finds endlessly stimulating and inspiring.

In 1970 the ISB premiered a work with the intriguing title 'Logos I' (1979). As with 'Emmaus Journey', a similar inspiration seemed to have struck two composers at the same time, the two pieces seeing light of day at the same Albert Hall festival, with Box Hill Band from Australia performing Leslie Condon's 'Song of the Eternal'. Fortunately the two pieces shared little in their musical content. For 'Logos I' Ray again turned to Negro spirituals, placing a biblical narration before each movement. In his programme note for the festival he explains his thinking:

> 'A work on this theme has long been in the composer's mind, but in a quite different form. The subject is far from inexhaustible and the composer, not having abandoned his original intention, begs to append a numeral to the title. Extensive use of song material will, it is hoped, make the substance of this music readily approachable. In the first and last of the three movements the hymn "All Creatures of our God and King" enjoins all creation to praise him. In each movement a Negro spiritual is prominently featured: "He's Got the Whole World in his Hands", "He Never Spoke A Mumblin' Word" and "Ride On, King Jesus". These relate to three considerations of "The Word": 1 The Creation; 2 Made flesh; 3 Crowned and glorified.'

With extensive use of song material it was ideal for the addition of a large chorus for a welcome return to the Royal Albert Hall in 1979 and again at the 1990 International Congress Composers Festival in Wembley Arena. The darkly brooding second movement begins with a misty slow fugue, creeping by semitones, evoking a mind-numbing sorrow, dissolving evocatively into the spiritual: 'They crucified my Lord, but he never said a mumblin' word, not a word, not a word.' This is interrupted by a fanfare interestingly conjured from 'When I Survey'. Continuing with the lament, music like this can only come from deep within a composer's soul. The last movement bursts forth in jubilation, the composer showing an increasing fondness for compound triple time. The spiritual 'Ride On, King Jesus' blends effortlessly into 'All Creatures of our God and King' for one of his finest 'big-tune' moments – a

(Above) With Leslie Condon and Howard Davies,
Christmas 1977.

(Right) With 'Rachie' in Resolven, South Wales;
Ray is holding a picture of her grandfather Caradog
Roberts, who named the hymn tune after her.

(Below) The Music Editorial team Ray left in 1980:
Maurice Ozanne, Ray Bowes, Doreen Rutt,
Peter Ayling, Les Condon and Kevin Norbury.

(Above) Downtown open-air meeting in Sydney, 1982.

(Left) Christmas carolling in London, 1984.

(Below) Awarding prizes as the President of the National College of Music in its centenary year, 1990.

(Above) Conducting Enfield Band, with Bandmaster James Williams
as cornet soloist, 1987.

(Left) Leaving *Hen Felin*,
the cottage at Ystalyfera, for a
'specialling' engagement.

(Below) With poet Colonel
Catherine Baird, 1985.

(Above) Ray, Rosemary and Barbara in a family trio at Ray and Joy's
Golden Wedding, 1991.

(Below) Ray and Joy with members of the Japan Staff Band
during the ISB 120 celebrations, 2011.

final 'He's got the whole wide world in his hands' bringing the music to a thrilling conclusion.

Premiered at the same 1970 festival was a fascinating work, by its very nature destined to obscurity. With its scoring for grand organ, fanfare trumpets and band, 'Chorales and Tangents on "A Blessed and Glorious King"' was hardly likely to find many performance opportunities. In his description the composer said: 'The four movements cannot accurately be described as variants. Although the basic theme (the hymn tune "Moscow"), or part of it, is never far away, the tendency of the movements to go off at a tangent has led the composer to select the geometric term.' In *The Musician*, Max Wood of Michigan, USA, was thrilled by the premiere, describing it as 'a new concept in composing... a unique sound that was thoroughly enjoyed'.

Significantly, the composer acknowledges one of his most distinctive aspects – his ability to absorb material into the fabric of the music leaving only a passing flavour or essence. It is not immediately obvious from studying a score how this is achieved, but careful listening can reveal a watermark imprinted below the music's surface. Indeed, Ray will readily admit a sense of satisfaction if song material is absorbed naturally into the surrounding texture. One must not expect this process to be his only *modus operandi*. Using a whole range of approaches, he will only sometimes choose exhaustive 'thematic transformations', but for another work he will delight in seamlessly welding together a diverse and contrasting range of material.

As editor of subscription music journals, RSA could be painfully aware what genres were in short supply. He noticed that bandmasters often returned to Eric Ball's prewar classic 'The Triumph Of Peace', a fine work with a kind of substance that belies its modest length. Ball originally classed it as an 'overture' but such a classification was not allowed in the 1930s, so it was published as a tone poem. 'The Warrior's Psalm' (1974), a compact, concise form, exactly filled the void. Its one well known tune, 'Armageddon', associated with the words of Francis Ridley Havergal, provides the title.

> Not for weight of glory,
> Not for crown and palm,
> Enter we the army,
> Raise the warrior psalm;
> But for love that claimeth
> Lives for whom he died;
> He whom Jesus nameth
> Must be on his side.

An example of classical sonata form, its two contrasting original subjects are symphonic in style: the first an heroic triplet march, the second, continuing in the same tempo, a spaciously lyrical cornet solo, underpinned with a sweepingly contrapuntal bass line. Building to an inevitable triumphant conclusion, 'The Warrior's Psalm' is remembered by some with affection.

It is perhaps characteristic of the composer's later period that he had no further need to be particularly innovative, leaving him the freedom to express himself freely and profoundly. Always present is a desire not to seem dated, dull or predictable. One might only guess how much of a personal statement is 'The Lord is King'; might it in some way be his equivalent of Richard Strauss's self-portrait *Ein Heldenleben* ('A Hero's Life')? Although RSA refuses to be drawn on Peter Graham's description of it as his 'crowning glory', he quietly agrees with surprising detachment: 'I like that, I like what it does,' adding that he may have achieved his ideal to 'make the tune part of it'. Challenging and arresting, taut in structure, brilliant in colour and orchestration, 'The Lord is King' takes its rightful place at the pinnacle of Salvation Army brass band literature. Malcolm Bale, reporting on the ISB's performance at the Royal Albert Hall, described it thus:

> 'The main contribution of the International Staff Band was a work which is undoubtedly the most ambitious yet produced for an Army band and possibly even for brass bands generally. To call it a symphony (as the British Commissioner did) is not by any means to over-rate its importance. "The Lord is King" is the title Ray Steadman-Allen has given to this magnificent music, which takes its inspiration from song 887' [in the 1953 songbook] 'and its thematic material from the Welsh hymn tune associated with those words ("Llangollen") and the chorus, "He Died of a Broken Heart for Me". Its form is really of a symphonic tone poem and it paints three vivid sound pictures to express the idea that all aspects of human life can "have their place and serve his will in God's economy". An exciting first movement portrays "My Joys"; the second, "My Toils", is sombre and suitably laborious, while in the final movement, "My Craftsman's Skill", the clamour of machinery and the hustle of the workshop are caught in a fugal fury of activity before the final *maestoso* restatement of the theme.'

It is a work where the principle of 'thematic transformations' is evident at all levels, yet one suspects this is nearly always intuitive. The tune of 'Llangollen' is superficially simple but on closer inspection reveals an unusual structure[21]. The material is absorbed into the composition without overemphasis, yet there is the feeling of a close audible link. It is clear from the initial bars that there is a mood of celebration. The first actual statement of the tune is actually quite simple, its final phrase extended by metrical implication. Between the phrases an apparently unrelated motif appears, destined to assume considerable importance throughout the work, in particular the second movement. Could it be this is RSA's personal motto?

The second movement contains some of the composer's most profound thoughts, alternating a disturbing sequence of unresolved chords devoid of melody over a throbbing bass, with a long lyrical melody woven from the 'RSA' motif. Imperceptibly the chorus, 'He died of a broken heart', is introduced and the restlessness returns, throbbing turns to hammering and 'died of a broken...' is heard repeatedly. Response is indeed a personal thing, but in this context, an evocation of the crucifixion cannot be ignored.

The last movement, as well as being a tour de force for the band, tests the skill of the composer in welding together melodic fragments with sustained energy and progression. Immediately a new figure is thrust forward, being an assimilation of Leslie Condon's affectation to drum on the desk this distinctive rhythm – 'Be dum dum!' It appears that the whole process of this movement is to draw together all the different strands towards a glorious restatement of 'Llangollen', which points towards further development of an exhilarating coda, pausing briefly to remind the listener: 'He died of a broken heart for me.'

'The Lord is King' stands as a prime example of RSA's mature style, combining profound expression, epic statement and consummate skill in handling a complex symphonic structure. It is tempting to speculate that there was little more to be said.

The duties of Editor-in-Chief of The Salvation Army's music were much more than expressing himself in major works for the finest bands. Voluntary donation to the Army of composers' own cherished inspirations inevitably leaves gaps in the regular subscription journals which have to be filled by the Editor and his staff. To balance these needs and the wide range of Salvationist music requirements was, for years, a self-sacrificing duty of Ray Steadman-Allen. It is sobering to peruse the entire list of all his music to put his most creative work into context. But still the demand for new works for special band tours and occasions continued to flood in. As he observed somewhat quizzically in the 1973 *Musician* interview: 'We have created a climate of desire for novelty which is to our own hurt, very often because in the quest to play the latest, some works get overlooked... If we are not careful we could find that we inculcate a sense of living for novelty rather than quality.'

In spite of that, the International Congress, held in London in 1978, saw Ray contribute a bewildering array of new compositions. Festivals took place simultaneously at Wembley Arena and at the Royal Albert Hall. The suite 'Battle Honours', written for festival chorus, band and trumpets, is one of the few of his large occasional pieces to be repeated. Celebrating 90 years of junior bands there was also a new piece, 'A Call to Action', played by massed young people. At the Royal Albert Hall massed Staff Bands from Melbourne, New York and London premiered 'Daystar'. Again largely in RSA's now preferred favourite compound triple time, 'Daystar' presents the listener with little uncompromising language, often juxtaposing his inimitable lyrical style with music of a joyous, celebratory nature creating a profound sense of praise and exaltation.

Norman Bearcroft remembers: 'The magnificent arrangements of "Fairest Lord Jesus" and "Lord of all Nature" which appear several times in the work, are, to me, so moving that I cannot express the emotion I feel as the music unfolds.'

If there is a sense of anticipation that awaits new works, similarly there is a sense of expectation in the ISB band room when a manuscript appears for the first time. However, 'On Ratcliff Highway' arrived on their music stands with no accompanying explanation. Anticipation turned to incredulity as the players sight-read this extraordinary music. True, Erik Leidzén said: 'If a Salvationist composer has to explain his music he has failed in his task,' but this was programme music of the first order. Subtitled 'Victorian Snapshots', it was written for simultaneous presentation by the Melbourne and International Staff Bands at the Congress's two major venues. To gain inspiration for the work, Ray had visited London's dockland area, now changed beyond recognition from Victorian times, but it was enough. Hardly remembering how or why he wrote, Ray quickly conjured up a most vivid picture of early-day Salvationists marching through London's colourful, cosmopolitan and decadent East End. Into this highway, strewn with human wreckage and detritus, marches the fledgling Salvation Army. In the composer's own words:

> 'Snatches of old-time songs such as "Champagne Charlie", "What shall we do with the Drunken Sailor?" and "Genevieve" evoke an atmosphere of river fogs, steam trains, horse carriages and dockside life. From up river there comes the sound of the Westminster Chimes. The original themes are bitter and coarse with mournful or vicious overtones – all the emotions of human wreckage. A street fight occurs. Over all broods a recurring, passionate theme suggesting divine yearning for these sad souls. The approach of the band is represented by the tune "Hold the Fort". There is a clash with roughnecks in the road where the Christian Missioners (SA forerunners) were indeed beaten up, and in the collision of tunes we are reminded of the courage of the early-day warriors and honour them in the song "We'll Be Heroes".'

The truth is that, given adequate introduction, a piece of this nature with its 20th-century compositional techniques, usually anathema to musically more conservative Salvationists, can be evocative, descriptive and inspiring. Weaving together fragments of Victorian street calls, the distant chimes of Big Ben and music hall songs with cross-rhythms, obtuse counterpoints and bitonality, the composer reached into Army history and produced a work of great strength and character. The story is told of a performance in Preston by the Melbourne Staff

Band, eloquently introduced by Norman Bearcroft. It so captivated one lady that, at the point where 'Hold The Fort' comes to an abrupt halt, her previously unnoticed vocal contribution suddenly became a solo!

Relocation to Australia did little to stem the tide of band music, and when Camberwell Band (Melbourne) approached RSA for a piece to play on their forthcoming 1982 tour of the UK he was happy to oblige. Returning once again to one of his preferred forms, he fashioned a suite, actually described as a sinfonietta, 'At the Edge of Time'. If Salvation Army musicians and congregations were now familiar with sounds of a more contemporary nature, there were still new ones to be found. No more the restless atonalities of the 1960s; now there is fascination with extended diatonic harmony. From its title one would expect the subject matter to be somewhat apocalyptic. Returning to the majestic tune of 'St Magnus' (a masterful hymn tune setting was published in 1969), a suggestion of which is heard in the opening bars, the first movement is mainly martial in character. Trombones and then cornets declare a strangely naive and pompous march tune built only from two different notes. A second verse of 'St Magnus' gently intervenes; the pompous march draws closer, its ranks proud and confident, but halted by a third magnificent statement of the hymn tune. The music that follows in the second movement, by contrast, is simple, tender and supremely beautiful. Introduced by clusters of muted cornets and trombones, an ostinato horn figure pervades the entire movement. A lone cornet pleads sorrowfully – the ostinato moves on to cornets and the lament is found to be a counterpoint of the lovely children's song 'When He Cometh'.

Bursting forward as if from the very depths of a shattered earth, apocalyptic music tears apart the peaceful atmosphere to begin the third movement. An ungainly march, taunting, leering; an alarm sounds and an upward-thrusting gesture similar to that heard previously in 'When they Crucified my Lord' and 'Lord of the Sea' takes on significance. There is brief comfort for the faithful as the Zulu tune to the words 'Never Fades the Name of Jesus' is heard.

Returning, the torment is greater, building until the veil is torn violently and the faithful realise their utter hopelessness in the penitential words: 'We have not known thee as we ought... Lord give us light to know thy truth.' Yet there is still no respite; all are caught up in an upward surge of struggling humanity. Softly the 'torn veil' gesture breathes its last. The music leads to the one and only place – the foot of the cross of him who alone can save: 'The head that once was crowned with thorns is crowned with glory now.'

Astonishingly, the end is not yet. The tumult returns more ferocious than ever, hammering, tearing, screaming... the head spins, the ears ring. There is sudden stillness, emptiness. A lament plays. Can it be that there is no comfort, that the gut-wrenching, final chords are not victorious? As Ray and Joy Steadman-Allen made their way to Australia in 1979 the world stood teetering on the brink of superpower conflict over Afghanistan. What is the message of this music? It is not a vision of the end of time but a vision of the edge of the abyss. Conflicts have come and gone but terrorism, global warming and even financial meltdown still threaten complacency. In 'At the Edge of Time' Ray Steadman-Allen has provided eloquent warning!

The world of Salvation Army music has undergone attrition, unimagined in the immediate postwar years. No longer is it true to say that most towns and many villages have at least one and often more full-sized Army bands; in reality there are now very few, even if the very best would be the envy of their forebears. The world of Salvation Army bands is now a shadow of its halcyon days; young people with greater opportunity and knowledge than ever before move to a different beat, sing a different song. Looking back on the composer's vast, prolific output, one realises that much of it is now neglected for no other reason than the lack of opportunity to present it. But still the restless, creative spirit of Ray Steadman-Allen pours forth music for all Army uses.

Technology carries music with a fidelity and capacity never dreamt of even 20 years ago. Recorded music now penetrates the heart and soul through tiny earphones – and with it, classics from the pen of RSA. With the relaxation of Army regulations, Salvationist publications are now available to anyone, regardless of religious affiliation. Apart from his purpose-written competition pieces, various RSA Army pieces have been used as such, including 'On Ratcliff Highway' which was a National Brass Band Championship regional test piece in 2009. In 2004, a recorded historical survey of brass band repertoire by Elgar Howarth and the Grimethorpe Band included 'The Holy War'. YBS (Yorkshire Building Society) Band under David King recorded a series of CDs with the title *Essays In Brass*, including 'On Ratcliff Highway', 'The Holy War' and 'The Lord is King'. The same band and conductor paid a personal tribute with an entire album of Steadman-Allen music entitled *Alpha And Omega*. It was subsequently voted *British Bandsman* CD of the year and in 2011 listeners voted 'The Lord is King' into Classic FM's Hall of Fame!

Undeniably, the Salvation Army brass band music of RSA has, for many years, made a considerable impact on thousands of listeners. It is extraordinary that the composer has remained surprisingly detached and objective about his output. Perhaps that is the reason he has continued to produce music of such creativity, innovation and depth. Post retirement, he has continued to feed into the Army music world, now quite changed from his boyhood, music of integrity and value. One is tempted to feel that the message of it all has left him aloof and unmoved. Yet nothing can be further from the truth. In 1985, as Norman Howe was planning his series of Bible studies for the National School of Music at Cobham Hall, he hit on the idea of asking RSA to write a work that would complement his thinking musically. Always cautious of writing directly representational music, Ray's aim was to evoke the essence of Romans Chapter 8. For this he saturated the work with song material, making direct or closely related references in nearly every bar. In more formal times the music would have been classed as a 'selection', for it is certainly a medley of song tunes, but that classification would tend to misrepresent the nature of this wonderful music. Kevin Ashman, now of the Music Ministries Department and cornet soloist of the ISB, then a student at the music school, recalls that every member of that year's school was deeply moved and impacted by the music. Norman Bearcroft, the course director, describes the first presentation to the whole school by the A Band[22]:

> 'As the work came to a close, absent was the good-natured banter that usually follows a number played by the A Band at music school, and all present were aware that the Lord was standing there, standing with us. Nothing more was said or sung as, one by one, the students quietly left what had become for all a holy place.'

Stylistically there is little in common with 'The Holy War' but interestingly they are linked in two respects. The notorious cluster chord that offended some so violently in 1965 returns in 'Romans 8' as a gentle mist, almost imperceptibly forming and then dispersing. The former work was built entirely on the chorale 'Ein Feste Burg', but now RSA takes mainly the final phrase associated with the words 'His Kingdom is for ever' and scatters it through the entire piece. If RSA has, on occasions, doubted the wisdom of not providing a gallery ending for some of his works, there should be no doubt about the ending of 'Romans 8 – A Brass Celebration'. In the final moments, there is a tremendous build-up, created from 'Ein Feste Burg', climaxing with Stainer's majestic hymn tune 'In the Cross of Christ I Glory'. The ensuing *morendo* is an affirmation that the final notes speak surely and simply: 'His Kingdom is for ever – Amen.'

At a festival given by the ISB and the ISS at the Fairfield Halls in Croydon to celebrate RSA's 85th birthday, those same bars ended a night of celebration in eloquent benediction to a life dedicated not to Salvation Army music alone but to the message that had inspired, motivated and equipped Ray Steadman-Allen. Deeply moved by the music he stepped forward to thank the participants, testifying simply and sincerely:

> In the Cross of Christ I glory,
> Towering o'er the wrecks of time;
> All the light of sacred story
> Gathers round its head sublime.

Dudley Bright is currently Principal Trombone of the London Symphony Orchestra and Professor of Trombone at the Royal Academy of Music. He is a well-known international trombone soloist and Salvation Army composer. He made his debut aged 14 as a soloist with the ISB playing a piece written for him by RSA called 'Suite on Original Christmas Carols'.

Chapter Notes

1. International Staff Band known as the ISB. Originally comprised of employees at International Headquarters, it became the benchmark for all bands. Entrusted with the preparation of new music to be presented for approval to the International Music Board (now UK Territorial Music Council).
2. Dates given are of publication unless indicated otherwise.
3. Scores for each issue of a subscription journal written by members of the department contained introductory notes introducing the music and then giving helpful hints to aid performance.
4. *The Musician* was a weekly magazine for Salvationists catering largely for bandsmen and songsters.
5. Evangeline Booth's 'Streams in the Desert' was the first tone poem, as suggested by Eric Ball who was responsible for the band score.
6. The pentatonic scale can be heard by playing the five black notes of a piano. The scale is typical of much folk music around the world.
7. A term coined by Dr Ronald Holz in his introduction to the CD *Alpha and Omega – The music of Ray Steadman-Allen*.
8. 'The Immortal Theme'.
9. Something like a Salvation Army version of the Mothers Union.
10. *The Musician* 7 July 1973 'Matters of Composition – Part Two'.
11. Probably the most famous example of this is the 1st movement of Beethoven's 5th Symphony.
12. 'Via Dolorosa' is the Latin for 'Road of Sorrows'.
13. A publication for small and junior bands scored largely in 4 parts with an optional euphonium.
14. Eric Ball resigned as an officer and Bandmaster of the ISB in 1945.
15. See p 43 for discussion of names.
16. A system of composing in which all 12 different notes of the chromatic scale are arranged in a row without repetition and used as the basis for a composition without a sense of key.
17. Arthur Rolls was a cousin of Maisie's and continued to serve in the ISB until his retirement, despite a heart attack in 1962.
18. A full appreciation of this piece is included in the Appendix.
19. The daughter of Commissioner Booth Tucker thought she had a section of choruses by her father, which RSA had to inform her were actually by others, only copied in her father's handwriting. Getting a little irate she began to criticise 'this awful band music' citing 'In Me, Lord'.

20. Common chords are built from the key note plus a third and a fifth above. Added note chords have other notes added, in this case the second and the sixth.
21. The first half is made up of two equal three-bar phrases, the third four and a half and the last two and a half. The basic simple rhythmic pattern is three beats long over a duple time signature.
22. The elite band formed from the best students.

Chapter Eighteen

Music In Mufti

Paul Hindmarsh

Paul Hindmarsh surveys the music Ray Steadman-Allen has composed for non-Salvation Army purposes.

IS Ray Steadman-Allen the most played brass band composer and arranger of all time? Possibly, since, in addition to his many hundreds of compositions and arrangements penned for Salvation Army use, his *100 Favourite Hymn Tunes* [or *120 Favourite Hymn Tunes* in the enlarged 2001 edition] which he arranged and edited for the publishers Wright and Round is used on a regular basis by the vast majority of non-SA brass bands of all standards and sizes in the United Kingdom and further afield. Although RSA's original work for the wider band movement is not as well established in the repertoire, the collection is both substantial and varied, ranging from test pieces and other 'bespoke' commissions to shorter concert items, some with a spiritual message and some composed for secular entertainment. They add dimensions of received creative expression and technical exploration that add to his stature as one of the brass band movement's musical 'adventurers'.

That spirit of musical adventure was evident in some of RSA's earliest important compositions. The revised finale of 'Lord of the Sea' from the 1950s includes flashes of harmonic dissonance, incisive colour and sea-shanty imagery that sets this work apart from the norm of Salvation Army publications of the period. The fact that it was originally composed as a secular work is a significant contributory factor, but even some of his devotional works stretch the harmonic and textural conventions in intriguing ways – for example, the dramatic contrapuntal and rhetorical moments in that fine symphonic poem 'When they Crucified my Lord', especially the opening, and the more searching quality of its sadly neglected Easter companion-piece 'Via Dolorosa'.

The quest for an accommodation between personal expression and a more contemporary approach to matters of harmonic, textural and rhythmic complexity on the one hand, and the demands and functions of hymn/song-based writing for The Salvation Army on the other, lies at the heart of much of RSA's most ambitious and substantial brass band music. Yet even when he is at his most adventurous, he never loses touch with the core of his language, which is founded on the traditions of English hymnology and counterpoint. In that respect RSA could be regarded as an heir of Vaughan Williams as much as his Salvation Army exemplars like Eric Ball.

As a young teenager in the 1960s, I became fascinated by the way RSA, Leslie Condon and Wilfred Heaton in particular were 'bending the rules' by introducing techniques and sounds from the 20th-century mainstream into their Salvationist work: extending but never breaking the boundaries of tonality, brightening up the sound of the brass band with more vivid colours (a counterpart to the way Gilbert Vinter was transforming the sound of the band on the contest stage), more incisive rhythmic energy and, above all, being prepared to be flexible with the 'given' content – personalising it, if you like. In RSA's substantial music of the late 1960s and 70s, this became evident in a flexibility at the joins between musical episodes and in a freedom of stylistic and contrapuntal treatment. Writing in the programme notes of the YBS Band's *Alpha and Omega* CD, the noted musicologist and brass band historian Ronald Holz encapsulated the RSA style in one sometimes overused word – eclectic. In this case, I think it is an entirely appropriate summation of Ray's approach to composition, which over the decades has embraced pop and jazz idioms as well as the more rigorous techniques of the 20th-century musical mainstream.

His musical adventures might have been frowned upon by the traditionalists, but there were many, including myself, who responded to what I perceived as a rebellious spirit. The dense dissonances of the climax of 'The Holy War' became my favourite brass band moment for its visceral energy. A work that I didn't know at the time but have come to admire in more recent years is the suite for trombone, 'The Immortal Theme', composed in 1962 for Maisie Wiggins. Is there another work in the Army literature that opens with a 12-tone row?

The work where RSA began to take a more determined and consistent adventurous direction remains in manuscript. 'Chorales and Tangents' (a 'modernist' 1970s title if ever there was one) has received just two performances since it was composed in 1972. The premiere performance at a Royal Albert Hall Army festival was a memorable one for me. The brilliance and clarity of the writing for brass and the imaginative ways in which the composer manipulated that great hymn tune 'Moscow' remained with me for decades. After that single outing, the piece seemed to sink without trace. For one thing, it was never really finished off. Since RSA conducted the performance himself, he did not write out a complete full score. However, when a long-held ambition of mine to engineer a second performance presented itself at the 2006 Royal

Northern College of Music Festival of Brass, for which I have the honour of serving as artistic director, I was able to prepare a full set of material, including a full score. During that editing process, I became even more convinced of the importance of this work in the RSA canon.

'Chorales and Tangents' may be based on a hymn tune, in time-honoured Army fashion, but the tune is used, as J. S. Bach might have done, like an objective 'quarry' for musical material rather than as an aid to worship. This concise nine-minute work is in effect a *concerto grosso*, a work of 'absolute' music, in which the tune is subjected to a mosaic of transformations. It becomes the subject for strands of modal counterpoint, for angular fragmentations, for 'early music' dances and for brilliant fanfares. RSA is working with much freedom and taking many musical risks, most of which come off. This is his summary of the piece:

> '"Chorales and Tangents" has something of the *concerto grosso* about it, in that there are two groups and an organ involved. It was written in the early 1970s for a Salvation Army concert in the Royal Albert Hall, London, and was performed by the International Staff Band of The Salvation Army (ISB) with organ soloist Michael Clack. A set of fanfare trumpets were featured in the concert and it seemed an appropriate occasion in which to bring the forces together.
>
> The music is a suite of movements broadly based on the hymn tune "Moscow". (I think I must have planned more chorales!) The "tangents" are departures or "strayings" from the chosen theme.
>
> 1. *Maestoso*: the full ensemble presents the theme.

2. A brief *scherzando* for brass quintet with a snare drum ostinato. It follows loosely the theme contour.

3. A slow chorale, with the trumpet group initially holding the stage, yielding to the band and finally joining it in a full tutti.

4. *Allegro vivace*: an energetic 5/4.

5. *Carillon*: organ solo, with a medieval flavour, enhanced by touches of percussion.

6. *Finale*: Pre-eminently organ at the outset, with some fanfare elements, culminating in the theme *grandioso*.

At the age of 50, RSA had reached, it seems to me, a point of new departure, which led to the crop of Salvation Army works that represent his most individual creative contribution to The Salvation Army – works such as 'On Ratcliff Highway', with its imaginative Charles Ives-influenced collage construction; 'The Lord is King' (a masterly technical and expressive tour de force, head and heart in perfect accord); and the powerful sinfonietta 'The Edge of Time'.

Some years ago, in a BBC documentary featuring professional musicians who are active Salvationists, Ray made clear that his 'priesthood calling' as a full-time Salvation Army officer and his 'creative calling' as a composer were not conjoined. While his life as a Christian minister was 'fundamental', his composing was separate, rooted by conviction to The Salvation Army but not exclusively locked into it. As he explained: 'Faith and musical composition are two distinct elements and may well combine to influence and motivate.' Consequently the music he has composed in retirement from full-time ministry for the wider brass band world has embraced both the sacred and the secular, serious and diverting. Given that the music profession and the brass band community is full of both active and former Salvationists, it is hardly surprising that his craftsman's skills were soon much in demand.

On 5 September 1987 at Manchester's Free Trade Hall a gala evening entitled the 'Concert of the Century' was staged by the *British Bandsman* magazine to celebrate its centenary. Included in the festivities was a four-movement symphonic suite specially commissioned from RSA, 'The Beacons', performed by IMI Yorkshire Imperial Band, conducted by James Scott. Given the nature of the celebration, his title and the expressive sub-text were most appropriate. 'The Beacons' was the first major non-Salvationist work that Ray had conceived since the original version of 'Lord of the Sea' in the early 1950s and thus the first for more than 30 years not to include any hymn- or sacred song-based content or references. Instead the composer imagines how, centuries before the days of newsprint and mass communication, 'hill-top beacon fires blazed across the land signalling important happenings or warnings of invasion. This music tells no specific story, but the titles of the four thematically related sections are a guide to the ideas.'

'The Beacons' has something of the character of the march, and the fanfare, spirited and tightly driving, promises most of the thematic material of the work. 'Far Horizons' is largely tranquil and is thinly scored with solo passages. 'The Invaders' has the most dramatic potential; its energy and conflict subsides to a lament and a tolling bell before a vigorous rounding off. 'Celebration', appropriately, is in a merry-making mood, and the jubilant music concludes with fragment statements of the main themes.

'The Beacons' is one of RSA's most integrated and symphonically framed works. It lacks the immediate lyrical appeal of some of his Salvationist pieces, but teems with invention. Textures and moods seem to be in a constant state of flux, the music's momentum and cohesion being supplied by short, memorable motifs based, like many of his non-Army works from this later period, on fourth- and fifth-based gestures that underpin the whole work. The brief first movement presents a kaleidoscope of images, from pithy fanfares to the jubilant pealing of bells and his trademark dancing cross-rhythms. The changeable, expressive quality of the music and the way short motifs are used to bring it all together reminds me of the way the great Danish symphonist Carl Nielsen 'painted' his musical canvases.

After the energy of the first movement, the second movement paints a much more restrained, enigmatic picture. This is a tricky movement to bring off. The contours of the solo lines which weave their way through the band present technical and expressive challenges, especially the leaping octave exchanges and high-lying decorative arabesques. The gentle, lilting pulse that has provided the underlying unity of this haunting movement is brusquely swept aside by aggressive transformations of the main fourth- and octave-based ideas in 'The Invaders'. Over his long composing career, RSA has proved adept at conveying images of violence and conflict in his writing. Think of the searing climax of 'The Holy War' or the dense, polytonal layering and jagged rhythms in 'On Ratcliff Highway'. The sense of threat and urgency – barbarism, even – in the music of 'The Invaders' is conveyed through brusque interjections from trombones and leaping contrapuntal lines that build inexorably towards a vigorous battle song. As the sounds of battle subside, a deep bell tolls in 'Lament' while the victors celebrate. 'Celebration' is less complex, combining simpler cyclic transformations of the core material in joyful dancing rhythms, with a reprise of the main ideas from the first movement, to provide affirmative resolution and structural balance. 'The Beacons' was dedicated to Eric Ball, a former editor of *British Bandsman*, who was a strong musical influence early on in RSA's career. The piece was used as a competition test piece for the 1990 regional qualifying round of the National Championships, but has rarely been heard since, with the notable exception of a vivid recording by the YBS Band conducted by David King [*Alpha and Omega*, SFZ 126].

RSA's next major non-Army work, 'Seascapes', has fared even less well. It was commissioned by Boosey & Hawkes for the 1988 National Brass Band Championship finals in the Royal Albert Hall. Subsequently, it received a broadcast performance on BBC Radio 3 early in 1990 as part of the BBC Festival of Brass by the winning band, Desford Colliery (under James Watson), since when this colourful and challenging work has languished on band room library shelves. Sitting in the Royal Albert Hall for the premiere performances in 1988, I was impressed with the array of scintillating colour and texture that RSA extracted from the band. The constantly changing fabric and the impulsive ebb and flow of moods were audibly projected through the cyclic thematic content and underpinned by strongly characterised rhythms. Reading the score later, when I came to broadcast the work, those impressions were confirmed and it struck me that no band in 1988 really reached to the heart of this music – the contrasts between energy and lyricism, dancing rhythms and evocative *rubato*.

Each movement takes its inspiration from a verse of John Masefield's famous poem 'Cargoes'. The first opens with a gentle, exotically perfumed modal tune, with open fifths and gently lapping accompaniments: 'Quinquireme of Nineveh from distant Orphir, Rowing home to haven in sunny Palestine.' The lilting melody, with its simple, memorable contour, is the suite's principal motif.

After the opening section has displayed much embellished detail, it is transformed into a wild and extended dance, highly exuberant and packed with detail. The momentum it gathers dissipates in thunderous percussion. There is just enough musical energy for a few bars of exhausted reminiscence of the exotic calm of the Orient that we heard in the opening section.

In the second movement, it is an image of Masefield's stately Spanish galleon sailing through the tropics by palm-fringed beaches that RSA's elegant music is intended to convey. The underlying dance rhythm here is of the baroque *sarabande*, but the composer allows himself considerable freedom and flexibility in the degree of 'written in' and implied *rubato*.

It is beautifully realised music, the subtlety of which passed all the bands by, even the winners, as I recall from 1988. Although the tempo slows marginally for a middle section of concerto grosso-like duets, the music, paradoxically, sounds faster or at any rate more active. The Spanish musical accent has become more obvious, with flashes of flamenco, hints of castanets and, at the climax, the musical equivalent of an 'Olé' from the whole band! When the *sarabande* returns, it becomes partially engulfed in waves of added textures and surges of activity in the basses.

The finale is, for me, the most impressive movement in purely compositional terms. Here is vividly portrayed the 'dirty British coaster with a salt-caked smoke stack, Butting through the channel in the mad March days'. There is no room for elegance and exoticism. Echoes of sea shanties and hornpipes prevail. Typical RSA flurries of activity butt up against them, and the somewhat elusive character of the principal themes is transformed into jovial songs and marches.

III. Shanties and jovial song transformations

In the middle of the movement RSA conjures up a wonderful image of fog in the channel. The music fragments, harmonies bend into elusive polytonal combinations, a ship's bell (whose inclusion caused much consternation in 1988) sounds out eerily from the muffled textures. However, the sky soon clears and 'Seascapes' ends with the main motifs resounding in jubilation.

RSA's eclectic acquisition of technique and style has enabled him over the years to tailor his music to the needs of its intended performers or function without a sense of compromise or of 'writing down'. He is especially adept at writing imaginatively for younger and less experienced performers. A work like the suite 'Stantonbury Festival', for example, commissioned by Milton Keynes Borough Council for its local youth band to play in the 1980 festival, combines simple, attractive folk-tune treatments with hints of contemporary colour while remaining well within the capabilities of a youth or a community band in the Fourth Section. Despite its enigmatic title, 'Amaranth' was a more abstract work than 'Stantonbury' and both technically and musically much more demanding. It was commissioned by Sandwell Youth Band (conductor Keith Watts) and was first performed by them in West Bromwich Town Hall in May 1989. The title is a reference to a mythical purple flower, as RSA explains, 'mysterious in that it never fades or dies. In an extended single movement, the music explores the colours and textures of the band.' In 1992 'Amaranth' was chosen as the test piece for the National Brass Band Championships in the Third Section. Similarly, the tuneful suite 'The Journeymen' (1993) has found a welcome niche in the concert and contest repertoire of youth and Fourth Section bands, with its attractive ingredients drawn from light and popular styles from both sides of the Atlantic. Each of the four miniatures takes a distinctive musical image. 'Wayfarer' is purposeful and perky. 'Pilgrim' takes on a more meditative, 'period' flavour with its flowing 'question and answer' melody and mock Renaissance dance. 'Sundowner' clip-clops along like something from a B-movie Western, while 'Commuter' takes on the manner of a piece of British light music – with its catchy syncopations and bustling beat.

The early 1990s was an especially productive period for non-Salvationist commissions and publications. In 1990, the Norwegian brass band Manger Musikklag recorded a trio of Norwegian-inspired works. The simplest is a setting for flugelhorn and band of the folk song 'Astrid'. The most substantial is 'Expressions', a complex work for championship-level bands in three compact movements, contrasting the simplicity of its folk song-like lyrical invention with the rigour of the RSA 'modernist' style.

Arguably more musically and emotionally satisfying is a nine-minute meditation on a beautiful Scandinavian children's song 'Ingen er så trygg I fare' ('Children of the Heavenly Father'). Originally commissioned by a Salvation Army band, this extended treatment follows the conventions of the Army meditation in outline. The three contrasting 'verses' of the song are linked by developmental episodes and framed by a freely composed introduction and a coda. The music flows seamlessly between the various sections, with subtly inflected chromatic harmonies and shifting textures providing a fluid and at times impressionistic backdrop for the given melody. Like the much older meditations of Wilfred Heaton, with which this lovely work shares some characteristics, notably the restrained, tonally ambiguous opening, 'Children of the Heavenly Father' (or 'Divine Comfort' as it is now entitled in the published edition from Gobelin Music) lifts the humble hymn-tune meditation into an altogether more sophisticated expressive plane. Manger has continued its connection with RSA. In 1993, the band recorded 'Paskemorgen' and as recently as 8 September 2011 premiered 'Magnificent Thunderbird', which had been commissioned in 2009. This expansive 23-minute concert suite is inspired by the paintings of the Norwegian expressionist painter Edvard Munch. The writing juxtaposes popular and 'period' styles including jazz, blues and dance music of the 1920s and 30s, with the occasional medieval inflection added for good measure – with serious and satirical elements.

In 1991, almost 20 years after 'Chorales and Tangents', RSA fashioned a second set of variations that infuses his 20th-century voice with a 'period' flavour. Composed as the test piece for the Second Section finals of the 1991 National Brass Band Championships, 'Chorales' is also based on a familiar tune from the Christian tradition, in this case the 15th-century German carol melody 'Es ist ein Ros entsprungen' ('There is a Rose that Bloometh'), as it appears in the *Oxford Book of Carols*. The same harmonisation, originally published in *Musae Sioniae* (1609) by Michael Praetorius (1571-1621), is set in *The English Hymnal and Songs of Praise* to the English words 'A Great and Mighty Wonder'. As RSA modestly explains in his programme note: 'Following the introduction and theme there are four variations and a finale, during the course of which the chorale undergoes a number of transformations. The musical language, while not directly rooted in the period, reflects something of earlier styles, and elements of the chorale are never far away.'

These are the bare facts, which do not convey the full flavour of this tightly composed and joyful work. The introduction, with its brusque off-beat chords set against rapid semiquaver flourishes and fanfares, establishes an extrovert setting for the chorale theme. The spirited scherzo which follows 'plays' with elements of both the introduction and the carol in a changeable contrapuntal canvas that introduces plenty of dancing rhythms and leaping intervals, particularly fourths, fifths and octaves, right across the range. In the second variant, the carol melody is set in an elaborate weft of counterpoints and harmonies – a 'call and response' manner, where a phrase of new invention is answered by lines from the carol over a sustained harmonic 'resolution' rather like a miniature chorale prelude. The third variation transforms 'Es ist ein Ros' into a feather-light dance that gradually gains momentum and harmonic intensity as the entry of fanfare figures derived from the introduction propels the music to an abrupt finish. The atmosphere then calms for a lilting pastorale, whose siciliana-like character is conveyed by gently falling and rising scales, more evocative colours, especially on cornets at the end, and a warmer, chromatic palette of harmony.

It has become something of an unwritten rule that test pieces of this kind, whose major feature is a memorable melody (either original or applied, as in this case), should come to a big finish with a resounding full version of the tune, overlaid with all manner of musical pyrotechnics. This is the way in which RSA himself has brought many of his most substantial Army and non-Army offerings to an end. However, in 'Chorales' he has taken a different approach. The finale begins full of vigour and determination, generating rhythmic figuration from the first line of the chorale, over a pounding bass. The lydian or raised fourth characteristic of this section is amplified in the central paragraph, where the third line of the chorale becomes the subject of a harmonically ambiguous dance, its 'period' quality refracted through a modern 'lens'. The energy inexorably builds to a final tutti elaboration of the chorale's last two lines, before the work dances to its joyful conclusion. While the level of technical difficulty and musical adventure in 'Chorales' would challenge the very best of brass bands, it would sit very well in the First Section as a test piece as I write in 2011.

Those familiar with RSA's many and varied musical adventures will have their favourites. For many, the innocent charm of 'Lord of the Sea' is as compelling now as it was half a century ago. Then there will be those for whom 'The Holy War' remains the iconic landmark in Salvation Army brass band writing of the 1950s and 60s. Others will undoubtedly look to the period when RSA was attempting to find a rapprochement between the hymn-based traditions of Christian expression within the Army and the pull of the 'classical' mainstream. Works like 'On Ratcliff Highway' or 'At the Edge of Time' would fall into that category. The meditative expression in devotional works like the timeless selections 'In Quiet Pastures' and its companion piece 'By Love Compelled' or the scriptural inspiration of 'Romans 8' are also high on the list of many. I retain much affection for a pair of light-hearted 'Sunday afternoon' pieces, the concise variations 'Walk in the Light' and the sharply-etched suite 'The King's Minstrel' – two fine examples of Army music in the British light music tradition.

However, the one work that arguably stands at the pinnacle of RSA's prolific body of original work for brass bands of whatever persuasion is 'Hymn at Sunrise'. Commissioned for the 1996 All England Masters Brass Band Championship, this five-movement symphonic suite is RSA's most expansive work for brass band. It also integrates many of his stylistic and technical preoccupations into a united whole. Although it is an abstract symphonic work, its textures and character will evoke images on many levels – spiritual, emotional and pictorial. On a technical level, the music is full of RSA's characteristic restlessness and energy, but there is a greater coherence to the musical paragraphs and moods than in some of his other, larger canvases. The density of his thematic approach in works like 'The Beacons' and the more varied stylistic approaches in 'Seascapes', 'Chorales' or 'At the Edge of Time' seem to come together without contrivance.

'Hymn at Sunrise' is beautifully scored from the evocative opening – a lonely soprano cornet and single B flat bass – to the majestic final bars. It was written as a competition piece but, like all the best of that particular genre, it wears the contesting conventions lightly. What comes first is the creative intention or idea, not the function. Thus the exposed solo passages, of which there are many (the flugel horn part is especially taxing in this regard), are integrated into the musical fabric. For me, 'Hymn at Sunrise' is as intense and personal a work of purely musical expression as 'The Holy War', but so much more refined in its compositional craft and commanding in its expressive and textural range. The chorale 'Ein Feste Burg' lay at the heart of the earlier work. In 'Hymn at Sunrise' an equally well-known hymn is employed. It was composed in 1567 by the great composer from Tudor times, Thomas Tallis, and is usually referred to as 'Tallis's Canon', although RSA does not exploit this aspect to a large extent. RSA's own synopsis is as revealing as any he has written and deserves to be quoted here in full:

'The idea of this work was slightly prompted by reading a poem "Hymn Before Sunrise" [Samuel Taylor Coleridge, 1802], which describes the majesty of a mountain in darkness, the plunging sounds of a nearby waterfall, and so on. Nothing came of exposure to these pictures except for general thoughts about dawn of day and the choice of a series of movements expressing a personal response to the wonder of creation in an imaginary moment of time.

Let there be no mystique: the initial idea sparked by the title and the headings of the movements were added afterwards. These headings may be helpful and are intended to underline a prevailing sense of worship,

195

wonder and exultation. The music is pure, not pictorial, though listeners may conjure their own images as it progresses. Although an evening hymn, "Tallis's Canon" was chosen for its association with the words of Bishop Ken, "Glory to thee, my God, this night, for all the blessings of the light".

1. Thanksgiving: A short prelude in two parts. First a brief passage of 'dawn music', during which the E flat bass introduces a motif that reappears from time to time throughout the work. Things become more vigorous and clear-cut. Fanfare material ushers in the trombone section playfully presenting the Tallis tune. A broad full-band version concludes the prelude.

2. De Profundis [Out of the Depths]: A slow movement shot through with anxious questionings (featuring flugel horn and trombones). The mood lightens a little in the central episode (featuring soprano cornet). The short reprise ends serenely.

3. Celebration: This is the most extended movement, characterised by rhythmic drive [and changeable moods and virtuoso solo content – PH].

4. Invocation: Melodic in nature and sober in mood, the first section is a series of solos mingled with chorale-like statements. Centrally placed is a chorale-prelude style presentation of the Tallis tune [see 'Chorales', above – PH]. The third section reintroduces the earlier solo material by the full ensemble, dissolving without a break into the last movement.

5. Paean: There is much fun and rejoicing in this concluding anthem of praise. At the outset the trombones enunciate the main theme of the work and this is followed by passages of thematic development, including the Tallis Canon. Then comes a gentle passage with cornet solo leading to a reprise of the fanfare music. Two recitatives [euphonium and cornet] lead to a brief coda that brings all to a sonorous and exultant conclusion.'

While the vast majority of RSA's instrumental works have been composed for brass band, there is a small but significant body of work for various chamber ensembles and for symphonic wind band. RSA's idiomatic versions of Holst's 'A Moorside Suite' and John Ireland's 'Comedy Overture' brought two masterworks for brass band from the inter-war years of the 20th century within the compass of the wind band, while 'A Cambridge Triptych' is his only original composition for wind band.

On a smaller scale there is a brass quartet entitled 'Images' and an entertainment for tuba and piano based on the song 'Dashing Away with the Smoothing Iron'. More substantial is a suite for the unusual combination of solo oboe and solo trombone with a ten-piece brass ensemble entitled 'Wansbeck Suite'. This remains unpublished, as does a collection of brass band commissions, 'Noah's Carnival' for piano and band (for the Chicago Staff Band), 'A Conwy Suite' (for Conwy Band), 'Corunna Suite' (for Regent Brass),

'The Spire at Cowholm', a musical portrayal of the events surrounding the history of Norwich Cathedral (commissioned for the 1988 East Anglian Brass Band Association Spring Contest), 'Centre Point', based on the hymns of Martin Shaw (for Birmingham Citadel Band) and concert marches for Canterbury City and Freckleton Bands. In 2007 RSA completed a short virtuoso trombone solo for Brett Baker, based on the tune 'Monk's Gate' ('He Who Would Valiant Be'), entitled 'Faith Encounter'.

There are two further brass band works of substance that deserve mention. The idea for 'Variants on "The Triumph of Peace"' came about through a conversation during a car journey between RSA and two luminaries of the wider brass band world, Bram Gay and David Read. Bram was looking to make a tribute to Eric Ball at one of his gala concerts staged the day after the British Open Brass Band Championship at Symphony Hall, Birmingham. RSA takes up the story: 'Uninvited I picked up the ball and ran with it. Part of the piece was played in Birmingham, but the fact that some movements were omitted caused the loss of the overall effect.' This unusual 15-minute work juxtaposes passages from Eric Ball's concise symphonic poem from 1938, 'The Triumph of Peace', with RSA's own re-creative tribute. The end result is a curious joint composition than spans some 60 years. At the outset Eric Ball's martial first subject is followed by RSA's reworking – in effect a re-composition of the principal motifs in the passage. The second movement begins with some passionate rhapsodising suggested by Ball's second subject. In the fleeting third movement RSA seems to take complete ownership of Ball's primary and secondary material, while in the sonorous fourth movement he reviews Ball's uplifting hymn of peace – the original second subject of the tone poem. There is no mistaking the energetic, quixotic RSA temperament in the fifth movement, with Eric Ball very much in the background. Ball surfaces again in the dramatic finale, which reviews the opening of 'The Triumph of Peace' and its wonderful second subject by way of an audacious modulation that only RSA would dare to include!

And finally, 'Starmaker'. This three-movement suite was first performed at the same concert in which the full version of 'Variants' was first heard [Boscombe Citadel and Foden's bands, conducted by Dr Howard Evans, and recorded for posterity on SPS 235CD]. It was many years in the making and, given the complexity and difficulty of the writing, it is understandable why this work, intended for Salvation Army performance, took so long to 'tame' and was actually premiered by Foden's, one of this country's elite contesting bands. Now available from SP&S, 'Starmaker' is a work of 'praise to a supremely creative God'. While it doesn't reveal anything new in terms of the RSA style, the degree to which he extends his tonal palette places it on the same level as works like 'The Lord is King', although 'Starmaker' is arguably the tougher challenge for the band. It is a major addition to the brass band repertoire, and indicative that the irrepressible inventiveness of Ray Steadman-Allen belongs to the entire brass band community. As he commented after hearing 'Starmaker': 'This has not been planned as a test piece, but maybe one day...'

Paul Hindmarsh is a music producer, publisher, journalist, editor and author specialising in British music and brass bands. He was appointed features editor of the British Bandsman *in 2010 and serves as artistic consultant to the RNCM Festival of Brass and the Manchester Midday Concerts Society.*

Chapter Nineteen

Encounters with Ray Steadman-Allen

Contributions, all written in 2011, are from Maisie Ringham Wiggins, Robert Redhead, Brian Bowen, Trevor Davis, Kenneth Downie, James Williams, Stephen Cobb, James Curnow, Howard Evans, Doreen Rutt, Peter Graham and Edward Gregson.

Maisie Ringham Wiggins
Maisie is an Honorary Associate of the Royal Academy of Music and was appointed MBE in 2011 for services to music. In 1944 she was offered a place in the Ivy Benson Band but turned it down as she felt it would conflict with her Salvationist values and commitments. Maisie was invited by Sir John Barbirolli to join the Hallé Orchestra where she went on to become principal trombone. She has been an international trombone soloist. Until recently she was a brass teacher at Harrow School and is still involved with both swing and big bands. She is also a member of her local Salvation Army band.

IT is with great pleasure I write these few words as a tribute to Ray Steadman-Allen. He is one of the great masters of compositions written mainly for The Salvation Army. His whole life he has dedicated not only to ministry as a Salvation Army officer but also to ministry through music. Over the years we have appreciated his masterly compositions for the brass band. As a soloist I have been so humbled that he has written music for me.

There is 'The Eternal Quest' which he wrote for me to play on the occasion of the International Staff Band's Diamond Jubilee celebration at the Festival Hall in 1951. Then in 1962 I had the privilege of playing 'The Immortal Theme' at the Royal Albert Hall. That also was composed for me to play at that event. I don't think that solo has actually been published and unfortunately it hasn't been performed too often. That is probably because of its length, but it is a fine work.

When I was preparing for my world tour for The Salvation Army in 1965, I contacted Ray requesting that he compose a solo I could take with me, as one

199

always likes to take a new composition on a tour of that nature. I suggested that the solo could be based upon a Salvation Army song and written in such a way that it could be suitable for use in devotional gatherings as well as festival events. Ray did just as I requested and I am honoured to say that it has become my favourite solo. When the time was drawing near for my tour I asked him for a title, as I was being pressed from places around the world for my programme. Ray sent me a telegram simply saying 'Walk with Me' and my reply was: 'I'd love to, thank you.' I used the solo extensively on the tour and I have played it on innumerable occasions ever since, including funerals. Indeed, in November 2007, at my request, Dudley Bright played it at my dear late husband Ray's thanksgiving service. To quote the words of the song: 'Walk with me, my Lord, walk with me. All the way from earth to Heaven, Blessed Master, walk with me.' I will be forever grateful and privileged that such compositions have been written for me.

Ray Steadman-Allen is a legend in his own lifetime, and I recollect that he became a Doctor of Music long before The Salvation Army began to recognise such honours as it does now. I am happy to pay this tribute to Ray and also to his dear wife Joy who has always been such a great support to him throughout his career.

May God bless both Ray and Joy.

*** *** ***

Robert Redhead
Colonel Robert Redhead is a Salvation Army officer and composer and former colleague of Ray's in the International Music Editorial Department. He was a past bandmaster of the Canadian Staff Band and the International Staff Band.

I WAS appointed to the IMED in August 1970 and don't remember having met Ray prior to that. We shared the next six years together and became very good friends. Often at lunchtimes we would go for walks discovering the history of St Pancras. We discovered the grave of one of the 'lesser Bachs' in St Pancras Cemetery, which for us, as musicians, was quite a find, but the rest of the SP&S population was not impressed! I think we even signed a petition to prevent an historic building being demolished and won the day. Ray enjoyed being involved in issues; and there were some at SP&S, particularly with the lunchtime arrangements. If I remember rightly Ray, as a department head, could eat in the nice public restaurant, whereas the rest of us had to eat 'lesser' meals in the staff canteen. So he joined us, much to the annoyance of the leadership! But of course he then complained loudly and often about the lack of quality of our fare compared with that of 'the restaurant'!

One of our 'triumphs' was the formation of a male-voice quartet – Ray Bowes, Howard Davies, Ray and me. It was at a Sunday morning holiness meeting in the lounge at Sunbury Court with the SP&S officers (of whom there were many) under the leadership of Colonel Bernard Adams and a guest preacher who was a commissioner. We stood under the beautiful chandelier. Ray and I were tall, and Howard and RB were 'shorter'. Ray started to get enthusiastically into this 'holiness' song, moving his head, only to discover that he and I were bumping into the chandelier, creating a musical tinkling accompaniment to our meditative song. We got the giggles, and our quartet's tonal quality began to deteriorate very quickly, except for RB who sang right through to the end at fortissimo to cover us, which, of course, heightened our hilarity. We were never asked to sing again, and our wives were very relieved!

As a musician he was a great mentor. I remember struggling with a modulation which was too 'grandiose'. Ray studied it carefully for me and then suggested that I simply move straight into the new key. It was perfect. I learned a major lesson of composition that day and have, over the years, appropriately minimised the modulations in my music to great advantage.

As a friend he was very understanding. Early on in my tenure I went through a difficult time for a few months when, having lost my mother a year before, my father died in our home. Ray didn't offer advice, trying to 'put things right' – he simply recognised my pain and listened 'to my heart'.

I will always hold Ray in the highest regard, as a superb musician but also as one passionate for the Lord with a heart to care.

*** *** ***

Brian Bowen

Brian is a composer, conductor and music editor. He is currently associate editor for Eulenburg (Schott) Study Scores and freelance editor for other music publishers. He has been a member of the International Staff Band, bandmaster of the New York Staff Band and a Salvation Army corps bandmaster.

SOMETIME in my teens I received a letter with a piece of manuscript attached from Albert H. Jakeway, then Head of the International Music Editorial Department (IMED), in response to a little song I had submitted. He had thoughtfully given it to Ray Steadman-Allen to work over and show me how my faltering effort could be improved. Little did I realise that some years later I would have the opportunity of working alongside my boyhood hero in the IMED. It was in 1963 when Charles Skinner was Head of the Department. He occupied a separate office from the rest of the staff, which then included RSA, Leslie Condon and Doreen Rutt (who was the secretary and music copyist).

RSA seemed rarely to do anything slowly. He walked, talked and wrote as though there were not enough hours in the day. I had the impression his mind was teeming with a variety of thoughts and ideas and, at times, it felt as though a whirlwind was passing through. Not only was he fluent in musical expression, he also revealed a facility with the written word that was exercised with grace and distinction. Sometimes, however, the typewriter would almost overheat as he rapidly produced a withering attack on an ill-considered opinion he had come across in a periodical. After testing other opinions in the office, he would furiously type an amendment. Several drafts might appear before the whole effort was finally abandoned and normality restored. These outbursts always appeared to be cathartic.

For many years, Salvation Army officers were discouraged, if not actually prohibited, from using their creative talents in non-Army publications and 'outside' performances. To the exceptionally creative spirit, such restraints on artistic freedom could seriously limit the acceptance and affirmation of a far broader group of peers. RSA, being a 'son of the regiment' and a faithful officer, accepted the rules, yet it appeared he sometimes found justifiable ways of circumventing such strictures. It was said that his suite 'Lord of the Sea' was first heard in a competition for new original brass band works, when it was entitled 'Neptune's Diadem'. I also discovered that he had tested, outside The Salvation Army, a particular style of songwriting when he showed me published copies of songs under the thinly disguised pseudonym Len Rayal (before he lengthened his surname by deed poll). If memory serves, these were in response to a publisher's request for Christian songs in a more popular genre of the time.

In 1964 The Salvation Army decided to encourage new songs that could be termed 'with it' and a special concert was held in London's Regent Hall to showcase some examples. RSA had written a song in a light jazz idiom called 'Glory to His Name' for vocalist, trumpet and piano, and it was presented at this event. June Mingay was the vocalist, RSA himself was at the piano and he asked me to play the trumpet part. (Incidentally, with Bernard Adams and Charles Skinner present – ISB Bandmaster and deputy respectively – it unexpectedly led to my becoming a member of the International Staff Band.)

I have no idea how many compositions RSA completed during my six years in the IMED but it seemed he was constantly working on something new. Even so, he was engaged in the routine editing and proofreading of other people's music for publication and in offering expert advice to up-and-coming writers. It was not unusual for Charles Skinner to hand RSA the full score of a brass-band manuscript to sight-read at the piano, something he would do intuitively.

He was also pianist for the Vocal Music Board, which met periodically to approve new songs for publication. Board members sat in a separate room following the lyrics as RSA played the music in the general office. Following this, the Board deliberated behind closed doors while a couple of us in the general office poured them cups of tea. RSA was ever willing to assist in this menial task, and on one occasion when the tea was spilt into the saucers he took out his somewhat soiled handkerchief and proceeded to wipe around the tops of the cups and saucers. The tea probably never tasted better to the unknowing Board members.

In February 1964, RSA was scheduled to visit New York at the request of the New York Staff Band. The visit was to include the first performance of a work he was writing for this occasion, the 'Fantasia for Piano and Band: Christ is the Answer', also featuring him as piano soloist. During the composition, as with other works, he shared ideas with us as they were taking shape. He clearly wanted to relate the new piece to the band, so chose for its theme the well-known chorus 'Christ is the Answer', written by the band's executive officer, William Maltby. Another link would be a florid passage designed for the band's celebrated cornet soloist, Derek Smith. As work progressed, I tentatively asked RSA if it might incorporate the singing of the band, for which it was well known. He agreed and placed the male voices at the heart of the work in a dialogue with the solo piano. This ground-breaking composition was performed the following year in London with RSA once again the soloist but accompanied by the International Staff Band in the Royal Albert Hall during The Salvation Army's Centenary celebrations.

It was during those celebrations in 1965 that another major work was presented to a vast audience in the same venue. This was 'The Holy War', a tone poem based on the book of the same title by John Bunyan. RSA was requested (probably by ISB Bandmaster Bernard Adams) to write something substantial to mark this very special year and in the office we became aware something was brewing. It was my impression sketches already existed for a work on this subject even before the request was made, as RSA was clearly revising or rewriting existing passages in the months leading up to the initial performance by the ISB in Scotland. Following the stunning performance in London at the Royal Albert Hall, Alfred Gilliard, reporting in *The Musician*, compared the effectiveness of this brave new music quite unfavourably with the pop-style songs of the new Army group the Joystrings. Some of us in the office felt that Gilliard's remarks were short-sighted and possibly hurtful to RSA, so I tried to defend his music in a letter subsequently printed in the same magazine. Regardless of the controversy some of his compositions have generated – often by those unable to understand or accept the need for advancement – he maintained his originality and time has surely justified his forward thinking and artistic integrity.

There were many light-hearted moments in the office. On one occasion we challenged RSA to play the piano backwards, ie, with his hands behind his back. He did so with little trouble, so a sterner test was required: to play the piano with his toes. Off came his shoes and socks and he made a valiant effort. I was present a number of times when a recurring in-house joke played out between him and Leslie Condon. What sparked these exchanges is no longer clear to me but they began with RSA exclaiming teasingly: 'Duke Street!' to which Les retorted:

'Gladsome Morn!' To understand this humour it helps to know that 'Duke Street' was Les's first published march (in 1947) and includes the hymn tune in a rather four-square setting, about which he had become a little self-conscious. RSA's earliest march (published in 1945) was 'Gladsome Morn', containing a peppy upbeat version of the chorus 'There'll be no sorrow in God's tomorrow'. In sharp contrast, Les had used the same song slowly and wistfully in his later selection 'Peace of Heart'. Touché! I always felt this good-hearted banter was indicative of their respect for one another. At the funeral service for Leslie Condon held in Croydon Citadel in 1983 there could be no more impassioned prayer than the one offered by RSA on behalf of his dear friend and colleague.

During those days in the 1960s, RSA and I took some lunchtime recreational walks from the office in Judd Street, King's Cross, to Camden Town Library and back. This two-mile journey took us past St Giles-in-the-Fields burial ground in St Pancras, where RSA showed me the grave of the composer Johann Christian Bach, youngest son of Johann Sebastian Bach. It was also during our lunch breaks that for a period I received counterpoint lessons from RSA (insisting he accept at least a modest payment). I had suggested a course in free counterpoint but he decided the discipline of 16th-century counterpoint was the place to start, and so we proceeded. One time I was taught quite unwittingly a very different lesson. RSA's wife, Joy, sometimes came into the office (always looking good) and on this visit she appeared with a new hairstyle. After she departed, I thought a compliment might please RSA so I said something like: 'Joy's hair looked good today', to which he responded: 'Well, doesn't it always?' He was serious. I tried to make amends but it was too late. In the background I could see the others in the office trying to suppress their amusement at my discomfort.

When RSA was appointed Head of the IMED in 1967, he naturally moved into the next-door office. Now he was responsible for selecting all the music for publication, corresponding with composers and authors and overseeing his staff of editors. That same year Enid Weaver (née Hardwick) joined the department and, in August 1968, Leslie Condon departed to become the National Bandmaster, his replacement being Ray Bowes. It became his honour to occupy the desk at which RSA had worked under three previous heads of department – Bramwell Coles, Albert Jakeway and Charles Skinner.

Following his promotion, RSA remained encouraging and stimulating, never allowing his position to alter the personal friendship I enjoyed.

My employment with the IMED ended in 1969 when I left to take up a post as music editor for the European publisher Schott Music in their London offices. The knowledge and experience I had gained working alongside RSA and other colleagues was to prove invaluable in my new job. The camaraderie we had shared was uniquely rewarding and a fond memory.

*** *** ***

Trevor Davis

Lieut-Colonel Trevor Davis is a Salvation Army officer and has been a divisional commander. He is a composer, past Head of the UK Territory Music Ministries Department and Music Secretary in New Zealand. Until recently he was the executive officer of the International Staff Band.

AS a teenage Salvationist musician growing up in the orbit of summer music schools and the like, I regarded the then Captain Ray Steadman-Allen with respect and almost a touch of reverence.

In subsequent years it is hard to believe that the words 'friend' and 'colleague' could ever have become part of my vocabulary regarding Ray, although the respect and reverence has never dissipated! To have come to know Ray and Joy so well, not to mention Barbara and Rosemary, has been a great privilege, sharing company and fellowship in many musical situations and even spending time together in Australia when Ray and Joy were working there and my wife Margaret and I were serving in New Zealand.

However, I have been invited to comment in relation to my association with Ray as the Head of Music Editorial. Many others will write analytically of the scholarship he brought to his editorship, and of the spirit and motivation he brought to the selection of music which was to enhance the worship and Christian service of many others around the world.

I could write of his constant personal encouragement – undoubtedly beyond my compositional deserts – of his humour, his compassion and his desire that the Army's ministry would be effective and relevant.

He held on to his good judgment, though! One of my first compositional submissions to RSA, having had one or two songs published in *The Musical Salvationist* by his predecessor, was a short and simple setting of 'My Life must be Christ's Broken Bread', much-loved words by Albert Orsborn. I thought my setting was beautiful! I felt it captured the soul of the sentiments expressed in the poem. To date – I was all of 24 – I thought it was my best work yet. Ray's reply was simple, friendly but direct: 'I am sorry that I cannot use this at the present time.' The blow of that letter was softened shortly afterwards when I learned that Ray had been trying to secure my services for the Editorial Department, without success, a privilege which was to wait another 15 years.

When I, in turn, became Head of Music Editorial, I kept that rejection letter on my desk, reminding me that being fair and honest in judgment did not cause people to go out and lose their soul!

Ray's final appointment was to return to Music Editorial in the mid-1980s and, with a very small team, complete the revision of the Salvation Army tune book. That was the period when I actually worked side by side each day with Ray and the task, which had been a long time in preparation, was finally completed.

At the time of writing, now as a retired officer, I have been drawn back into the Music Ministries Unit to help co-ordinate the next revision of the tune book of The Salvation Army. It looks like a big job. Come back, Ray!

*** *** ***

Kenneth Downie

Dr Ken Downie is a composer of both Salvation Army and non-Army brass band music. Among other eminent positions, he has been creative consultant to the SA Music Ministries Department with special responsibility for the nurture of promising young composers.

I AM heavily indebted to RSA for his encouragement to me as a young composer. Starting off life in Greenock in Scotland, and later moving to Southport in the north of England, the bright lights of London, where all the Salvation Army luminaries were based, seemed a long way off to me then. I did not know any composers personally and actually felt nervous and intimidated when I was eventually introduced into that world as I started to write music.

These feelings were eventually allayed by the warm, appreciative reception RSA gave to me. Not only did he supervise the early publication of my first contributions, which was a massive confidence-booster, he also positively encouraged me to be myself and not feel any need to be 'safe' in my writing. My *Festival Series* prelude, 'Towards the Victory', written while I was a student, would never have emerged without his support. He embodied a new climate of creativity and invention when he assumed the role of Head of the International Music Editorial Department.

It was exciting for me when he took what was to be my first brass publication, the march 'Greenock Citadel', to use on a visit to America in the late 1960s for a workshop with the New York Staff Band. At some stage later I was asked by the Music Department if I could provide another set of parts, as the original ones had been lost. (This was in the days before photocopiers.) As a rather stroppy student by this time, I refused to copy them again. Quite soon afterwards I received a letter saying that my march was to be published. RSA had quietly organised a staff member to accommodate the unco-operative student by copying out the parts. His kind, fatherly behaviour made a strong impression on me, and was typical of our relationship in the days to follow.

I have looked through some correspondence from him that I have kept, dating back to 1967. Almost invariably an official note, usually a copyright assignment form, has an accompanying personal note scribbled beside it: 'A fine work', 'I immensely enjoyed listening to this' and 'There are occasionally songs that make me wish I was still a Songster Leader. Yours is one of them.' They define RSA: the wonderful encourager.

*** *** ***

206

James Williams

Originally a Grenadier Guards musician, James was once deputy bandmaster to RSA and for many years was himself the well-known bandmaster of Tottenham Citadel Band and its successor, Enfield. He is also known as an international cornet soloist, conductor, lecturer and brass band contest adjudicator. Bandmaster Williams was appointed MBE in June 2002 in recognition of his service to the brass band movement and The Salvation Army.

EARLY in 1955 the then Captain Ray Allen was appointed as the bandmaster of Tottenham Citadel Band. I was the deputy bandmaster of the band at that time, and for several weeks, until they were able to move, my wife Elsie and I picked up the Allen family – Ray, Joy, Barbara and the very young Rosemary – at King's Cross Station and transported them to Tottenham. They were very memorable days and we had a lot of fun together at that time.

The band had been going through a very difficult time and Ray brought a great feeling of humility, a great sense of musicianship and, even more importantly, a realisation of the spiritual impact a true Salvation Army bandsman can have. The character of Ray and his great musical ability were soon felt in the band and its spirit was greatly enhanced by the influence and sincerity of the new young bandmaster.

As the deputy bandmaster I learned a lot from Ray Steadman-Allen, especially the meaning of Salvation Army bandsmanship.

We were greatly privileged to witness the creation of many great works of musical artistry and were allowed to broadcast and record a large number of these works – in those far-off days recordings were a one-off take on 78 rpm Regal Zonophone recordings. For five most interesting years we had the benefit of the leadership of a great musician and a fine Salvation Army officer, and to this day we have memories of a wonderful example from which we still benefit.

I personally never forget Ray's wonderful words of advice and encouragement given to me, which have helped me over the years that I have served in the band. In 1960 I was appointed as the bandmaster of the band, and both under the name of Tottenham Citadel and latterly Enfield we have played and recorded many of Ray Steadman-Allen's works, and I know that his great influence on the band and on me personally have helped us to plumb the depths of his very fine scores.

We are forever in his debt.

*** *** ***

Stephen Cobb

Dr Stephen Cobb was bandmaster of the Salvation Army corps band at Hendon for 29 years, and has been bandmaster of the International Staff Band since 1994. Since April 2001, Dr Cobb has also been serving as Territorial Music Director for the United Kingdom Territory, overseeing all aspects of SA musical activity.

IT'S a huge privilege to add my voice to this collection. I can remember, as a child, my father coming back from ISB rehearsals talking about 'The Holy War'. Although then I wasn't able to absorb it musically when I heard it, I had a sense of it being film music. There were aspects of it I didn't understand, but there were moments that excited me as a young kid.

I have known Ray initially through the interaction of our families – we were all at Hendon Corps – so because of our familiarity with him, I felt I knew him when playing his music. We went through a cornet solo he wrote for my father Roland Cobb, 'Love's Vision', and that gave me an insight into his music. And what I have appreciated in my more mature years as a conductor is that I could go to Ray and ask: 'How would you like this done?' Invariably his humble reply would be: 'How would you like to do it?'

For players, Ray's music is always physically demanding. For conductors, his music is musically demanding. If, as a conductor, you have got your radar on as a player – and I still think like a player – his scores are very challenging. They have an almost symphonic feel about them. His scoring is rich. I have always felt that there's more he wants to say, that the Army brass band *genre* hasn't been big enough for all he wants to say. Yet one of Ray's greatest gifts is his ability to write across the range of abilities, from small ensemble pieces to full band concert works.

The player-composer dynamic is a critical one, and one determines the other. He has kept pace with changing technical ability and been ahead of the game stylistically. If you play 'Sparkling Slides' now, all the kicks are in the right place. 'The Holy War' made use of atonality 50 years ago. He's always on the cusp of 'what's next'; 'At the Edge of Time' is Salvation Army film music, 'On Ratcliff Highway' is a cinematic piece.

Bringing it up to the here and now, Ray is still full of ideas aged 90. He visited the Music Ministries Unit* recently and you would never have thought conversationally that he was that age. His greatest gift is that he still looks forward and is burning with creativity and innovation.

The MMU became a department when the UK became a territory. It embraces what was the IMED.

*** *** ***

James Curnow

James Curnow is a prolific composer for concert bands and brass bands and vocal and instrumental ensembles at every level. He is Music Publications Editor for The Salvation Army's USA Southern Territory; Composer in Residence, Emeritus, Asbury University; and President, Composer and Editor, Curnow Music Press, Inc.

THINKING back to my early years progressively as a member of the young people's band, senior band and songster brigade, I recall the excitement of receiving a new piece of music with the name 'Ray Steadman-Allen' printed in the prestigious, upper right-hand corner. As Salvation Army band enthusiasts we knew we were in for a treat and couldn't wait to explore his latest creation. We looked forward to his seemingly inexhaustible creativity, the sought-after challenges and the deeply spiritual dynamic of the music. We were never disappointed.

Ray's ability to put his thoughts into music motivated us to work and grow as musicians. We wanted to be better so that we could meet the next challenge that would flow from his pen. By example, Ray taught us the importance of striving for excellence as Salvation Army musicians.

I now realise that I knew very little of the true contribution he made, as editor, to all the music that was available to Salvationists. It is only after 30 years as a music editor myself that I am beginning to appreciate Ray's influence upon Salvation Army music.

Through his commitment to excellence, Ray ensured that the gospel message of Salvation Army music was presented to the highest possible standard. The unmatched quality of the Army's printed music during his years as editor left an indelible impression upon me, a young musician hoping that my efforts would bring glory to God.

Ray has helped thousands of musicians worldwide understand the beauty, responsibility and privilege of being a Salvation Army musician. Ray taught us that only our best – our greatest effort – is worthy of dedication to God. I thank God that he made it possible for our paths to cross and that I now can count Ray as a musical, artistic, spiritual mentor and friend.

We owe thanks to God for Ray's gifts and brilliance as a composer. We owe thanks to Ray for his willingness to work to develop those gifts. Ray's example taught us that any 'prestige' associated with having your name at the upper right-hand corner of the printed page truly lay in the struggle, craftsmanship and labour required to produce a gift worthy of dedication to God.

*** *** ***

Howard Evans

Dr Howard Evans is a pianist, teacher and conductor. Performance lecturer at Salford University, he is a former ABRSM examiner and was formerly the Musical Director for The Salvation Army in the Netherlands and bandmaster of the Amsterdam Staff Band. He is currently serving as a Salvation Army bandmaster at Boscombe.

IT is with great pleasure that I recall my earliest dealings with RSA, as we all affectionately refer to him. From my earliest days as a young Salvation Army musician in the young people's band, his was a name spoken of in revered tones and with great interest, and so to get to know both him and Joy has been a privilege over the years.

When I began my earliest efforts at writing for bands Ray was in Australia and so I never received one of those letters from his hand in the International Music Editorial Department! As a member of the Bands and Songster Brigades Department at NHQ from September 1981 to 1982, I often heard Ray spoken of and he provided the usual massed songster item for Norman Bearcroft for the annual Bandmasters Councils Festival in 1982. I was a participant in that festival which included the first performance of his work 'At the Edge of Time' by Camberwell Band from Melbourne, Australia. For me it was a thrilling experience to hear this work on this very special occasion, little realising the contact I would have with the composer later on.

By the time I came to my own commissioning as a Salvation Army officer in May 1982 Ray and Joy were back in the UK and he was serving as the Editor of *The Musician*. For the usual commissioning pageant at the Royal Albert Hall in the evening, music and drama had been put together for the occasion and it fell to me to come up with some music for the devotional chorus incorporated into that event. It was actually a very simple chorus entitled 'You Don't have to Do it on Your Own'. The best encouragement I received for my efforts was from Ray. He got in touch with me after the event and suggested that he print the chorus in *The Musician*. His knowledge of the IMED meant that he knew it was too short for publication in the usual songster material, but felt that it would be worthwhile to give it a wider audience, and so my first publication was not in the band journals or *The Musical Salvationist* but in *The Musician*! – thanks to Ray.

Our contact over the next few years became a little intermittent, but this was to change very quickly in 1988. On commissioning I served as a corps officer and was with my wife Heather at Camborne Corps early in 1988 when it became clear that we were to move to London for me to return to the Bands and Songster Brigades Department with Lieut-Colonel Norman Bearcroft as Secretary for Bands and Songster Brigades. There was a British Congress planned for July that year. Norman's duties with the International Staff Songsters meant that he was due to be away on a Scandinavian tour during the period of the British

Territory (as it was then) Congress. Who was going to take charge of the music for the events that were to happen in London at the Royal Albert Hall?

Heather and I moved to a temporary quarters in Romford a few days before my appointment as National Bandmaster began. I shall always remember that first day of the appointment. It was not typical for a new job! I met Norman and Ray at the bottom of the M11 near Ilford and we travelled together in the car to Norwich for our first massed rehearsal for the forthcoming grand event. I was sitting in the back. Norman handed me a folder and said: 'There's your music for tonight!' Ray and I decided who was doing what – ie, which pieces we were to conduct and which pieces we would accompany for each other in the rehearsals.

After the first few rehearsals, once everything was up and running, Norman left Ray and me to it. For the next few months we travelled over the British Territory rehearsing the massed choruses in their geographical locations for both the Saturday festival and the Sunday meetings of the Congress. It usually meant meeting up somewhere by lunchtime to travel with plenty of time for an evening rehearsal, and then the late-night journey back home together. We obviously shared many moments together on those journeys.

Our conversations on those journeys allowed me to get to know this man I had heard of since my early days. Ray was a brilliant musician and composer, but those hours spent travelling together revealed to me that he was also far more than that. His breadth of experience, knowledge and understanding in so many other facets showed him to be quite a remarkable person. We did enjoy many discussions about music, but also covered far more widely-reaching subjects. I always loved those journeys and the chance to be together and converse. For me this was the start of a friendship which I have always valued immensely and both Ray and Joy have always been very kind.

My time in London through to 1992 meant we were often in touch and Ray was often to supply works for our national festivals and special events. However, by the end of 1997 my own personal difficulties and situation meant that I was to resign my Salvation Army officership. Since then, a number of conversations with Ray have revealed his great understanding of the huge cost of making such a decision and its personal conflicts. His perspective and the conversations we have had about this have been most illuminating.

One of the great opportunities over recent years has been to continue to champion Ray's work. In connection with my doctoral studies Ray gave me the opportunity to premiere his 'Variants on "Triumph of Peace"' – which had been given a truncated performance on its first outing and was therefore incomplete. I also spent some considerable time trying to encourage him to finish a work I knew he was in the process of revising in 2008 – 'Starmaker'. This was premiered in a concert I was able to put on with Boscombe Salvation Army Band along with the famous Foden's Band, where we also finally gave 'Variants' its first full outing.

In this way my personal reflection is that things almost came full circle. Ray encouraged me in my earlier years when we first met. Part of one's retirement years seems to engender the feeling that one is no longer part of what is going on or needed in quite the same way. I know that Ray has sometimes felt this way. I have therefore felt a sincere responsibility to want to continue to encourage Ray, that there are those of us who value what he has done and what he still can do! I champion his works as much as possible in my programming, and am currently reviving 'The Holy War' with Boscombe Band as I write. In my recording of the meditational literature of the Army on the recording *Sanctuary* with Boscombe Band, we also had opportunity to rediscover his meditational study 'Emmaus Journey', long forgotten by many.

I am sincerely grateful to know him and to count him as a friend, despite the years that separate us in age! He is a vastly talented man in all respects, not just for his music, and I have always found him to be most stimulating and encouraging. I hope that over these last years I have been able to give a little something to him in return for all that he has given to me and to many others.

*** *** ***

Doreen Rutt

Doreen Rutt was one of the Army's leading pianists and was a colleague of RSA's in the IMED for many years. I remember her sitting in the corner of the shared room where individual desks were pushed up against one another, so there were lots of opportunities for quick wit and banter as well as interchange of ideas. I asked her to add her voice to this collection of memories – BSA

IN 1953, fresh from music college, I entered the sacred portals of the Music Editorial Department in Judd Street, London, where the Head, Colonel Albert Jakeway, introduced me to the staff and I first met Lieutenant Ray Allen, whom I dutifully addressed by his rank for quite a while!

Being the only female on the department at that time I soon realised this was the job of a lifetime and we all formed a great rapport with each other, humour mixed with hard work and dedication.

I cannot really remember many individual incidents 50 years later, but one of my memories is listening to extempore piano duets played by Ray and Michael Kenyon with great musicianship and verve. I also remember Ray playing the piano with his feet!

I remember experiencing the hectic preparation before a Royal Albert Hall bandmasters councils, copying band parts for the International Staff Band to perform their 'big' numbers and, of course, Ray's inspirational music, on which he spent so many hours.

I have always been grateful to have worked in a unique and wonderful department with its comradeship and humour. I shall never forget Ray's friendship and his wonderful God-given music.

*** *** ***

Peter Graham

Professor Peter Graham is an award-winning composer, Chair of Composition at the University of Salford and co-founder of music publisher Gramercy Music (UK). His music for brass and wind instruments is performed worldwide.

THE music of Ray Steadman-Allen has been part of my musical background for as long as I can remember. As a youngster listening to my father play euphonium in Hamilton Temple Salvation Army Band I was struck by one particular piece which seemed to stand out from the others. It had a vitality and what I could only describe as a 'busyness' (which much later I recognised as counterpoint). Quizzing my father, he told me it was a march called 'The Scarlet Jersey'. What an evocative title – and being a fan of the TV show *Captain Scarlet* this was a connection which for me put the icing on the cake!

As time passed my interest in brass music increased and with it an appreciation of the large-scale works by this legendary Army composer. Before it became fashionable to release dedicated composer recordings, I had compiled cassette collections of RSA blockbusters – 'The Holy War', 'Go Down, Moses' and the latest masterpiece 'The Lord is King'. This was a symphony for brass band – music which challenged and moved in equal measure. The ethereal beauty of the second movement, 'My Toil', is one of the composer's greatest achievements.

I began dabbling with composition around this period and was encouraged to submit my very first effort for publication to the Music Editorial Department, headed up by RSA himself. Even if the work was not suitable, I explained in my letter to the colonel, would it be possible for him to have the piece reviewed and to suggest any improvements? Almost 40 years on I now recognise the audacity of that request. Reviewing is a time-consuming process, and with a busy publishing schedule a piece with no hope of making it into print is an unnecessary distraction. Nevertheless a few days later the manuscript was returned with comments and suggestions from both RSA and his colleague Leslie Condon. This remains the best lesson in scoring/orchestration I ever received and still forms the basis of my own teaching on the subject.

I now consider RSA a friend and colleague, having over the years had the privilege of working with him in Music Editorial. Following my appointment to the University of Salford I was thrilled to be able to persuade him to teach the best final-year composition undergraduates for a period. All were overwhelmed by the privilege and by his knowledge, enthusiasm, empathy and encouragement – including a former Principal Director of the Royal Marines who still proudly cites RSA as one of his most influential teachers. As I do. Thank you, Ray.

*** *** ***

William F. Himes

Composer-arranger Bill Himes is in international demand as conductor, composer, lecturer and euphonium soloist. Since 1977 he has been music director of The Salvation Army's USA Central Territory and, in this capacity, he is also conductor of the Chicago Staff Band. Bill was awarded the Order of the Founder in 2000.

IT is impossible to fully assess the breadth, meaning and influence that Ray Steadman-Allen has had on Salvation Army music. His impact as composer, arranger, editor, author, educator and mentor is incalculable. In each of these areas he has excelled, with the sum of accomplishments far exceeding the parts.

As a chronicler of Army music works, having created databases of most of its instrumental and choral publications, it is quite easy for me to prove that RSA is without peer, with more than 270 band works and 140 choral settings to his credit. But more than quantity, what sets him apart is the depth of skill, the exceptional knowledge of his art, his willingness to take risks, push traditional boundaries and explore virtually all musical genres that will be a lasting influence on present and future generations of Army composers.

While some instrumental composers are known for their marches, hymn settings or major concert works, when one looks at the list of RSA's output it is clear that he cannot be stereotyped.

Consider these forms and just a *few* representative titles from his pen: variations ('Go Down, Moses', 'The Lord is King'), selections ('In Quiet Pastures', 'His Guardian Care'), marches ('The Scarlet Jersey', 'The High Council'), solos and ensembles ('The Ransomed Host', 'Rhapsody on Negro Spirituals', 'The Veterans', 'The Eternal Quest', 'Gone My Care', 'Fantasia on "Christ is the Answer"'), tone poems ('The Holy War', 'On Ratcliff Highway'), suites ('Lord of the Sea', 'At the Edge of Time'), meditations ('Floodtide', 'Blacklands'), song settings ('Bethany', 'Whiter than the Snow') and classical transcriptions ('Melodies of Dvořák', 'The Last Spring'). Regardless of form or genre, RSA's contributions are more than representative – they are *definitive*.

The same could be said for Ray's choral works which range from toe-tapping ('Whosoever Will') to contemplative ('Remember Me') and esoteric ('Humbly I Wait') – to say nothing of those 18 epic works written at the request of his friend Norman Bearcroft for the annual band and songster festivals in the Royal Albert Hall. Such epic works as 'A Childhood Suite' and 'The Age of Rockets'

214

were truly one-off works, calling for a chorus of 1,000 voices, accompanied by the International Staff Band, Michael Clack at the pipe organ and everything but the kitchen sink!

The thing about RSA's seemingly endless creativity is that it comes from a musician who was not content with his considerable natural gifts. Instead, he has followed a lifelong passion to pursue its formal disciplines and academics. His interest and enthusiasm for past forms and future trends is almost childlike – he never seems to tire of the quest to learn more. It is indicative that, following retirement from active service as a Salvation Army officer, he pursued and earned his doctorate in music!

But to dwell solely on RSA's personal musical achievements would be to miss the breadth and depth of the man. Those who know him only by his name in the upper right-hand corner of a publication could easily conjure up the image of an eccentric recluse, sitting at his desk day after day, producing an endless flow of quavers and crotchets on demand. Nothing could be further from the truth!

Since my first interactions with RSA as a teenager, I found him to be an encouraging mentor, merciful editor and a lifelong friend. Any conversation with him is likely to be on any current topic and is fast-paced, stimulating and constantly infused with humor! Any personal concerns shared are sincere and thoughtful. Regardless of his monumental talent, he is truly a humble man. All of this comes from his lifelong quest to be like Jesus. Of all the titles one could bestow on Ray, the one that means the most is 'Christian'.

The 120th anniversary celebrations of the International Staff Band in 2011 included a Sunday united worship service in London's Westminster Central Hall. The highlight was an inspirational message by the Army's world leader, General Linda Bond, who concluded with an invitation for people to come and pray at the mercy seat. Very soon I saw one of my bandsmen resolutely step out and kneel at the altar – and the first person to come alongside to join him in prayer was none other than my boyhood idol, constant mentor and lifelong friend, Ray Steadman-Allen. Just a small example of how much more there is to this man than his music!

*** *** ***

Edward Gregson

Edward Gregson is a composer of international standing, whose music has been performed, broadcast, and commercially recorded worldwide. His commissions have included, among others, orchestral music for the English Chamber Orchestra, the Bournemouth Symphony Orchestra, the Royal Liverpool Philharmonic, the BBC Philharmonic and the Hallé, with performances by many other orchestras and ensembles around the world. He retired as Principal of the Royal Northern College of Music in 2008.

215

I FIRST met RSA when I was a teenager. I was living at that time in Manchester, where my parents were Salvation Army officers. I had already written a fair amount of music (most of it fairly rudimentary and 'undeveloped' from a technical standpoint) and was studying for my A levels. I had just had my first song ('Soldiers of Salvation') accepted for publication by The Salvation Army and felt very proud when I saw it in print a few months later. RSA was already known to me by name, of course. I was then playing euphonium in Manchester Openshaw Citadel Band and had played and heard many brass band pieces and songs by him.

Even then, and before I had acquired any real technical knowledge, his music sounded to me very different from other Army music. It was original, colourful, seemingly quite complex and certainly highly technically accomplished, and I remember having a conscious desire to try and write music as good as his one day. In parallel, my musical horizons were already expanding quite widely and the music of Beethoven, Brahms, Stravinsky, Bartok, Hindemith, among many others, was expanding my musical intellect. But always there was RSA's music in the background as a constant challenge to my development as a composer, particularly of course in the process of writing for bands.

However, to return to my first meeting with him: I had gone to London to see my brother Bram, who is 11 years older than me and was then principal euphonium in Tottenham Citadel Band. He had kindly promised to try out a new brass quartet I had just finished with some of his fellow bandsmen after a band rehearsal. The conductor of the band at that time was RSA, and Bram had already mentioned my name to him some time before in terms of: 'My kid brother has started writing music – would you be interested in seeing some?' To which, of course, RSA replied in the affirmative. And so it was that I got to meet the great man for the first time after that band rehearsal; but I was probably too awestruck to say anything very sensible to him!

Then in 1963 I went to London to study at the Royal Academy of Music and was able to meet and talk to him on many more occasions; and he continued to be tremendously encouraging and supportive to me. For the next three years or so I wrote mainly non-Army music; however, as I was still in the Army at that time, I continued to write occasional music for the Army, including some solos for soprano voice and piano, and my first (completed) brass band composition – the march 'Dalarö'. Interestingly enough, although I wrote this march in 1964 it was not published until 1970, by which time RSA had taken over as Head of the International Music Editorial Department; so it was that 'RSA the progressive' started to exert a more significant influence on Army music.

The year 1966 was significant for me in that I wrote a new work for the National Songsters ('In the Beginning') and a 'Concertante for Piano and Band', commissioned by Regent Hall Band for a festival weekend of new music. RSA heard both of these works and was most complimentary about them, and indeed wrote a review of the 'Concertante' after I performed it in 1966 at the Royal Festival Hall with the ISB conducted by Colonel Bernard Adams. While an earlier review of the Regent Hall premiere by another writer (*The Musician*, 14 May 1966) had commented: 'One is reluctant to give personal reactions to innovations; however, I would suggest that it might be too big a step at the moment,' RSA in his review (*The Musician*, 29 October 1966) commented: 'Eddie and his contemporaries have things to say; if they are benefiting from a new (albeit occasionally reluctant!) enlightenment within our own circle this is good. I do not believe that the freedom so hardly-won for them will be misused. This is a review not a crusade, but let those who tend to reach wrathfully for their pens after each "first performance" have second thoughts and "encourage each other in the Lord".'

Of course, besides commenting on my music in those terms he was really commenting on his own history of 'difficulties' with conservative elements within the Army. The 'hard-won' freedom he referred to was in fact his own struggle and eventual success (at least partial) in overcoming the prejudice against so-called 'modernist' tendencies which his music provoked in many people. For example, Ronald Holz commented on the premiere of the 'watershed' tone poem 'The Holy War' in 1965: 'When first played this music shocked many Salvationists, one of whom wrote to the SA magazine *The Musician* to say how the experience had made him physically sick! Three decades later this brilliant score can be appreciated not for any shock value but for its marvellous invention, colourful scoring and compact formal symmetry.' Agreed! Indeed, it is one of the masterpieces of the 20th century's brass band repertoire.

Music has always seemed to flow from his pen with consummate ease and this has been demonstrated time and time again through the sheer fluency and virtuosity of his compositional technique. Of course, the prerequisite of including at least one hymn tune in his Army works could be seen as restrictive from a compositional point of view, but he often cleverly circumnavigates this, or at least enhances it, by either just hinting at a particular tune, or by adopting a process of continuous variation, often without stating the theme in full – all within a quasi-symphonic structure. One also has to recognise that his music mirrors his deep religious faith, and for this reason, as much as any other, it has an added spiritual dimension for those who share that faith. Intellect in conjunction with a religious (Christian) goal – J. S. Bach would have been proud of him! Along with Wilfred Heaton he is, in my opinion, the finest and most original Salvation Army composer.

I remain to this day a great admirer of his music, from his early set of variations 'Go Down, Moses' (1954) and the suite 'Lord of the Sea' (1957), to his most prolific and successful period of writing through the 1960s and 70's, exemplified in works such as the suite for trombone 'The Immortal Theme' (1962), the tone poem 'The Holy War' (1965), 'On Ratcliff Highway' and 'Daystar' (both

1978) and 'The Lord is King' (1975) – surely one of his finest creations – to his later works such as 'Seascapes' (1988) and 'Pavilions of Praise' (1995). Some of his works are both unfairly underrated and underperformed, while many have entered the mainstream of the band repertoire, both inside and outside The Salvation Army. If only the newly enlightened attitude of the Army towards its own composers had come earlier in RSA's career we might have had many other works from his pen which embraced a wider musical landscape. In any case, like all fine composers, his music will go on being performed and will continue to bring huge satisfaction to countless people in the future.

To sum up my admiration for RSA, and to mark this special moment in his life (not many composers make it to 90 and beyond!), I can do no better than quote the elegant words which my brother Bram penned in his notes to a CD recording devoted to Ray's music which he made in 1995 with his Intrada Brass (Canada): 'His output as The Salvation Army's most prolific composer has challenged bands to stretch performance levels to new heights both technically and musically. His compositions offer such variety; his mastery of form creates a wonderful sense of balance and homogeneity; his total understanding of the brass band medium exploits the full range of tonal colours available; there is emotion but never does he wear his heart on his sleeve; and underlying his Salvation Army music there is a conviction to present the message in which he so fervently believes. The Salvation Army has been blessed indeed, as has the brass band movement, to have this luminary and celebrated musician enrich its musical repertoire.' And so say all of us!

Chapter Twenty

Engagements With The Contemporary

In his time at the IMED, Ray was already communicating with those in the wider Christian music world who wanted to introduce more contemporary hymns to the Church at large. These included Patrick Appleford and Geoffrey Beaumont among others who formed the 20th-Century Church Light Music Society in the 1960s. Within The Salvation Army two strands were emerging – the 'pop group' and the musical. Joy Webb and John Larsson tell their own stories of Ray's engagement with the contemporary.

Joy Webb

I AM astonished to find that I can remember quite clearly the very first time I actually met Ray. I was 14, going on 15, to parody a very famous song! My father Burnal's health had finally broken down during our stay at Swindon Citadel Corps and he and my mother had been sent to the Army's convalescent home in Beckenham for him to regain his strength. I had been left behind in the care of two lovely people – John and Grace Snook, soon to become officers, known and remembered by so many in Great Britain today – to take some exams. My mother then sent a train ticket and I finally rejoined my parents 'in convalescence'.

As you can imagine, it was hardly a laugh-a-minute place to which I went, filled as it was with 'war-weary' corps officers, some of whom, like my parents, had finally succumbed to the long years of danger and horror that had accompanied them during the excessively hard challenges of Great Britain at war.

There was almost nothing for me to do, but the large old house did boast a croquet lawn fitted with hoops and supply of mallets. I, of course, had never seen a croquet set in my whole life, as it was hardly to be found on any self-respecting quarters furnishings list in those days. So when my mother suggested I might like to have a go one afternoon, I wandered out on to the lawn with no great enthusiasm. I picked up a mallet. 'What do I do next?' I wondered. Did the ball have to go around the hoop, over it or through it? I had no idea and stood for a while pondering what to try first.

Suddenly, from behind, a hand came over mine. A voice said: 'No! You don't hold it like that. It's this way.' I turned around and looked into the face of a young man. I had no idea who he was or that I would come to think of him as one of the greatest musicians God was to give to the Army in my lifetime. 'I'm Ray,' he said. 'And you are?' 'Joy,' I said. 'Come on!' he encouraged. 'You can do it! Let's try!' Well, try I did, and after many endeavours finally got the ball through a hoop – just once.

I am sure Ray has forgotten all about that first meeting but it has remained with me. Ray's parents were also at Beckenham at that time and so we saw quite a lot of him when he came to visit. In the evenings, sometimes, the officers would all gather in the large lounge which had an old piano in it and they soon realised that Ray was a most accomplished pianist. He would sit down and someone would call out the name of a song. He would then play it for us. Often they would join in and sing. I, who had had my fingers smacked for wanting to improvise at the piano when I was a little girl just beginning to learn, was fascinated when he would go on to improvise on the tune in a fascinating way. I would sneak a look at my dad and wonder if, after this, I could get away with it again! I must say that being able to play 'by ear', as it is strangely referred to, has stood me in good stead many times when more qualified pianists than me have had to move from the piano stool and let me take over.

Eventually my father recovered and we moved out to a new life with my father's appointment to International Headquarters in London. It was a number of years before I saw Ray again. By the time we met again we were both officers. He had come back to the Music Editorial Department from being a corps officer and I had been recalled to the International Training College. My life was undergoing a 'sea-change' known as the Joystrings and for the first time in my life I was having to write songs – and not songs such as I had known them in the Army all my life, but songs with new words, new ideas aimed at the unchurched young people of the 'swinging London' of the 1960s. It's hard to try to learn to songwrite when you have a great corporate enterprise like EMI waiting for your next 'hit' to be produced!

I have to salute people like the then Colonel Charles Skinner who was the Head of the Music Editorial Department and Ray who was working alongside him. I remember one morning the phone rang and I heard the colonel's voice saying: 'Joy, could you let me have a copy of your music for "Open Secret" please? We have been asked to prepare copies for publication.' I remember stuttering words like: 'I only write down the melody. We improvise the arrangement until we get it right!' What on earth that must have sounded like to either the colonel, or people like Ray, who were schooled in the good Army tradition of every note being scrutinised and all harmonies vetted thoroughly, I have no idea. The upshot was that those poor souls had to listen to the single discs again and again to try to make out what we were playing and set it down in a singable kind of format together with a pianoforte accompaniment so that all the Salvation Army youngsters in Great Britain – joined by thousands of other church young folk – could actually sing it for themselves. I salute them, I really do! For me to say that things were in a state of 'ad hoc and flux' must be the understatement of the century – well, that century, anyway.

I have never had a chance to ask Ray what he thought at that point, but my mind was actually paralysed by imagining this giant of our Salvation Army music scene poring over our first attempts at a religious pop style which had swept into the secular charts, as it were overnight. Of course with hindsight I realise that he himself knew just what living at the cutting edge was all about. His advent on to the scene of Salvation Army music-making had certainly thrown up many and varied comments, as we had not really had such brilliantly conceived and 'modern' work for our Army bands before he arrived and he must have known what it was like to be a 'first'.

They do say that 'fellow feeling makes you wondrously kind', and I have to say that his understanding of where I was having to come from has always been just that – 'wondrously kind'. In later years, when I had learned a great deal and was capable of so much more, I have found him gracious and generous in his appreciation of what the Lord has gifted me with, personally. I often wonder whether it was what he had had to struggle through before some people's complete acceptance of his gifts to the Army that helped him to understand just what we had to contend with in the early days of life with the Joystrings.

To put it bluntly, during some of those rather difficult early years of pioneering contemporary music in The Salvation Army I always felt that he was 'on my side' and that was something for which I have never ceased to thank the Lord. Goodness only knows, we certainly needed support in getting those early groups up and going and getting the young people the acceptance in the many corps where the advent of guitars, drums and microphones – oh! especially microphones – filled folk with quite a degree of horror. My heartfelt thanks to him.

Of course, sometimes, as with everyone, I didn't really know what he was actually thinking and then something happened, quite out of the blue, that confirmed the sense of his 'one-ness' with what I was trying to do for the young folk of our territory.

We were both in attendance at a meeting in the Assembly Hall of the training college. I was seated in my usual place at the piano on the platform and we were waiting for the entrance of the leaders and guests for the afternoon. Looking around I spotted Ray seated almost at the top of the platform seats. He caught my eye and smiled. Then, suddenly, he was on his feet and rushing over to me. I thought that perhaps he had been asked to lead a song in the meeting and was coming over to check that we had the correct tune or to say something about the tempo he might want when leading the song. No! I couldn't have been further away from the truth. He reached the piano and leaned right over it. I waited. 'Joy,' he said, 'I just wanted you to know that I think you are a wonderful Salvation Army officer. If I don't say it now I might never say it.' So saying, he rushed back to his seat. Our leaders entered, and the first song started with me playing the piano with my mouth still wide open with shock. That, purely and simply, is the kind of man he is.

Thinking about what I might write about him led me to recall that he and I have yet another much newer bond in the fact that we were both admitted to the Order of the Founder one after the other, myself in 2004 and Ray in 2005. I must say I wished that the years had been the other way around – much more suitable, I think, if I could ever feel that it was suitable for me. I thought it might be interesting to discover what other fellow officers in the years gone by had been awarded this tremendous honour in connection with their individual work for the Kingdom through music in the great Salvation Army. It is always humbling to discover in whose musical footsteps you are treading. I certainly did not expect what I found. Brindley Boon in his book *Play the Music, Play!*, published in 1966, listed many *non-officer* Salvationists down the years who had been admitted to the Order for their work and witness through music, and then says, simply: 'The *officers* to receive the award in recognition of their services to Salvation Army Music are: Lieut-Colonel Richard Slater (1923) and Colonel George Fuller (1942).'

I was slightly surprised to find that by 1966 only the founder of Salvation Army music and one other officer had been so honoured, the Order having been introduced by Bramwell Booth in 1917, the fifth anniversary of William Booth's promotion to Glory. I then remembered that in my lifetime Colonel Bernard Adams, the Staff Bandmaster for many, many years had also received this honour and that this had been given in 1975.

Surely there had been others? No. The Roll of Honour names just two others – one after the other in 2004 and 2005 – my name and the name of Colonel Ray Steadman-Allen. How could that 14- going on 15-year-old and the young man so recently released from the Royal Navy ever have anticipated that a meeting over a game of croquet would ever result in their names being so closely linked almost fifty years later? The divine plan is sometimes so extraordinary that it almost beggars belief!

What can I say except the obvious: 'Ray, I have never said this to you, but I think you are a wonderful Salvation Army officer and, as you once said to me, if I don't say it now I may never say it! There – I've said it!'

Major Joy Webb is a Salvation Army officer and has been a pioneer and innovator in the areas of pop music, drama and other forms of contemporary communication. She received the Order of the Founder in 2004.

General John Larsson (Retired)

MY admiration for Ray Steadman-Allen began literally from afar – from as far as Buenos Aires, Argentina, where my parents were serving as officers in the 1950s. As a teenage bandmaster in that city I avidly read *The Musician* as soon as the next edition arrived from London, and from its pages got to know the musical personalities of the day – and was first introduced to Ray. As my collection of 78s began to grow, Ray's music frequently flooded our home. I often wished we could get hold of the sheet music so we could play some of those magnificent pieces – but in those days economy dictated that we had to rely on old journals. So my relationship with Ray in those days was one of admiration, bordering on worship, for his creative skills – but from afar.

When in 1956 I entered the International Training College in London I would catch the occasional sight of Ray and, as a young officer, I met him from time to time. But with the 16-year age gap between us, Ray always belonged to the next generation up – so it was still admiration from afar.

It was the musicals that brought us together as a working team and as friends. When John Gowans and I were planning our first musical, *Take-over Bid*, I asked Ray if he would write a band overture for the work. The first public performance was to be on the grand scale, with a full band taking part in addition to the small pit orchestra and a large songster chorus augmenting from time to time what was being sung on stage. Ray readily agreed – and, what is more, agreed to work from the vocal lines only (supplemented by chord symbols), as in those days I did not write out the full piano accompaniments for the various songs until I was sure they would survive the rehearsal and try-out stage. The magnificent overture to *Take-over Bid* was subsequently succeeded by a series of band overtures for our other musicals, even though we abandoned the idea of using full bands in the actual performances of the musicals.

When it came to the publication of the first musical, I wondered whether our newly established teamwork and friendship would come under stress. There were due processes to be observed. The International Music Board had to approve all new music. The National Drama Council had to approve all new drama. But to which of these bodies should the musical be submitted? The Music Editorial Department, which belonged to International Headquarters, prepared all music for printing – but scripts were not their line. Salvationist Publishing and Supplies Ltd, which was also part of International Headquarters, printed and published all music. But at the time SP&S did not consider that there was a market for musicals.

The road ahead seemed unclear – until Commissioner William Cooper, then the British Commissioner, flexed his administrative muscles. He decided to cut through all the red tape and informed us that, as a territorial commander, he was going to exercise the right of every territorial commander in the world to publish music and drama without reference to any international body. He then announced that the Youth Department at National Headquarters was going to publish *Take-over Bid*, and informed us that everything was now approved and would we please get on with it.

All of this was rank heresy in those days! All the normal processes were being bypassed. At a stroke I found myself a one-person music editorial department and had to write out the music by hand in 'camera ready' form for the Youth Department to publish. What would the reaction of the International Music Editorial Department be? The reaction, personified by Ray, was one of total graciousness and co-operation! Ray could not have been more helpful – and I will always be grateful to him.

This arrangement lasted for the first two musicals – *Take-over Bid* and *Hosea* – but from then on everything got back on proper procedural tracks, with the Music Editorial Department attending to the professional setting of the music and SP&S handling the publication of the musicals. This meant that for the next four musicals – *Jesus Folk, Spirit!, Glory!* and *The Blood of the Lamb* – I worked even more closely with Ray. Working with Ray on these projects was always a delight. I still stood in awe of his professional skills, but noticed with what courtesy he accepted what I had written without trying to 'improve' the product – as he could so easily have done. It boosted my musical self-confidence – and is another reason why I will always be grateful to Ray.

What started out as admiration from afar gradually became a friendship – with admiration from close by. I don't need to document Ray's brilliance and incalculable worldwide influence on the Army's music – and therefore its ministry. That has been eloquently done by others, including in the pages of this book. But when I was the General-in-office I was glad to be able to initiate the award to Ray of the ultimate Salvation Army accolade for his services to Army music: the Order of the Founder. Nothing could be more eloquent than that.

John Larsson was General of The Salvation Army from 2002–2006. He succeeded John Gowans with whom he had written ten full-length stage musicals between 1967 and 1990, John Gowans providing the lyrics and John Larsson the music. It was as much a new medium for The Salvation Army as the pop group. John is also an accomplished author.

Chapter Twenty-one

An Interview with Ray Steadman-Allen
Reprinted from the magazine SA Bandsman *(2011) with permission*

The interviewer is Andrew Wainwright

In 2010, after a spell of just over two years with Virtuosi GUS Band and contributing a number of compositions and arrangements to the band's repertoire, Andrew was appointed as their Composer and Arranger in Residence. Andrew works for Salvationist Publishing & Supplies and World of Brass as a graphic designer and teaches brass in his spare time. He is also Editor of SA Bandsman *and is a regular reviewer for* British Bandsman.

AW: *Can you tell us something about your upbringing in The Salvation Army?*
RSA: My parents were Salvation Army officers who spent the majority of their active service on what is termed 'the British Field', ie, at corps centres. This naturally led to my involvement in their youth programmes and shaped the expression of my faith. My father could play the trombone and concertina (then popular with officers), my mother learned piano, but there was no strong family musical tradition.

At what point did you decide you wanted to compose? Was there any particular moment or piece of music that triggered your interest in composition?
I would date 'creative stirrings' to around age 13. It was not until the family went to Barnsley that I started cornet and piano at age 11. Following our next move I soon changed to a trombone and was pianist on young people's band programmes. In those days the general rule expected 'Army' music so I transcribed a march or two for piano. Hence scores came into my hands and I began to try my hand, relying on a combination of what I could glean plus intuition but without the skills or capacity to complete anything. An excellent school music curriculum widened my horizons.

Some new hymn tunes, such as 'Crimond', were becoming popular but no printed SA arrangements yet existed. My father asked me to score one or two of his old-time favourites. Though up to then I had no tutorial guidance other than textbooks, hearing what I'd harmonised and scored was a spur, so listening and learning were the alternatives that were enjoyably beneficial. I might mention that the Novello textbooks were invaluable and I also had a book on band instrumentation by a man called Vincent – now out of print.

There are various reasons why composers write music – some as an act of worship, others for commercial reasons, or simply as a pastime. Many will say they 'just have to write' when an idea comes to mind. As a young man what would you say your reasons for composing were?

Those first feeble experiments, more or less doodling on the piano, became firstly a fascination with improvisation and then a deeper creative compulsion – I just had to express myself in music but with no particular end in view. It meant exploring and trying to unravel the technical secrets – the language, the grammar, the designs. Why did I instinctively react to what appealed to me as convincing and satisfying or challenging because I sensed rather than understood? In the absence of tutorial guidance, textbooks and actual music printed, listened to or played were the only way forward. As a bandsman I found rehearsals informative where passages were broken down into their component parts. The creative pressure was within and anything that aided it was grist to the mill. As with taking any project seriously, there was (and is) an ongoing demand on mental grip, energy, concentration, self-criticism, reaching out with self-criticism and – at the end of the day – hopefully (but not always) achieving. This is a rather roundabout way of getting to the basic answer. I wrote SA music because that was my music-making context. In late adolescence I got into orchestral writing and had some encouragement in a BBC competition. My LTCL examination was in Glasgow with Sir Granville Bantock. As a director of Paxton, the publishing company, he gave me his card but died before I was demobilised. I had brief aspirations towards film music, but postwar Britain had to accommodate returning professionals in all walks of life. Then it was that the Head of the SA International Music Editorial Department, Colonel Bramwell Coles, gave me a post on his staff. Composition was a part of the work and of course it changed my whole life.

What were your musical influences as a young man? Did they extend beyond the SA?

The SA musical influences were not that deep, though they provided sound examples of design, episodical construction and the scoring of choral and keyboard idioms. For SA purposes, models in the selection and balancing of suitable song material were valuable. The three bands I played in up to 1942, when I joined the Navy, were good-average, but my experience of the best work of people like Ball, Leidzén and Marshall were not until I joined the ISB in 1946, by which time I was 24 and maturing. The choral repertoire seldom contained progressive language and styles. So, turning to other influences in chronological order it would be first Sullivan and Vaughan Williams at school. Then in teenage years I learnt about Beethoven in the home of our 2nd trombone player at Harlesden on occasional evenings – he was a great lover of Beethoven's music. Then I played Haydn and Mozart in a piano trio. On the piano at home I played Bach, Debussy, Schumann, Brahms, Ireland; and at the other end of the scale Billy Mayerl, Eric Coates and contemporary light pieces. As for recordings, there were the usual classics, plus Constant Lambert, Roussel, Walton, Holst, McDowell, Ives. In my early 20s I developed an interest in ballet, jazz and swing, and I haunted the second-hand bookshops which were then in Charing Cross Road.

And related to the question above, where would you say your compositional voice developed from? Is it often linked to the music you are listening to at that particular moment in time?

It's difficult to trace any clear chronological sequence. It's probably unwittingly shaped by a love of English music from Renaissance onwards, together with working through loads of textbooks, including two excellent books on 20th-century harmony. When briefly stationed in South Africa I had counterpoint lessons and my foundations were strengthened by a diet of Brahms. A degree course made me develop by exploring and imitating a variety of styles. Subsequently I consciously wrestled with systems like Hindemith and Schoenberg; though – as most of us are, or used to be – raised on a traditional tonal diet I can be swept away by the dissonances and techniques of others but am not always comfortable with my own! I'm not consciously aware of derivative influences on anything I'm chewing over, but I do take note of something that strikes me when listening and often seek to analyse what made it effective. When working on a particular passage or situation I have sometimes recalled a parallel in someone else's music and perhaps this may nudge my thinking. I would normally shun a conscious look-alike. I think most creative people hate being told their prized effort is like something else!

Were bands and music leaders always encouraging in your early days as a composer, and did you ever receive criticism for what you were doing? If so, was this something that spurred you on to greater things?

Following the Second World War, affected countries were ready for resurgence, including SA musicians who were returning to civilian life with widened horizons. Additionally the SA has always thrived on the new and the novel. Even so, there was initially some conservative reaction and negative attitudes tend to be more vocal!

Bands, audiences and individuals appeared to be encouraging about my first productions. The official printed voice of feedback and report was *The Musician*.

A correspondence column is naturally a typical cross-section and sometimes attitudes were prompted or encouraged at the varying personal approach of the editor. Some editors sought to stimulate controversy but I'd be less than honest if I pretended to have welcomed criticism, especially if there was a suspected hidden agenda.

I'm informed that, years ago, a chap had on his car a sign that read I HATE RAY STEADMAN-ALLEN – but I have been pretty fortunate. Mostly comments from quarters I valued were kindly but a differently-angled viewpoint (if informed, constructive and balanced) can have value and is a pill more easily swallowed if graciously expressed.

A particular personal favourite of mine is 'Victorian Snapshots – On Ratcliff Highway', and it will certainly go down as one of the seminal works of its era. If ever there is music that tells a story, this is it. Can you tell us what the inspiration was behind the piece? Being so original in construction and different from anything that had come before in SA music circles, what was the general response of people when it was first heard?

Thank you for your personal reaction – I appreciate it. When I was reading Brindley Boon's book *Play the Music, Play!*, I came across a small reproduction of an artist's impression of Whitechapel Band marching through the Ratcliff area. It caught my imagination and I looked up the original in an old *War Cry* (the SA weekly). The centenary of SA bands was arriving (1978) and those early days of banding activity was a promising subject. With family members I walked that blitzed and decaying docklands area, soaking it all in. I studied old maps to try and trace the pictured spot.

In 1933, my parents were the corps officers at Worthing where there had been riots 50 years before, an aspect much featured for the corps jubilee. So the 'persecution' angle must have been embedded in my mind. In the atmosphere of a concert celebrating the centenary of SA bands the audience mood was positive. Melbourne Staff Band, under Colin Woods, premiered it – a courageous thing to do in the home of brass banding – and they acquitted themselves excellently. A heartening spin-off was when I later met someone who had been a boy in that London area and he told me it recreated his boyhood.

Can you describe the thought process you go through when starting out on a new composition? Where does your inspiration come from?

As these questions are in an SA context I'll stay with that. The subject matter (not the musical ideas) usually is a spontaneous thought sparked by a song, Scripture theme, maybe an article headline, a sermon or testimony comment. Occasionally it is a title or phrase in a book. The musical ideas are often a mental by-product of physical activity, like walking. Usually they are unexpected and a 'shape' or phrase just pops into the head. Mostly it can't be forced, though the moment of getting an overall idea can spark off something promising. I rarely remember when and where. I do recall getting the germ of the 'big tune' theme for the last movement of 'Lord of the Sea' when walking home through Cunningham Park in Harrow. When I was writing 'The Holy War', I was stuck and need a fresh beginning at one point. I had to leave it, until one day, as I stood on a King's Cross Underground platform, the hoped-for idea pushed its way into my consciousness. The trick then is to hang on to it, as often these things tend to turn up at inconvenient moments when one can't write them down. There's little mystique about this – the same sequence must happen in all walks of life.

Each composer has a different way of formulating ideas; some will generally have a clear idea of where they want the music to go in a particular piece, others will let it develop organically as they go along. The film composer, John Williams, has said that he often starts by writing the end of a piece so that he knows where the musical material is going to land and develop. He will then decompose it and take it apart, so to speak, so that individual strands can be exposed singularly and then collect together at the end of the work. Do you always write chronologically or do you tend towards the Williams model of planning out clearly the destination of the music?

My wife insists that my best ideas are the first ones. The older I've become the more I have tended to revise and work over – hopefully not to death – and normally the basic drift is clear; I don't proceed in straight lines. The opening seems to spring forward at the time of getting the first ideas. I don't normally envisage the endings, though I imagine that in some contexts the finale is a summary and could be vital if you want to ensure an excited audience reaction like Tchaikovsky's '1812'. But it could turn out to be an epilogue (though other than devotional music, quiet endings can be an act of courage!). There's food for thought there. I don't blueprint very well, or maybe I feel it's too calculated. But there again, developing musical ideas is mostly a mixture of calculation, labour and feeling. Latterly, I've become rather indecisive – especially with openings – and tend to rework.

How would you say the advent of technology has changed the process of composition? Is it something you make use of or do you prefer the tried and tested method of writing out everything by hand?

The three PC positives for me are: 1. You can change your mind or make alterations without having to rewrite pages or cross out. 2. Provided your playback is adequate you can listen away from the visual score (but the playback of brass band on my kit is terribly reedy, like massed accordions, and rather thick!). 3. Part extraction is helpful.

I began computerising with Sibelius's first model – the Acorn. Having gone to Cambridge for a demonstration by the Finn brothers I was hooked by the sound of playback. Though basic, the Acorn was adequate for my purposes. Consequentially, though I moved on to Sibelius on Windows, the method is somewhat different and seems more complicated and time-consuming. The frustration and time spent has sometimes tended to send me back to handwriting, which, in any case, feels more 'direct' than a computer keyboard.

We have in The Salvation Army a wealth of music that could be described as 'timeless' – music that stands the test of time and will continue to be played and enjoyed for years to come. What would you say are the elements that go into creating a piece of music that does just this?

It would be untrue to respond that music with an immediate appeal tends to have a shorter shelf life. But with some exceptions, especially marches and attractive solos, SA bands have been raised on regularly-spaced new issues of journals, novelty and the next 'winner'. Also (ideally anyway) so much of our output is intended – like preaching – for communication on a spiritual level with a spiritual response. It's unsafe to guess what may survive and it doesn't always include the most immediately attractive. 'Developed music', which may often reveal more concentrated depth, takes time to assimilate and carries the risk of band-room dismissal on grounds of difficulty or immediacy. So some music with strong survival potential may never get off the ground. One reason for this is that the stampede for a newly-released popular item can cause other deserving items to be neglected. Commercial recordings help to popularise, but even there composers' chances are at the mercy of the personal choices and tastes of a microscopic handful of bandmasters. An important function of the International Staff Band's constitution was to familiarise people with music in the publication pipeline. I've noticed that 'going back' to earlier music seems usually to choose the 'favourites'. I yearn for more researchers who will give the 'what could have beens' a go.

There are a number of challenges to being a composer in the SA – one of these is balancing the aesthetics of the music to create a satisfactory musical account with that of portraying a spiritual message. Have you found this to be a particular challenge in your own compositional life, and if so, how have you managed to find a balance?

This is a penetrating question. I am glad you refer to me being 'a composer in the SA'. I have occasionally suspected that a label like 'SA composer' has led some to expect religious undertones in every piece of one's music whether written for the SA or not. Faith and personal outlook are from within which does not necessarily extend to every item being a manifesto. Shostakovitch, for instance, had political pressure on his music, and while we have the 'Leningrad Symphony' his output isn't constant versions of 'The Red Flag'. I've wrestled with this question, and the best I can come up with is (where appropriate) to view the challenge as a stimulus to ingenuity, and to discipline the style or language of the moment to be compatible with the whole piece. Even that's not quite satisfactory, as for a particular reason or effect one might choose to distort the traditional concept of a song melody. I've sometimes thought that we are a bit like Palestrina, who was assigned the task of simplifying Church music while avoiding losing its beauty and strength. Some may query our treatments. As far back as 1977 I addressed and illustrated for a bandmasters councils relative to a published letter which read: 'We have now commendably advanced from solos to concertos, rhapsodies, chords ancient and modern... counterpoint and countermelody and every clever musical device that composers can muster appears in such compositions... I wonder if, to mix metaphors, we run the risk of blinding by science to the extent that we cannot see the musical wood for the trees.'

There are bound to be occasions when the free spirit lets its hair down. I don't want to get into motivation – the readers of these replies will know the score in that direction – but as the very act of creation has a degree of ego-expression we may sometimes need to look within and take stock. We are serving a Higher Power and thus may need to modify our musical language, but within any parameters our musical judgment and craftsmanship are inevitably challenged and tested.

What advice would you have for any aspiring young composers in The Salvation Army?
If you have a gift, don't be too easily satisfied, work at your art, develop your skills, avoid overloading your work with cramming too much in at one go, and keep the character of the piece you are working on consistent with itself. If you are fortunate enough to have a kindred spirit to share with, you may find it mutually helpful. Be true to yourself. While role models are helpful – even essential – be selective about fashion but not its slave. While creative expression is often just for the joy of it, in SA terms there is an end purpose, even if that purpose is not always 'heavy'. Have a clear view as to a specific and how the character, design and handling of your material will best achieve it. The SA does not exist just to keep creative people happily occupied, so be prepared for the fact that the editor may not always be euphoric about your new masterpiece. He may already have a drawerful of that genre. Be basically grateful for your ability to build from within, though most of us have our dry and desperate times. Try to stay balanced about yourself; it makes sense for us to be humble enough to learn from others – there are usually new challenges and widening your awareness can be stimulating. We have to learn the hard way that we won't please everyone. If some of your work does, that's great. Rejoice, but be prepared for climate changes. Try to condition yourself to criticism and be streetwise to recognise a hidden agenda. You are there to put your 'twopenn'orth' into the scheme of things. So are others. Jealousy is a killer and shadows your work. Follow your

star – you have been entrusted with a gift, you are accountable for it and I hope you will have the encouragement and opportunities to share it.

And finally where do you see SA band music going in the future?
The question acknowledges that, in our Movement, almost the only things that stay the same are the spiritual facts of life. Congregationally the harmonic language has renounced many of the traditional harmonic patterns together with giving a welcome to a pentatonic Celtic folk flavour. In our arrangements swing (daring in my youth) finally became acceptable. From what I am encountering, rhythmic elements, underlined by percussion, have strengthened considerably together with, at the moment, the whirling factors of excitement. That is a fair reflection of today's world. However, at local level the technical resources are nowadays frequently far from capable and I have never changed my mind that we have more to offer than excitement. But I recognise that all SA outreach music serves its 'present age', which of course challenges awareness and creative response. So who can tell? I am glad to note that we have composers who can not only still major with poetic and expressive ideas but are also taking the trouble to hone their techniques to make those ideas effective. I am concerned as to today's listening capacity when I learn that programme planning may avoid anything longer than six minutes. It's years since I argued as an editor that the stopwatch is not the yardstick of interest, though perhaps conditioning is hastening that kind of approach. I never dreamed that our bands would implode so quickly though I am aware of some reasons. Rock has become a universal catch-all language; the classical world remains aloof and maybe we have to accept a continuing sub-cultural role. On the positive side there are very many enthusiasts who, I hope, are determined to stay that way.

PART THREE

Humanity

Ray Steadman-Allen –
The Lighter Side

Ray finds an outlet for frustration in writing parodies of that which has 'got him going', but this is not the only springboard for his love of words. He has written several poems, some of which are humorous but are still in themselves a comment. Other poems are deeply reflective, provoking an emotional response. He has requested that we include this aspect of his creativity. This kaleidoscope illustrates both his wit and his engagement with life.

YEARS and years ago – I was probably a captain at the time – we were beavering away at our editorial tasks when in came a group of cadets. Part of officer training was to visit the various social work and administrative establishments which included the trading company of Salvationist Publishing and Supplies Ltd. One earnest young man said to me: 'It must be wonderful working with these God-given songs with their inspirational words.' I was a bit at a loss to answer, as for us in the department words were lines to be scrutinised, worked upon and checked. How penetrating he was, though. I have often looked back to those active days where matters technical shared honours with theological and experiential statements. It was just a part of the job. Yet so many lovely songs have passed through one's hands, songs which have ringed the world and brought thousands nearer to God.

I had little tolerance for the trite and cliché-ridden. It seemed terrible to offer the Almighty the cheap and throwaway doggerel. Often, though, that may have represented a best personal achievement and could well have been costly to its originator. That is why, in the editorial chair, I tried to accompany necessary rejections with a tender and, where possible, encouraging response. I'm afraid I have an irreverent but non-malicious streak when encountering pomposity and have a reaction to broken pledges.

The tape recorder brought possibilities for serious work, but I also found a kind of relaxing fun in doing spoofs. When the girls were younger we used to put together taped 'Army meetings' dubbing in old 78-rpm historically-recorded voices, including the Founder. At least it inculcated a sense of roots! Somewhere I have an old tape of when I had a rush of blood to the head in performing (not in public!) an impromptu solo-voice-plus-keyboard 'setting' of the letter to Philemon, really going to town on the rhythms of 'Please keep a guest room ready for me'.

During our term in Australia country music was strong in the service of popular evangelism and that was enjoyably fine. A diet of that style together with colloquial translations occasionally drove me to tape record improvised material in that genre. Another safety valve!

Born again

Come runnin'

(Peter...ran to the sepulchre Luke 24:12)

Then, in the wake of *The Message* paraphrase of the Bible, I had the notion of a colloquial *Real Cool Bible* which, of course, I could never get off the ground, but I expect someone else has done or will do it.

The following is obviously a penned cartoon.

Peter Makes a Splash

'WELL, take me to a Samaritan knees-up!' exclaimed Peter. 'Just look at the Master walking across the water to us. He must want to tell us something important or he would have waited till morning or at least till we got back ashore.' He was thinking about this in his own steady way when he could bear it no longer. He just had to know what was going on.

'Come on over!' cried Jesus. 'Don't worry, the water's fine!'

So Peter jumped in, full of confidence. If Jesus could do it, so could he, and he was on his way. Or so he thought.

The water failed to hold him up. His feet just sank and, as they did, so his legs (being attached) followed suit. A heavy man, Peter sank like a stone. Fortunately his life as a fisherman had made him a skilled and experienced swimmer. He trod water, he did his breast strokes, gasped and bubbled.

'What's the problem?' asked Jesus. 'Don't lose faith, put your believing bonnet on.' But Peter was in too deep and didn't hear it.

After rescue, a good towelling down and a good swig of Galilean pick-me-up, he felt his old self again. The local council heard about it and put up a lifebelt. But even they couldn't understand it. 'Why would the Nazarene walk on the water?' they wondered. Why couldn't he take a boat like everybody else? More to the point, who gave him permission? Surely there was a bye-law forbidding it. Typical troublemaker, they thought. So, a lifeguard being expensive, they not only put up a lifebelt, they also called a special meeting under the chairmanship of the mayor, and had a big sign painted which they fixed on the seashore. It read NO WALKING ON WATER.

Peter

RS-A ... RS-A

When you walk with the Mas-ter on the wa - ter, Don't get cold feet!

Poor old Pe - ter start-ed to sink Al-most ere his feet had left the brink, So un

less you've faith you hadn't ought - er Walk with the Mas-ter on the wa - ter.

A Chocolate Cake

THERE is little quite so humbling as doing for oneself in the dear one's absence.

The dear one is holidaying for a few days. She phoned at teatime on Thursday to say that the weekend roads may be busy, so return will not be Saturday morning as planned but after the evening meal on Friday. Notions of a leisurely bit of lawn-mowing on Friday, followed by a duster flick on Saturday, have entirely imploded. Up early Friday (why did we move to a place with so much grass?) and a feverish go through the bungalow. Savaged by the vacuum cleaner, exhausted by noon, I decide on fish and chips in town.

Back, feeling so much more poised and somewhat virtuous, having spotted, and bought, some cheap jellies in the market. Then the disastrous idea. Make a cake for her return! I am a bit of a dab hand at a simple recipe fruit cake. Right: quick shelf inspection – no dried fruit. Get out the post-Mrs Beeton books. Thumb through. Ah, chocolate cake! Check the ingredients. Yes, we've got 'em all. Four ounces of this and a few drops of that. Will be a breeze. Better put the oven on. The book says 375F or gas mark four. Our oven is centigrade. What was that conversion formula again? C over 9 equals F minus 32. Doesn't look quite right. Better ring a mathematical or scientific friend. On second thoughts, perhaps not. No, perhaps it was C over 5. How does that come out? Rough calculation: looks about 200. That seems reasonable: go for it, switch on oven – almost the point of no return.

Now the ingredients. Sugar, marg. No problem weighing those out. 'Cream together with the vanilla essence and a tablespoon of golden syrup.' 'Cream together' – fancy way of saying 'mix'. Have you ever attacked a tin of syrup with a tablespoon? Only the spoon won't go in – the tin's a small size. So, get a dessert spoon and fill the tablespoon that way. Problem-solving? Nothing to it! Now the syrup has glued up teaspoons and a knife I scraped them with and is flowing down the sides of the tin and happily settling in the rim. The ants will be on the march again. So, scrub the tin, cutlery and anywhere else dripping with syrup.

'Until soft and light,' says the book. 'Sieve together the dry ingredients.' Just about to throw the carefully weighed ounce and a half of cocoa when a sixth sense cautions: 'Just make sure.' No, it was an ounce and a half of chocolate powder; only one ounce of cocoa. That was a close one! Another bowl used up. Sieve? I stir gently and stuff puffs all over the work surface. Egg beating uses a third bowl. Can't do it like the television; I bang them on the edge and wonder why there are bits of shell floating about. Pick most of it out. Stir the whole shebang together. Does 'alternately' mean alternate small doses? Too late now. Going great guns. But what's this? 'Add just enough milk to make it a soft consistency. Be careful not to make this cake too soft, for if you do, the weight of the golden syrup will cause it to sink in the middle.' Now they tell me! It's

The Order of the Founder

Instituted by Minute dated 20 August 1917

Presented to

Lieut-Colonel Ray Steadman-Allen

Both in active service as an officer and in retirement he has exemplified the highest possible standards of Salvationist spirituality expressed through creative musicianship, constant encouragement to others, both inside and beyond the Army, and through his preaching and teaching ministry.

I hereby appoint the said

Lieut-Colonel Ray Steadman-Allen

to be a member of The Order of the Founder *and direct that his name be inscribed on the Roll of The Order.*

Dated this 11th day of June in the year of our Lord Two Thousand and Five.

International Headquarters
London

General

Ray's surprise and delight at being presented with the Order of the Founder are evident. The award was made by General John Larsson and presented by General Shaw Clifton at the Gospel Arts Festival in the Royal Albert Hall on 11 June 2005.

First page of manuscript for *My New Day*

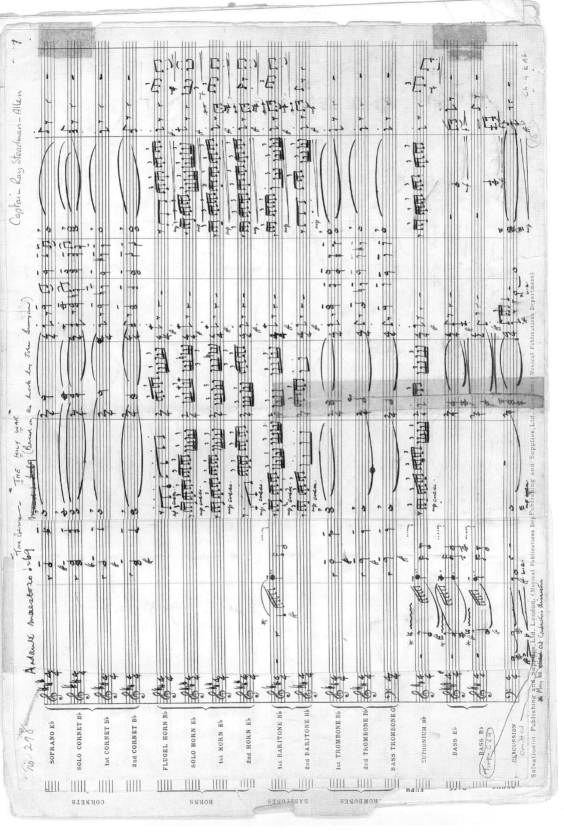

The beginning of *The Holy War* – with amendments and sticky tape!

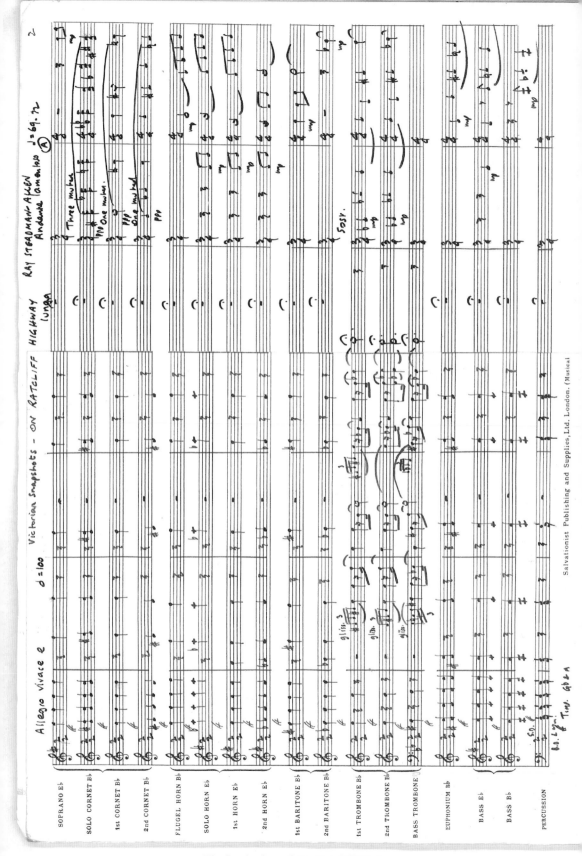

The beginning of *On Ratcliff Highway*

already soft without the milk. Déjà vu; last week I was mixing mortar for a bit of re-pointing. Well, it says 'milk'; ought to add some as they've mentioned it. So trickle in a token teaspoonful.

Now load the cake tin. I know this bit. You grease round and maybe stick a margarine wrapper on the bottom. So do this on the first cake tin to hand. Put the gooey mixture in with the now washed tablespoon, scraping the goo of the spoon with a knife. The knife also comes in handy for scraping bits off me. All done, pop it in the oven. Just a minute! Mix looks lost in there. Quick read: 'a seven-inch tin' (this book's too old to be metric). Mine's a ten-inch. Whip out of the oven. Try to lift the mixture by the edges of the margarine wrapper, naturally, and in abject conformity to gravity and Murphy's Laws, the goo – now further softened by the heat – streams over the sides. Happily not too much lost as I scrape off the side of the tin.

Never say die. Mind over cake mix. Pull out the margarine wrapper, pour the repulsive substance via bowl four into its original, wrong, hot, tin. Locate the seven-inch one, and – self-control thinning – transfer loathsome mix into tin two. Well done. I would have thought that by now I would have learned my lesson about reading the instructions before doing the job – especially after many years ago making sure the liquid paint stripper really worked by leaving it on too long. So I shouldn't have been surprised to find that I should have greased and floured tin two first. Which I hadn't. So I wearily tip it all out again and repeat the operation.

Incidentally, all this consumes so much time I had turned the oven off again. I forgot to mention that I originally put the sugar and marg in the processor. So there was that to wash, plus four bowls, a redundant cake tin, an assortment of cutlery and acres of work surface.

I've just taken out the cake. Looks OK. If I hadn't sat down to write this sorry tale and done a King Alfred, it might have been for the better. But it was only a tad scorched.

*** *** ***

239

Festival of Light
25 September 1971

I haven't the pen to describe
The unregimented, moving down Piccadilly.

Marching? More like a ramble really.
Partly in holiday mood, but with determined purpose.
No aimless shuffle; the gaiety in the step,
The radiance in the face:
Not Baptistry, nor Methodism, nor Salvationist,
Not Catholic or Protestant –
We are Christians! Nothing else is meaningful today,
(And likely to be much less important afterward).

The Army band is playing 'Onward! Christian soldiers'.
They have played it innumerable times –
Old Baring-Gould should have been here;
He would be thrilled. 'We are not divided, all one body we!'

Now the shout is 'Jesus':
'Give me a 'J': 'J' goes up the roar;
'Give me a 'E' – and so it goes on until
The Name is thundered out again, again:
'Jesus! Jesus! Jesus!'
With skyward pointing fingers, 'He lives!'
'God is dead!' from the pavement.
From the marchers the song begins:
     'Christ Jesus lives today,
      You ask me how I know he lives?
      He lives within my heart.'
The shouter's gone.

Nearing the park now,
And passing the paintings on the left
The crowd begins to thicken.
There were rumours that an opposition reception awaited.
We wondered what it would be like;
Violence is not a major feature of protests here in London.
We wondered; but no one seemed particularly bothered.

240

And now we see the beginnings,
The hippies, the Gay Libs,
The Maoists –
You name them.
Some to see the fun, others more deadly.
The band is still playing.
The Blood and Fire banners plough into the horde of sniggering sneering faces.

I can't evoke for you the faces. I haven't the skill.
The faces of the morally sick,
The old-before-their time,
The haunted,
The painted men.
Our pew-bound platitudes will not avail here.
Our faith confesses that only Jesus,
Only his Spirit could make any impact.
It's as basic as that.

I suppose these faces are as old as time.
There have always been these sick, ravaged, bestial faces.
Today they shout obscenities.
Yesterday it was 'Crucify him!'
Evil is here all right,
No doubt of that.
A hating face thrusts into that of my wife.

At this moment,
At this moment,
At this moment the witness.
Jesus talked about people like these;
On the lines that they would find
Their way into the Kingdom before some of those
Who rather prided themselves on their piety.
Probably because they are being themselves,
They are not pretending,
In their despising of hypocrisy there is hope.
But it's hard to go along with it here and now.

The burly city men carry the cross
Made of massive wooden beams.
Someone said that the city office ministry
Has yielded three thousand converts in two years.

Three thousand.
A number Peter would remember if he were here.
He'd remember three thousand all right.
Wasn't that the day of Pentecost?
He'd be right at home with all this rabble.
He'd heard shouting,
Seen the glaring faces,
Had the sneers, the jibes, the hate.
He wouldn't know what a Maoist was,
Or recognise 'Heil! Heil! Heil!' in time to Sullivan's tune.
Of course any call for clean-up or restriction
Is thought to be fascist.
Peter didn't know what a fascist was.
Mind you, he'd seen a fair bit of dictatorship.
But his answer would have been exactly what the youngsters were shouting:
    'Jesus! Jesus!'

Somehow the opposition seems to be melting.
All in the line of duty, an uninvolved
Emotionless line of policemen.
(Some are family men – most, probably.)
One sergeant in particular has been dogging Joy's footsteps.
I think he's making sure her evangelical zeal
Doesn't earn her an unpleasant experience.
She doesn't care.
There she is, in the front, right through them,
Arm upraised,
With an assortment of Christian war cries.
Is this feminine tornado of evangelical fire,
This alloy of Joan of Arc, Catherine Booth and Boudicca,
The sweet lady who presides at our meals and does the ironing?
Twice I have whispered in her ear,
'Don't start a one-woman war.'
But that's what she seems set on!

The band plays away.
Barbara and Rosemary are in it – bless 'em.
Lips like blubber, I shouldn't wonder.
But all to the glory of God –
And who'd miss this, having come? Here's the action.
The Sunday routine is nice and cosy.
It does good (so we tell ourselves);

And, to be fair, it really does. The witness on the street
Is vital. Today proves it afresh.
But to come out of the citadel, the chapel, the church and muster like this;
To see the face of the enemy; to get a whiff of the stench
From the gates of hell.
This is the action.
Right here, where they can get at you, as well as you at them.

The park, and we're there.
Was it worth it?
I wouldn't have missed the exhilaration,
The effect of seeing your opposition,
The wonderful sense of comradeship beyond the label;
The awareness that
'They that be for us are more than they that be against us.'
With Gideon we take heart in this.

I will not forget the gentle, dark-haired youth,
Coming to us and asking: 'How can I get up on to the platform
To speak to my people?
I must speak to my people.'
'Where are your people?'
(Thinking he had a small following in some esoteric cult).
Are they scattered in the crowd?
I took him to the small entrance gate.
'Tell me, who are your people?'
I hear again the so, so gentle wistful reply – an echo of another time,
Another place, another Heart:
'They are <u>all</u> my people.'
Simplicity of response, divine in the vastness of its concept.
I, who had sung 'Whosoever will may come',
'Christ for the world we sing', 'He's got the whole world in his hands'
And all the rest of it was brought up sharply with this breath of reality:
'They are all my people.'
I saw then he wore a crude sign.
It read: 'I am Jesus: who are you?'
A bit simple. Maybe.
Such gentleness. Such wistfulness. Such bewilderment
Because the steward wouldn't admit him to the enclosure.
I have wondered what he would have said.
Have we missed a revelation?
I suppose London's full of Messiahs, prophets, cranks and the rest.

Every city is.
But are our eyes any more aware
Than those who turned away a gentle Nazarene?
Who can say how the Prince tabernacles with his people?
Might he not be with his own on such a day?
What fancifulness!
A lifetime of disillusion beginning with the dissolution of Santa Claus
Makes cynics of many of us.
Perhaps we are the poorer for lacking expectation of the miracle.
If what we read be true, our rude, unlettered forefathers
Having no acquaintance with 'education'
Apparently took unworldly manifestations in their stride.

This day and all its influences
Would have made utterly normal any such manifestation.
Was this lad then a sign?
His deep concern,
His gentleness,
They were.
I must record a moment of emotion in that encounter.

'I am Jesus: who are you?'
Sometimes I wonder (don't we all?),
Quite often I don't greatly care for what I see in the mirror.
But I shall recall those two extremes which breathed
An atmosphere of the Realm of Heaven
In transcendence of the evil unity:
The jubilant 'Jesus lives',
The gentle word:
'They are all my people.'

*** *** ***

Through the Cottage Window

It's rained day after day,
but how quiet it is
except for the waterfall.
When we've left we'll not say
about the rain,
not at all!
But how quiet it was.

The cottage was Hen Felin, South Wales. This was scribbled in Biro on a fragment torn from the local paper – 14. 9. 74. And framed soon after.

Homesickness *(Hen Felin, Ystalyfera)*

Generous, impetuous, forgetful Cymric people:
Land of pubs and churches,
Rugby clubs and local gossip.
Far, too far away from here
you sleep under a Celtic moon.

I sit here in the hot sun
thinking about the waterfall,
the bridge, The Old Swan,
St Dai's, the springtime daffodils,
and the wild, careless green sprawl,
the bingo and the burned-out junk shop,
after-nine chips and an omnipresent grubby dog,
the back lane through to Gurno's
and the blackberries in season.
The family fun, the hills and peace of heart,
Nancy and Eric's hospitality,
Eunice and Wyn – and Hannah's rose bush.

But we shall see them again;
inhaling the orange blossom in the garden,
poking about in the shed for tool or brush.

Like music of a deep, developed kind,
life has movements, tempo changes,
modulations, threads of theme;
isolations, clustered, crowded, busy passages,
rests, silences, jarring discords.

But, after the turnabouts and counterpoints
of conflict,
of sometimes complicated joinings-up,
the music turns and comes back home.
And so will we.

New South Wales, Australia, 1981

Glory March

On rare occasions I go home
northward by Paul's cathedral.
One early evening, Friday-dulled,
trudging the churchyard route,
on impulse –
whimsical snippet of thought, no more –
I headed an imaginary march.
The lilt of music in my brain
would square the shoulders,
sharpen up the pace.

An idle fancy, scarce projected,
instantly in my mind created:
flags ablaze with God's tricolour,
And at the back of me
skilled musicians,
compact, clear, precise and crisp,
play martial tunes that lift the step.

Buoyant, silver-sparkling bands,
Salvation soldiers, numberless as the sands.
Past the grey church stones we swing,
reinforcements crowding in.

Saints and martyrs, loved, forgiven,
ransomed souls, task force of Heaven.
Holy colours streaming brave,
say 'Jesus lives, and lives to save!'

I left the church path, through the gate,
my spirit soaring, grown elate,
burning with a sense of mission,
glowing with a Patmos vision.

The Underground become a shrine
on the westbound Central Line.

All afternoon I had been on some official business at International HQ and was returning home to Barnet. My way to the Tube lay through St Paul's Churchyard. c1979.

Treasure In Botany Bay

Back from her early morning walk,
Like a dew child, bright-eyed,
Clutching two beach flowers
And three flat shells.
'Do you know
there's a penguin in Botany Bay?'

You nerve-taut greedy world,
Learn from her:
Real treasure's but a step away.

*** *** ***

For Years To Come

O Doctor Croft, O Doctor Croft,
I see you in your organ loft
Crafting your tune 'St Anne'.
Immortal Isaac's firm belief
Has voiced a nation's prayers and grief,
The mystery of life's span.
Three centuries of sober chant
Have humbly asked God's aid to grant,
Reveal'd the hopes of man.
A brighter page is set before us:
Tommy Walker's added a chorus.

I was editing some song material when I encountered an arrangement of Isaac Watts's immortal hymn 'O God our Help in Ages Past' set to the standard tune of St Anne (William Croft). A chorus was appended – a good chorus in today's terms, but the addition to a virtually national hymn surprised this Englishman.

Lost Innocence

This morning I wept for earlier days,
remembering the boyish zeal
for Saturday night open airs –
all weathers.
Knowing nor caring about pyramids of power.
In my innocence:
Every man a brother,
Every cause a crusade,
Every soldier a saint.

The years bring too much knowledge of littleness.
A vast darkness with here and there a few candles of selflessness –
it would be simpler to know less.
Why does one become cynical?
Pettiness and envy are not new;
the heart longs for a return to innocence.

But it is strength, it is wisdom to know the less in men
and, in the dignity of chosen dedication,
in the pattern of my Lord,
to spend myself.
The towel and the bowl:
these are not base
because his hands have touched them.

20. 6. 65

A Psalm of Praise

Let us praise him!
Let us stand within the sanctuary and let him have the full blaze of our
    glorious brass.
Let us give the drums and harps a real jolly day out.
Let the Levites say, the one unto the other, 'Wow, this is a real rave up and no
    mistake!'

Let us go up, even up to the place of rejoicing.
Let us proclaim the name of Elohim from Dan to Beersheba.
For we are indeed the children of Abraham.
Our fathers journeyed in the desert for forty years.
Lo, they moaned all the time and gave unto Moses a load of grief.

Publish it in the streets of Gilgal and noise it abroad in the valley of Hinnom.
Do not ask the Almighty why these two places: it is one of the unfathomable
    mysteries with which we have had to put up from the rising of the sun
    until the day break and the shadows flee away.

So let us fold our tents.
Let us be going.
For there is no rest to those who make their dwelling upon a bed of thorns.

To the tune of 'Old MacDonald had a Kibbutz'.

*** *** ***

249

Blood on the Doorposts

(Exodus revisited)

Old Moses said to Pharoah,
'Now let my people go;
We've frogs and flies and plagues besides,
You just won't want to know.'
But Pharoah only said to him,
'Oh no, no, no, no, no!'

    So there's blood on the doorposts
    And another little lamb is dead.

So the 'gyptians went through that routine
Of boils for high and low –
And all the things the Bible says –
But Pharoah still said 'no'.

    So there's blood on the doorposts...

There's been the time when wizards too
Had really been gung-ho.
Aaron beat them at their game,
But Pharoah still said 'no'.

    So there's blood on the doorposts...

The Lord had really to get tough,
He laid the first-born low;
Death's angel swept throughout the land,
So Pharoah said, 'Please go.'

    And there's blood on the doorposts
    And another little lamb is dead.

O agnus corpus est
O agnus corpus est
If those in charge had done their best
And Phaoah'd managed to pass the test,
Israel might never had gone west (or east),

So there'd never be blood on the doorposts,
Nor another little lamb got dead.

Which would really have wrecked the theology!

Harry Foster

When Harry Foster went to Heaven
And ceased Salvation fighting,
'Twas all of fourteen years ago –
Before I took to writing
Of this kind.

I see him and his slide trombone
With Dick and Jack together,
A forthright trio: men of years,
But out in any weather.
They didn't mind.

I see him on the Bexhll Road,
Our Rose and Barbara shouting
And 'Charlie, Charlie, chuck-chuck-chuck'
The anthem for their outing.
Their Dad behind.

And at the stop on the West Hill
From fruit to vests and woollies,
He stands there in his ice-cream coat
And kids he's down to his last pound note,
Till another one he'd find.

They say his was the generous hand
That many a soul in Stockton
Would keep the secret but had to own
The fact that Harry gave a hand
When times were poor
He was so kind.

1980

I am not a poet

(see chapter 10, Glasgow Musicians Councils 1975)

Open the Bible and you will see
Words of comfort for you and for me.
Words of salvation, words of cheer;
With Jesus to help me, why should I fear?

Shepherd divine, thou hast called me to be
A fisher of men till thy glory I see.
When in the storm and the loud waves roar,
Feed me with manna till I want no more.

When in the valley and my sight grows dim,
I will be his helper, I will walk with him.
Though my sins are many, he will make me clean,
'Neath his cross of suff'ring on his arm I'll lean.

Help me, Heavenly Father, as I seek the lost;
Come just now in power, as at Pentecost;
Then within the battle's heat, when the foeman stands –
I will be as helpless clay in the Potter's hands.

Now the fire descending, flowing o'er my soul,
Cleansed in love's baptising makes me fully whole.
Filled in fullest measure, powerful I'll be;
Firmly on the Rock of Ages permeate through me.

Like the woman at the well, off'ring me to drink,
Washed in the all-cleansing flood never will I shrink.
Like the boy whose loaves and fishes fed a multitude,
Let me ever follow thee, o'er waters rough and rude.

When my feet would go astraying, pilot me to shore;
As a bird beneath her feathers, open thou the door.
As in penitence before thee, here I bow the knee,
Come thou mighty Rock of Ages, roll right over me.

Though the way be darkness, though the path be bleak,
In the thunder, fire and 'quake, let me hear thee speak.
And when hell assails me, in the bitter fray;
From my place of safety, I will never stray.

As the fisherman his net, the craftsman's fashioning tool,
I with grief am quite resigned to live by Golden Rule.
Help me in my wand'rings; guide me in my sin;
Then before the Gates quite shut – beckon me within.

Written semi-humorously for a choral conference to demonstrate the importance of understanding the text of a song by using meaninglessly juxtaposed phrases from the SA songbook. Notice especially the mixed metaphors.

Pennine Chain

I have followed David's intention,
I have looked at the hills.
Not that I reckon God to be up there
More than in the city,
Because the people are in the city.
It is reasonable to suppose
That, like his Son,
He should be down
Among the hungry and the suffering:
The slaves of the tall chimneys
(higher than any Roman cross,
And – some would say –
Far more relevant
And important.
Pointing Godward, like the church spires;
But mammon-rooted
In the iron world that bore them.
The industrial incense
Falling in fine soot upon mean terraces,
A grimy blessing
Upon grey votaries.)

It may be I didn't look long enough.
True, the hills are quiet and solid-still;
With their crags and streams,
Lambs,
And dry-stone walls
(no petrol stations).

It may well be I didn't look long enough:
My heart didn't follow my eyes.
It was still in the dirty city,
Contaminated.
'He that is washed needs but to wash his feet'
Said Christ.

I have walked into polluted places:
      The God-revolting dustbins of respectability;
      The sewage of self-righteousness.
      The selfishness
      That crowds the betting shops,
      Sprawls across pub counters.
      The brutality
      That makes neglected children
      Sob hopelessly
      In the loveless dark.
      The greed
      That coshes old ladies;
      The lust
      That hangs about the dance halls;
      The stupidity (pathetic arrogance!)
      That maims the leather bodies
      Of ton-up boys.

I have walked in polluted places.
David himself
Was not untainted by his times.

I need to wash my mind in the mountain stream,
To find eternal values in the timeless skyline;
To be with myself;
With the Radiant Purity
That is God.

So I will go again to the hills,
And stay a little longer.

*** *** ***

Interlude: conversation piece on engaging with the 'contemporary' today

Barbara writes: This is a conversation Dad and I had one Thursday afternoon in January about the challenges of composing non-vocal music for Salvation Army congregations today.

Barbara: Do you find it challenging to write for Army congregations nowadays? They seem to have a decreasing corpus of music that might bring them 'blessing', shall we say, because they can't associate the music with the words of songs.

Ray: I'm not sure that they ever could entirely. You include at least one song that you hope they'll know, but when I was writing 'Wells of Gladness' few knew 'Streams that Never Fail'. I wonder if that's why they are now going more in the direction of a simple arrangement of something people know, though that approach is not new.

Barbara: I think the point is that once you were able to introduce a song into something. Think of the major pieces you've written: you've included 'In the Cross of Christ I Glory', 'The Head that Once was Crowned with Thorns'. Those are heavyweight, deeply stirring, theological hymns…

Ray: 'We have not Loved thee as we Ought'…

Barbara: Yes – you were able to introduce all those songs into pieces. They brought people to the mercy seat and therefore became significant in their spiritual experience. You knew you were going to be invoking the Holy Spirit because people were able to associate the songs with past experience. In a sense it's quite hard for composers these days because there's less of a common language.

Ray: There's a big part to be played by our meeting leaders too. They need to take hold of what the sections do, refer to the pieces, quote from them. It's part of the worship. When that happens, it presses home a point or the basic message of the music. It's possible to pick up the last chorus of a band piece like 'All my Days and All my Hours' and say: 'That's number whatever in the songbook – let's sing it.' To me, that's imaginative meeting leadership. I would like to see more meeting leaders utilise what their sections present.

Barbara: And it has to be that way round because the musicians can't just jump – they have to train and practise so that they can play the music properly.

Ray: Yes, it's not exactly off the cuff, is it?

Barbara: But the dilemma is, how do you write music for the 'now' that will last into tomorrow – especially if people don't associate words with tunes?

Ray: When Leslie Condon wrote 'I'll follow thee, deny thee…' and stops dead, everybody's brain used to continue, '…never.' We can't do that any more.

I don't know why not – maybe because we're getting so many new people in from different places.

Barbara: The language of Christian worship changes so quickly. You've been writing a piece to include 'King of Kings, Majesty' – that's become a bit of a classic now, but who knows what people will think in three years' time? You're writing a piece of music now which means something now but which may not have lasting endurance on paper like 'In Quiet Pastures'.

Ray: The onus is then on a composer or arranger to be doing more than knock a tune together with a few fancy gimmicks and to write a piece of music which, in itself, has got something of musical worth in it. When people listen to 'The Eternal Quest' they might not know 'Jesus is Looking for Thee' but I would hope that something would get through – the dramatic nature of things. We could listen to, say, Grieg's 'Holberg Suite' – there's something about the quality of the line – it's nothing directly to do with God, but if you've got that spiritual connection in you... For decades we've accepted the original passages of Army music as valid expression. Slater's 'The Stilling of the Storm' is largely pictorial. Some themes of larger works have had words added afterwards and become songs. The expectation is that there should be a sacred root.

Barbara: So now we're coming to the place where music has a language of its own irrespective of the words.

Ray: Yes, it always has had, to a point, but we're losing those extra building blocks. An instance that comes to mind is Bramwell Coles's descriptive selection 'Discipleship'. It is based on lovely and relevant song material, but it would be doubtful whether all the words were well known.

Barbara: It isn't a criticism, it's an observation of a trend – but how are we going to write stuff that is going to be played in two years' time with the same kind of meaning?

Ray: The only hope is to keep a certain amount of tradition alive – the Church of England doesn't just live on only what was written last year, does it?

Barbara: No, and I suspect that Army corps don't either – that it will always be a matter of careful and pastoral leadership in choosing music for meetings that enables everybody in the congregation to worship at some stage.

Ray: And that takes the challenge back one stage to the training college teaching the value of preserving some tradition as well as using contemporary material.

Barbara: Language and identity go together though, don't they? And with the changing identity there will be changing language, so what do musicians do then? England has always had an amazing track record in hymnody, so it's not just a matter of Salvation Army tradition, it's also a matter of Christian tradition.

Ray: Of course a lot of our Army tradition is Wesleyan anyway. I personally would be poorer without 'My chains fell off, my heart was free'.

Barbara: On the other hand, classics are being written now – the Holy Spirit didn't just inspire yesterday, he also inspires today. But then it's always going to be the nature of changing culture that there will be overlap – we didn't wake up one morning and find ourselves in a baroque era when yesterday it was Renaissance, for example.

Ray: I was encouraged by the fact that 'Amazing Grace' returned after 200 years.

Barbara: And Samuel Wesley's anthem 'Lead Me, Lord'. Perhaps the past is being rediscovered with contemporary accompaniment.

Ray: You could be right.

Barbara: I suppose the real question is: 'What is music for?' It's a big topic to address. Take this new piece you're writing for the 'I'll Fight' Congress (2012). What inspired you?

Ray: It was General Linda Bond's call to 'One Army, One Mission, One Message'.

Barbara: Why did you choose the tunes you're using?

Ray: I've stayed with popular traditional ones that I think a lot of people still know. I've introduced 'I, the Lord of Sea and Sky'; I've opened with 'The World for God' which people may or may not know; I've got 'Stepping on Together in the Ranks of Truth' which a lot of people know. The second song is 'Just Where He Needs Me' and the last ones are 'We Have a Gospel' and 'Cardiff', which makes the ending 'Amazing Love' and 'My Chains Fell Off'. They are all traditional Army ones which most people will know without the songbook – or did. This challenge is issued to the existing Army. After all, the General is saying **one** Army, **one** Mission, **one** Message. There has to be some simplification up to a point. And there is also the problem of cultural differences, as we are a worldwide Army.

Barbara: Was there more of a uniformity in the past or has there always been that kind of international cultural difference anyway?

Ray: It was uniform in so far as many people doing missionary work took songs which were largely common in the Movement. Some people went to Africa a couple of years ago and came back with a CD – and they're all singing these old-time Army songs that have died with us – they're marching around singing them!

Barbara: Is it now 'hand to mouth' as opposed to 'built to last' in this country?

Ray: We have a throwaway society where the thinking is: 'Don't fix it, get a new one.' Religious expression is in danger of going the same way. It seems that composers just cater to popular taste, only writing what they think people will use or in a currently prevailing style.

Barbara: Are we saying that craftsmanship can't be thrown away but that its impact might diminish if the words are not known so well?

Ray: Well, I wonder if it can be thrown away – because how many people sitting in the congregation know what craftsmanship is about? A cross-section of any congregation will reveal people who are more happy with a simple pop idiom song. And we have a whole area of people who have never been exposed to the songbook.

Barbara: That is the very point, isn't it?

Ray: Yes – locally we have lot of new people, and when we have an old-time song newly introduced they sing just as heartily – it goes with gusto. We sang 'I've Joined the Army of the Lord' the other week.

Barbara: Things come fresh to the palate.

Ray: They are doing so. If we think about something like 'The King's Minstrel' – I don't suppose a lot of people know those Victorian Bateman songs now, though I think most British and other Salvationists did when I wrote it.

Barbara: But this isn't a new thing, is it? I played 'True Life' as an early trombone solo. I don't think I know the words of the tune in that.

Ray: I remember when Black Dyke Band recorded 'In Quiet Pastures'. Stephen [Cobb] said to me: 'The band played it like angels – but they don't know what the words say.' We come back to levels of understanding – which applies to art generally, of course.

Barbara: That's going back to the point of what Army music is for. It gets right to the heart of it.

Ray: I'm beginning to think that it's starting to be seen (a) as an accompaniment to singing and b) as an entertainment to catch the ear – which it probably was in the first place, to stop the crowds from heckling. I think we developed, in those golden years, probably the 1920s to 80s. Our expanding into musical forms had early official blessing and offered a way of deeper musical expression. There's no question of the validity of pure music. However, with some critics – even the Army press at times – original band music has been regarded as suspect. I wouldn't go as far as 'subversive' but I confess I've felt its effects!

Barbara: This is only true of band music because, of course, songs are songs – they always have words anyway.

Ray: So when people sing 'Jesus Loves Me, this I Know' it doesn't matter if it was written in 18- whatever, it still comes over; but if someone plays it on the cornet they wouldn't know what it was unless someone told them.

Barbara: But do you think there's something inherent in the music if it's specially crafted under the guidance of the Holy Spirit?

Ray: It's a mystical area. Music is a language and what a composer says may sometimes just pour out, or be the result of hard labour. In religious music I don't see there can be any special claim of creative excellence on the grounds of spiritual state. But I wouldn't deny the possibility of insights.

Barbara: For a composer like yourself it's the construction of the music that matters anyway, isn't it? The reward is in putting together something which wasn't there before and doing it excellently so that it has a power of its own. And you're really not just writing for other people, you're writing from your own heart and experience.

Ray: Yes, and if it says something to me, then presumably people will pick up the feel.

Barbara: That's an interesting dimension – it's not just about giving it to others; it is about putting yourself into it before you give it to others.

Ray: At the end of the day, you've got to believe the Holy Spirit will translate the unknowable.

Barbara: That's a very excellent finish. Thank you.

(The atmosphere becomes suddenly heavy with emotion)

Ray: *(continuing)* If he's a teacher, then he's an interpreter, isn't he?

Barbara: Mmm *(pause)* – that's excellent.

Ray: We got there.

Barbara: We did.

Ray: *(continuing)*: As usual, at the end of the day, we're just tools in his hand and the way they're wielded – you do your best, don't you? I'm going to weep now... *(light laugh)*

Barbara: We must have touched a place of truth.

Ray: We have. You know, don't you?

Barbara: You do. Thanks, Dad.

Ray: Lovely. *(pause...)* Shall we take that stuff to the tip that we were going to – would you mind?

Barbara: Not at all.

So we went. But the afternoon had been tinged with glory and it had taken us all by surprise.

Plan B

The following commentary and snapshots are by RSA

I HAVE always been fascinated by the history, folklore and exploits of the early-day pioneers of The Salvation Army. I was confronted with it all as a child when I first encountered:

> Salvation Army, free from sin,
> All went to Heaven in a corned-beef tin;
> The bottom fell out and they all began to shout,
> Salvation Army, free from sin.

So while some of my poetic (doggerel) excursions have occasionally taken a wry look at the Movement, it's a Movement I love deeply, a Movement which, with a secure identity thankfully, was – and hopefully still is – able to laugh at itself. What follows was intended as a separate booklet, but I was persuaded by the General Editor that including this as part of 'The Lighter Side' was too good an opportunity to miss.

Those familiar with the poem 'For the Want of a Nail the Kingdom was Lost' will catch the underlying principle of these little tales. Sometimes significant events are brought about by politicians' planning or scientific research and so on, but there have also been times when some freak accident, encounter or incident has led to similar unlooked-for results. Or perhaps the two happen together. Conversely, as Scottish poet Rabbie Burns has reminded us: 'The best-laid schemes o' mice an' men gang aft agley.' Perhaps even God had his moments of frustration when a Jonah said 'No', or a Moses responded: 'You must be joking.' Usually such folks' better side came out on top and God had his way in the end. Which he will! There must have been quite a few divine 'plans B', however, and the following fanciful little historical rewrites of Salvation Army history from that angle are (a) not to be taken other than bits of fun, and (b) an underlining that when (often unlikely) people said 'yes' to a challenge or a need, something miraculous happened. It still happens.

1. GOLDEN BOY

The Salvation Army sprang from the Rev William Booth's summer 1865 encounter with a small band of missioners who were holding an outdoor service in the rough area of London's East End. His spontaneous acceptance of an invitation to speak resulted in his leadership role and the development of a movement to take the gospel into the 'highways and the byways', particularly the socially underprivileged areas. Plan B comes about when Booth, factually having walked

260

from Hammersmith, turns down the speaking invitation because he is physically exhausted, perspiring and wearing a new pair of killingly tight shoes. So no developments and therefore no subsequent Salvation Army...

TOO right it was a scorcher! Nearly every sober Londoner seemed in a good mood. However, the boozers just lay about somewhere sleeping off the gin, or crowded the thoroughfares waiting for opening time. And who cared about such riff-raff? It was a Sunday morning in July when respectable citizens (and their domestics) were in church (or chapel). All was quiet in the suburbs (apart from the odd dog or runaway horse), where the freethinkers put aside their intellectual meditations in favour of breakfast.

Despite the heat, a 30-something man walked at a swift and purposeful pace. He wore a black suit and a beard to match. Glad to be out of the house and away from his family for a little while, he headed east; furthermore his throat was a bit sore, the result, he reflected, of some pretty powerful preaching these last few days. (He shared the Victorian view that false modesty got nowhere with the Almighty.)

Now his shoes began to rub; if he walked much further he'd soon have sore feet. Then the sound of singing caught his ear. Better still, it was religious singing – he knew the tune, a hymn popular at the time: 'We're bound for the land of the pure and the holy.' Then he saw them. Just a small group of men and women dressed in the customary sanctified black. They stood in a ring surrounded by a number of curious bystanders. To give his feet a rest he flopped on to a nearby seat. Being in the evangelism business himself he felt rather sorry for the singers perspiring under their heavy Sunday-best serge. Undoubtedly a crown awaited each and every one. But that was sometime in the future. In the meantime they sweated and sang.

Then a man entered the ring and started to speak. 'Good carrying voice,' the weary walker thought professionally, 'but mediocre; his scriptural quotations heavy and dully delivered; their King James language over the heads of his hearers.'

Noting the interested listener in his stovepipe hat, someone hastened across. 'Would you care to join us and perhaps have a word?'

'Very kind of you, and thank you for the invitation,' the addressee croaked, 'but, as you can hear, I've got this throat; I think it must be the flu coming.'

'Some other time, perhaps,' responded the missioner.

Back at home his wife (after referring to the terrible afternoon she'd had) asked: 'Anything interesting happened to you today, dear?'

'Nothing much, my pet,' replied William Booth (for it was he). 'What's more, my feet are killing me – and have you any of those throat sweets left?'

Thus The Salvation Army was never born – not just then, anyway. 'Phew!' said God, 'and we had a nice little thing laid on there. That tent, Three Colts

Lane, Clapton Congress Hall, New York Temple, ALOVE – you name it. And I rather fancied yellow, red and blue. It's plan B again, lads – back to the drawing board!'

2. DEM BANDS

Music, though generally recognised as a powerful weapon in The Salvation Army's armoury, and indeed a public part of its identity, has never been without its critics, ever since the early missioners of Norwood objected to the appearance (and sound) of a big drum. Nonetheless, a mushrooming of thousands of musicians worldwide has ensued over a period of some 130 years. It started with Booth's use of the Fry family brass quartet as a means of supporting his ministry in Salisbury. Brass bands being a growing working-class phenomenon, instrumental groups just took off, encouraged by the Frys and lots of local brass teachers. In this episode it was all a non-event because on the chosen occasion one of the players couldn't find his mouthpiece. So they didn't do the job, didn't go round with Booth and didn't spark off the rage for brass bands (which in fact has not yet abated).

'LOVELY day, Martha – what weather!' The rich Wiltshire accent rang through the Salisbury builder's yard.

Came the female response: 'Where's the lads, then? They're usually blowing their heads off during their dinner break.'

'Ooh ah,' said the foreman, 'but they ain't here today, they be 'elping out, like. As it's a special do, the boss (that's Mr Fry) has let 'em go over to Fordingbridge. Well, I says special do – actually it's a wedding. And they'll get a few bob for it.'

'You mean that somebody's so soft in the head that they're going to pay for those dreary tunes they play?'

'No, they just do the hymn tunes for church and that; this time they'll be giving 'em quadrilles, waltzes and the Lancers, and that sort of thing. Very popular are the waltzes. And it sounds pretty good even on a brass quartet.'

'They must have improved a lot,' commented Martha, with heavy, somewhat acid humour.

'That's as may be,' said the foreman with partisan warmth (his daughter was courting the trombonist). 'And they practise a lot.'

'Need to,' came the predictable retort.

Early in 1879 Charles Fry and his three sons caught the attention of James Dowdle (remembered in the northeast by the term 'Sally Doodle'), who was running things at Plymouth and passed the word to William Booth – his supremo. 'Hmm,' thought Booth. 'Brass, eh! Wake 'em up in the streets, give the singing a lift – and keep the hecklers under control. We'll give it a go.' Well, it seems there was a theatre in Portsmouth where they were going to have Sunday services. 'Put the brass boys in and see how it goes.'

It all went well. The dockyard came to life, the residents had mixed feelings (the sale of earplugs went up), the police patrols were doubled, the singing was great and altogether it was a big success. Brass bands were all the rage, especially in the industrial north, and Booth had a big vision of what could be if the idea took on.

A fortnight later the Frys were wanted again, this time in Manchester, to support none other than Ballington Booth, second son of the top man himself. Into the big time? Maybe. Charles kept his cool. They practised hard (even fewer building jobs) and by Thursday they were ready. Friday came and nearly went when, just as Charles was off to the station to get the tickets, Fred said – in a kind of funny voice – 'I can't find me mouthpiece, Dad.'

They looked everywhere: through the tools, the bags of sand and cement. And there were a lot of bricks. 'Haven't you got another one?' asked father Charles.

'No, I ain't.'

Oh, the scene that night! Charles went spare. Mrs F. cried out: 'Leave the lad be, Dad.' A small crowd gathered outside. There'd been nothing like this since the Crimea and that was the best part of thirty years before. Nothing for it but to cancel; can't go with just a trio. Fortunately, they hadn't yet paid for the rail tickets.

Truth to tell, Ballington was rather relieved. He hadn't argued with the old man, but there was short shrift with another point of view (as the Methodists had found out). Ballington, a century ahead of his time, regarded the absence of brass as an answer to prayer.

Booth senior was less than happy. And it was no picnic in Heaven either. The Divine Opinion was strong: 'I didn't mind those Hebrews going on and on about the cuisine they'd left behind in Egypt. Our menus get a bit boring up here as well, but losing your mouthpiece is something else! A right brilliant idea down the drain on account of a bit of brass tube!'

The angels sat back; here it came:

(God speaking) 'I well recall that Vivaldi feller in Venice. Tight ship he ran. Two galleries in St Mark's and nobody lost mouthpieces or came up with a broken fiddle string. He wouldn't have any of that nonsense. Fined 'em, he did! So they watched it. Mind you, there was that time a second sackbut copy floated down on to the bishop's head. There was a lot of fuss about that. Viv and I saw eye to eye on the comedy (so did the musicians), which is more than the bishop did. The congregation didn't bat an eyelid; asleep mostly. I've known livelier occasions, like those false prophets jumping up and down in Elijah's time. *Gashing themselves with knives* the record puts it. Well, in those days there wouldn't be any forks, would there? Calmed down a lot now, they have, with the possible exception of some of those signs and wonders boys. The bishop should've been glad it wasn't the sackbut slide fell on his ecclesiastical nut!'

'Where's Venice?' a young angel asked – inadvisedly.

'Do me a favour,' said God. 'Even though some dude wrote a little ditty, "Angels Ever Bright and Fair", in my experience they might be fair but they're not all bright. Listen out. We're not getting far with this Army lot, they're a real pain when it comes to second guessing what they're gonna do. And don't anyone say "Plan B" before lunch! You know I favoured something a bit more up-market at the last committee meeting and here's proof. Lost his mouthpiece indeed! We've gotta move on. I think we should be looking at New Orleans. You wanna hear what those jazzmen can do with "What a Friend" – wait a minute, true they're up and running but those hot choruses haven't been invented yet. Give it time, say ten years. And until then – watch my lips – just keep it in mind, no one says "Plan B". Got it?'

Author's footnote: Sorry about Fred F! Hopelessly unfair. I could have picked another brother but Fred was the only name I had at the time. Actually he's a bit of a hero of mine as he worked in the first SA music editorial office under Richard Slater and I've been privileged to handle some of his efforts. I think he was a bit of a workhorse; his job was to produce inky duplicated music copies for sale; rather uninspiring and messy. Perhaps he preferred it to building. We shall never know. He has written widely used Army songs. He became a secretary to both William and Herbert Booth, moving to Canada with Herbert, and subsequently resigning when Herbert parted company with the Army. He finally returned to England where he worked in the Town Clerk's Department, Gillingham, Kent, was a Methodist lay preacher, died in 1939 and is buried not much more than a stone's throw from where these tales are being spun.

The logical minds among my readers will not fail to notice that tale No 2 could not have taken place unless tale 1 is disregarded, ie, there would have been no Army at that time to have any bands. And that goes for the rest of these yarns. As has been observed of a good raconteur friend of mine: 'He doesn't spoil a good story for the sake of the truth.'

3. GLAD RAGS

Early in the Movement that became The Salvation Army, Captain Cadman descended on Whitby with its link to St Hilda and events significant in the development of the English Church. Cadman was a colourful character (he was one of the first, if not the first, to array himself in military garb), and his posters proclaimed war on Satan in language reminiscent of the circus and its lion. It was evidently rather strong meat for the district and ultimately there was a closing and reopening of the local work. Plan B makes the most of Cadman's (imagined) brushes with the civic dignitaries. (Hopelessly far-fetched fiction about the businessmen – but the Army, in the quiet fishing village of Whitby, in the shadow of the ancient Abbey, was just not going to make it big in the church growth charts. Years later it was closed.)

'MAJOR' Cadman felt no end of a toff as he hurried toward the fishing boats moored at the water's edge. Whitby, he reflected, was just the place for his brand of showman-type evangelism. Yes, this quiet little town was going to sit up. Sit up for Jesus or he'd want to know the reason why! He had his flyers all printed for distribution: LIONS AND TIGERS – A GREAT SALVATION CIRCUS ON YOUR DOORSTEP! And much more besides. He felt that the printer of the local paper had looked at him a wee bit strangely when he read the copy, reaching automatically for his blue pencil in anticipation of the mistakes he expected to find.

Cadman was used to people looking at him strangely or even in alarm. His methods were a trifle colourful, but these were days when humanity was rushing headlong into hell and somebody had to warn them. He'd recently been called 'flamboyant'; it was probably a compliment – he must get somebody to look it up. Certainly he was not being ignored and he was sure that it was due to both the power of his message and his startling uniform. Topped by his military peaked cap (ex-Zulu War) he stood out in a crowd. And as to his message – only last night he'd preached on 2 Samuel 22:34: 'He maketh my feet like hen's feet.' After a prayer meeting in which precious souls were calling on the Lord, there had been the usual fault-finder: 'It's not *hen's* feet,' they said, 'it's *hind's* feet.'

'Rubbish,' answered Cadman. 'It must be hen's feet – look at the mercy seat!'

What was needed here was not that brainy stuff – they already had that available elsewhere; they needed the power of Christ to lead them from the darkness of sin into his most marvellous light. Trouble was, a lot of 'em couldn't catch on. They seemed to prefer the old quiet Abbey traditions to drumming Satan out of his evil kingdom.

In a very short time Cadman had gathered round him a small group of supporters. Perhaps they may not all have been the pick of the Whitby citizens, but they were all on fire and ready for anything – the more outrageous the better. And their leader definitely had no inhibitions about being outrageous for the cause. Soon they too were parading the streets of the little fishing town in a variety of self-assembled uniforms. Well, uniforms they may have been – of a sort – but uniform they certainly were not! Bowler hats and jerseys, helmets and military jackets were all grist to the mill. They followed their yellow, red and blue banner, singing words which were totally incomprehensible to most of the bystanders: 'Come on, my comrades in distress' or 'Fly, ye sinners, to yon mountain' and 'I am sweeping through the gates, I am washed in Jesus' blood'.

Someone had got hold of a penny whistle and played all the tunes in roughly the same scale; a highly individual approach which ignored anything so unnecessary as sharps and flats. To keep the time, a sister thumped a tambourine with more enthusiasm than skill and was often a greater source of nervousness to her companions than the scowls and threats of the publican's larrikins. So there they went, most evenings of the week, singing and ranting through the hitherto quiet streets. Sundays were special. After a red-hot morning holiness meeting they were raring to pitch into Satan and that could be even noisier. Whitby – hitherto a tolerant community – was under siege.

There hadn't been so much of a carry-on in Whitby since the blessed St Hilda ran things up in the Abbey. It couldn't last; well, not by any normal standards, but as the disturbances showed no sign of abating, something had to be done. So thought the solid citizens and so did the gentle, and rather less solid citizens. The citizens who lacked any solidity at all were also given to generous use of the rich and expressive language of their north-eastern heritage. The situation began to come to the boil until one day a group of influential business gentlemen knocked on the door and enquired for Mr Cadman.

They declined offers of tea and came straight to the point. 'Mr Cadman, we are well acquainted with your name; it is that of an illustrious cowherd monk who served in the Abbey over on that hill in the time of the blessed St Hilda. Our traditions tell us that St Hilda, though of the Celtic persuasion, hosted a great Synod of churchmen and that, contrary to her desires, a decision was taken to follow the path of Rome. Nevertheless, she and her side accepted the ruling without demur. For the 1,200 years since then, as before that, God has been worshipped with reverence and dignity. Our forefathers have seen the changes: through the Reformation and the piety of good King Harry, the regrettable shift of emphasis with the return to Rome, the conversion again to the Protestant faith, the divisions of the Civil War, the Wesleyan revival and the British Empire. Whitby has lived through it all and survived heart-whole; a close-knit and respectable community. (Though admittedly the Wesley times were not always to our taste and some don't reckon much to Mr Gladstone.)

'Now you come, another Cadman (is that why you were sent here?), with your "Hallelujahs!", your "Glory be to God and down with the drink!", your caterwauling in the streets and the unsociable hours in which you create your noisy disturbances. Indeed, your circuses of "lions and tigers" and "jumbos", and "getting Satan on the run", all in the name of religion, are driving this town insane. It has to stop!' Here the speaker ran out of steam and appeared to be about to have one of his 'turns'.

'Well, well, well,' replied Cadman. Opposition just bounced off him. 'Well, if you feel like that about it, why not fix us up with a barracks and we'll moderate it a bit.'

At the prospect of funding, providing real money, two more gentlemen turned white and a third began to shake violently. There seemed to be no meeting of minds, and so each camp retired, telling themselves that they had made a good showing. At any rate the Army didn't go away. Years later – about sixty-odd (and odd years they certainly were) – the corps was finally wound up. Long years of experience has demonstrated that sixty years could just about be the average for some administrations to implement a decision, assuming a decision has been reached. Be that as it may, Cadman and his colourful methods must have shaken quietly conservative Whitby town.

Up in Heaven God didn't exactly look sheepish. That couldn't happen and omniscience etc was on his CV as part of his job. However, he said to Archangel Gabriel: 'It really wasn't my idea; I was overruled at the committee meeting. If you recall we were having trouble down in Africa and I had a lot on my mind.' Gabriel looked across at Archangel Michael and winked. 'What's more,' continued the Lord (and the cherubim groaned), 'that Location Manager is definitely past his sell-by date. Look at that desert business with Moses. First it was "Fed up with manna", then "Sick of quails". They even moaned about the sand in their coq au vin. There's no pleasing some folk. Then they got themselves lost. Don't know why they didn't ring up the AA like anyone else. I had to send a pillar of cloud and another one of fire. What that did to our budget you just don't want to know. OK, here we go again: Plan B. Let's give Folkestone a go. We might get a book and a musical out of it.'

Which they did: Folkestone provided Edward Joy's anecdotes in The Old Corps *while the 1970s saw dramatisations of the incidents in* Glory! *(from the minds and pens of John Gowans and John Larsson). Cadman was a great warrior but a trifle too colourful for Whitby, where the Army never really flourished. It was my dad who told me the story of Cadman saying, 'It must be hen's feet, look at the mercy seat.'*

4. BIG APPLE

In January 1880, Commissioner George Scott Railton travelled to New York to open Salvation Army work. Actually there had already been some start, but this came with a headquarters blessing. Not only Railton came, though, but also seven Army lassies! Presumably suitably chaperoned – after all, it was the era of Sherlock Holmes, Jack the Ripper and Queen Victoria on the British throne. The fantasy concerns itself more with Mrs Railton, pondering her husband away in America and pouring it all out to Mrs Booth. Of course it wasn't at all like that. I'm pretty sure I've read that Mrs R was very supportive and it can't have been easy.

EVERYTHING was frozen. James Jermy looked out of his workshop, with its completed furniture, sawdust and tools, and saw nothing but snow. Here in Ontario he remembered Whitechapel which he had left in 1865, ten years earlier. He recalled the tall, bearded figure of William Booth and his powerful preaching in the East London tent meetings, the converts gathered from slum and gin palace. The testimonies, the songs: 'Oh, say, will you go to the Eden above?' So Jermy began to conduct meetings on a modest scale. In Cleveland he met a Methodist local preacher by the name of Joseph Fackler. Together they began a 'Christian Mission' and wrote to Booth for recognition and help. Booth was pleased but could not accept any practical responsibility. Then Fackler's health failed, followed by Mrs Jermy becoming ill. So in 1875 the work ceased.

It was early days and up in Heaven the Lord was full of ideas about a new movement, bubbling with love and fire. The Jermy thing had fizzled but, God reflected, you can't win 'em all, though, being God, that wasn't strictly the case. The committee went into session under the chairmanship of Archangel Michael, Gabriel being on a special mission to sort out some freethinkers and in particular under orders to try and get the hang of some chap called Darwin who'd come up with a theory about what he called 'Natural Selection' and which was rather putting the cat among the believing pigeons. The Almighty was just a bit miffed because people insisted on missing the point of Genesis and regarding whole chunks of the Bible from a scientific angle. So the possibilities of the new movement were on the back burner for a while. Plan B looked like a distinct possibility.

Then some four years later there was a turn-up for the book. A man called Shirley (his surname) emigrated from England to America and found a job in a Philadelphia silk factory. Back home in England was Mrs S and their daughter Eliza. All three were or had been on the soldiers' roll at Coventry, and Eliza had become a Salvation Army officer at 16. Eliza secured Booth's official blessing and she and her mother joined her dad in Philadelphia. They rented an unfurnished building which they named 'The Salvation Factory' after their home corps in Coventry. There hadn't been such shenanigans since the Civil War, which most people wanted to forget, and Abe Lincoln's assassination – which nobody was allowed to forget.

Up in Heaven there was a right to-do. The admin was in trouble. Though they were reluctant to admit it, the facts had to come out. The file had gone astray. The Records office had obviously bungled. It was no good blaming Beelzebub as in the good old days; no one swallowed that excuse any more. All weekend, while the saints were practising a new anthem, the Records staff was busy searching: under date, under name, under place. Then the answer came. The first thrust had been in Canada, had petered out and the restart was somewhere else with new names in charge. No links at all. They were so relieved! So was God. He looked along the ranks of the massive choir and, during a dramatic pause in the music, his Sinai-honed voice broke the dramatic silence (the angel-conductor later had a breakdown). 'This is Plan B Plus. I'm not looking to have it messed up. For one thing I have had too many Plans C lately; furthermore I'm getting some lobbying from the Jehovah's Witnesses.'

So things plodded along and cooked gently for a while and then Booth heard of the successes in Philly. 'Right,' he said, wiping the crumbs of toast from his beard and swigging down the last drops of his strong tea. 'Right. We'll put it all on a sound footing now. Songbooks and regulations, that's what they need. Nothing beats a good meaty set of regulations.' (Like many a visionary leader before and since, he'd never kept any rules himself but he saw to it that everybody else did.)

So the plan to invade the States went forward. It was decided to send seven women and a man: six women soldiers with a woman officer, no doubt as chaperone. The proposed man was Commissioner George Scott Railton. In a response to success reports from the other side of the Atlantic *The War Cry* (31 January 1880) bellowed: WE MUST GO! 'This news has come upon us like a voice from Heaven and leaves us no choice... the United States must... be overrun by Salvation desperadoes.' The proposed 'desperadoes' were the six women soldiers, a female officer and Commissioner Railton.

Mrs Railton was visiting her mother at the time so she didn't know about the proposal. And the commissioner, a workhorse if ever there was one, had a lot on his mind and forgot to mention it when she came home. When she read about it she went spare. 'Never home, you're not!' she cried. 'You just come in, pick up a pair of pyjamas and a clean shirt and you're off again. My mother warned me and I thought I knew better. But she was right!'

She wrote to Mrs Booth (the top one) and all Heaven held its breath. Plan B Plus down the gurgler? Mrs B soothingly said: 'I'm sure you're right, dear, I know how you feel. And if the press get hold of it they'll have a field day. One peacock and seven blackbirds. As a matter of fact I've been getting funny looks from the woman next door ever since that time we did the Exeter Hall Easter Monday last year. You remember? They covered the floor with two inches of sawdust. Must have thought it was going to be a bull-fight. I'd go with the flow this time. In any case, if it doesn't come off, William'll be like a bear with a sore head' (which was her real reason).

And up in Heaven they breathed again. 'Whoo!' said Gabriel, and uttered a sigh of relief, last heard from the lips of Wellington after Waterloo (the battle, not the railway station): 'That was a close-run thing!'

There is no factual reason to believe that Mrs Commissioner R was anything but lovingly supportive, but one would have liked to be a fly on the wall when the proposal was broached at home.

5. HAND TO MAN

A slogan The Salvation Army used to have was 'Hand to God and hand to man'. In this tale, it's a terrible night in London. William Booth and his son, Bramwell, come across down-and-outs and homeless people. Booth tells Bramwell: 'Do something!' As a former Nottingham pawnbroker's assistant, Booth knows all about deprivation and poverty. Thus began the social work of the Army: hostels, hospitals, children's homes, refuges, emergency response, help in national disasters, missing persons, services in war. In Plan B various reasons throw a spanner in the works and the social work doesn't happen. 'The men rejected him, he wasn't well...' Let it be noted that Bramwell must have done his job – the results are eloquent.

IT was a bitterly cold night. It nearly always was in the winter, and being Victorian London the city was wrapped in the thick fog coming up from the smelly river. Somewhere in that vast metropolis Oscar Wilde was rehearsing some one-liners for his next dinner date. Somewhere else Sir Arthur Conan Doyle was working on another Sherlock Holmes mystery. And so on and so on. A full list of these creative people would make writing a book very easy indeed. But databases had yet to be invented. Some people were still on gas – and some Salvation Army quarters would still be on gas well into the 1950s. This is a heart-warming tale, however, in which any negative breath – such as majors having lawn mowers while captains had to make do with garden shears – would be rightly regarded not only as sour and unworthy but as a misuse of the purpose of the tales. Also that makes far too long a sentence, though perhaps not by Victorian literary standards. Leaving such philosophical drivel we return you, gentle reader, to the bitter, freezing streets of London. High in the sky could be seen myriad stars (the fog must have lifted), and a little lower down could be spotted the pendant orbs of the pawnbrokers' establishments. Closed at this time of night, of course.

Two men pursued their way, only occasionally slipping on the icy pavement. One was none other than the Founder of The Salvation Army, the other his eldest son Bramwell, by a strange coincidence his Chief of Staff. They turned into a side street. There, on the ground, partially covered with rags or cardboard boxes lay some of the human wreckage of the city. Booth was horrified. They didn't see that in Hammersmith, Clapton or even pre-ethnic Brixton. 'Bramwell, do something!' he cried.

Yes, well, anyone can tell somebody else to do something, and Bramwell thought 'Yeah? I should chuckle,' but being loyal to his dad he didn't actually say it out loud. Off he went, while William, satisfied that he had launched something really worthwhile, proceeded on his way home, to his hot supper, slippers and cocoa with a lovely warm glow inside.

Two hours later young Bram also came home, chilled through, coughing and generally all in. 'Tell me,' demanded the General, 'did you do anything?' There was a slight pause. Up in Heaven they knew the score already.

'Well, Dad,' hesitated Chief of Staff Bramwell, 'you know how it is; it's not that easy. And anyway when I spoke to any of the men they told me to push off. In fact I was actually picked up for soliciting. Fortunately the sergeant knew me and I got off. But I don't think you could, in all conscience, chalk up any points tonight. In any case I've got a heavy day tomorrow. It's all right for you, all you do is preach in the big meetings and tell people to go thousands of miles away and start up a new territory. I only get the little meetings, have to calm the complainers and rebels and don't go anywhere exciting.' And on and on....

'Same again,' sighed the Heavenly Host. 'Back to Square One.'

'I blame that City of London School he went to,' said Peter. 'Get above themselves. I was comprehensive meself. Failed the eleven-plus – that Galilean Education Committee is prejudiced like you wouldn't believe.'

6. WHAT'S FOR AFTERS?

Many Salvationists will know that the Army concept of 'Self-Denial' (later to become 'Annual Appeal') was literally to cut down on some luxury for a week and give the money saved to the cause. Commissioner John Carleton set an example – in the spirit of Lent – by offering to deny himself his pudding for a year and give the money to the 'Lord's work'. Many of us try to follow that example. Be that as it may, in this total fiction we take it that John loved his pudding. Otherwise giving it up hasn't quite the motivational, let alone the spiritual point. I've never reckoned much to those films where the (usually pretty) nun packs it in to marry (or go away with) the hero, or the character who is knocked off his perch by some incident, loses his faith and... (I don't remember what he does after that, but it's a scriptwriter's must to ensure the faith gets dumped). Back to John C. Yes, he loves that pudding and I quote from the wording of the tale: 'The gates of hell will never prevail against the Kingdom of Heaven. But a British steamed pudding with a jugful of runny custard was something else!'

JOHN CARLETON loved his puddings. Jam roly-poly, spotted dick, apple tart, rhubarb crumble – so long as it came steaming to the table accompanied by a large jug of custard, John was in a state of bliss. He would wolf down his boiled beef and carrots, steak pie, fish and chips (with mushy peas), tripe and onions, toad-in-the-hole; none of your European fancy stuff for John – he had the healthy Victorian appetite for big meals (when they could afford them). Not to mention sausages and mash. And mutton stew. First course over, he would loosen his belt and waistcoat and then Mrs C would take his plate into the kitchen returning with the steaming and fragrant pudding of the day.

One day in January they had been on about a fundraising period called 'Self-Denial'. Not the most exciting or popular event of the Army calendar; it subsequently spread to standing on street corners or outside factory gates with a collecting tin; or else pushing envelopes through doors and going wearily back days later to collect them. There was always the risk of being snarled at or the dog being let loose. So Self-Denial, theoretically a spiritual exercise, could become something to be endured rather than enjoyed – though, mark my words, there were a few souls who reckoned they liked it. No one believed them, least of all the Lord – and he should know. His Son was on record as having had to fork out, but on that occasion they miraculously produced a coin from a fish. No such luck for most of the hardworking folk of John's acquaintance. No, Self-Denial was something the hallelujah soldier was stuck with and could only get out of if actually in a wheelchair or 'P to G'* (dead). 'Hallelujahs' were a bit thin on the ground, and for some reason – no one knew why – London Headquarters had settled on the winter month of February to do it in.

Now in the summer you can make do with a bit of salad. Spring and autumn the tummy tends to roll a bit if neglected for too long. But in winter? There just has to be that hot and solid intake or there is a fading away. Now some of the stories John was hearing about the underprivileged, starving and homeless made him want to do something. Give a little more? Yes, but how? Then he hit on it. Go to the basic reason of 'Self-Denial' and deny himself something. Something very special to his heart. That was it! A week of no puddings and give the money to the cause. It would come hard, but he was a man of strong principle and determination. He had decided. No puddings for a week.

All went well for two days. John would have been the first to admit that there was something not quite complete about mutton chops and nowt else till 'roll on teatime'. On day three he felt a little under the weather. By Thursday his insides were really in revolt. And by Friday he couldn't even face his cod and chips. Something was wrong. He went to see the doctor though he hated being 'on the panel'. The doctor quizzed him and soon heard the puddingless saga. John was instructed not to give his system so fierce a dietary change. 'Ease in, do it gradually,' said his physician.

'This is Self-Denial week,' wailed John. But to no effect.

Mrs C, for Saturday dinner, as ordered, produced a huge apple pudding, steaming, fragrant, drenched in glorious yellow custard. And the total sum saved for the cause was only fivepence ha'penny.

In another dimension, it might have been a different story. The idea would have caught on and spread to such things as abstaining from sweets and chocolates. It was not to be. In the Land of Bliss yet again it was back to the drawing board and another round of committee meetings (all that paperwork).

272

The word of God declared that the gates of hell itself would never prevail against the Kingdom. But a British steamed pudding with a jugful of runny custard was something else.

P to G – Promoted to Glory, the triumphant SA term for death

7. SILVER SCREEN

At the turn of the 20th century motion pictures were in their infancy. In Melbourne, Australia, a younger son of William Booth – Herbert, a fine hymnwriter – had his eye on the resource of the moving film. He set up a department and made a film about Jesus and the Early Church. When we were working in Sydney in about 1982, John Cleary and a team had been working on the film and some us were fortunate to enjoy a private showing of their restoration labours. Herbert Booth was well loved by the Australian Salvationists and didn't respond all that well to autocratic control from London. He was reappointed to Canada and eventually left the Army to become a freelance evangelist campaigner in the USA, travelling worldwide. I may just mention that when we served in Australia we became friends with two Australian senior officers who had been leaders in that great territory: the Scotneys. Mrs Scotney told me that she had played the piano for Herbert Booth when he again campaigned in Australia. Somehow that simple statement touches history. I have always venerated Herbert; his hymns are so personally honest. I am becoming a little serious in the present context and though I served fulfillingly in the London headquarters for many years, administrations are but human and could be sometimes negative. While I believe that 'man proposes, God disposes', our frailties must often send God back to his drawing board. At any rate the spirit of this fun series might be summed up in what I have unforgiveably credited to authority: 'Don't waste your time. Moving pictures will never catch on.' Up in Heaven, God said: 'Another good idea down the gurgler, but hang about; mark my words, sport; they'll come good one of these days... Put it on the back burner.'

THE world teetered on the cusp of the 20th century. Down in Melbourne, Victoria, the sun beat down, harshly unforgiving. A new age was dawning. Ned Kelly and his gang were history. Not yet were they to be promoted to glamorous folk heroes, winsome but driven to a sort of Robin Hood life of adventure by a repressive British establishment. But there was glamour. Glamour had moved on from mere static photography and was now to be seen in action, thanks to the moving pictures of the bioscope. No words yet; talkies would come later, the pianist pointed up the dramatic sequences of train robbers and elegant males, swooning under the maddening spells of beautiful painted sheilas.

'But,' thought Herbert Booth, the Commander, 'we may just have something here.'

273

'Bonzer idea!' said his aide dutifully. So the Limelight Department was instituted. It made movies. That is to say, the people who worked in it made them. Naturally they chose a religious theme and sensibly omitted to inform London. Which was another bonzer idea. A film was made, perhaps many more. A *Life of Jesus*, *The Early Church* and so on. It was a pioneer venture in a day when the whole Army was trying new things, some of which worked well and others, which looked no-hopers, were abandoned. Booth H was ecstatic. Finally he wrote to his dad, the formidable, hook-nosed, bearded prophet leader who dominated and terrified them all in the cause of the Prince of Peace and Love.

A succinct response came from International Headquarters. It read: 'Don't waste your time. Moving pictures will never catch on.'

Up in Heaven, God said: 'Another good idea down the gurgler. But, hang about; mark my words, sport, they'll come good one of these days. Of course, they'll have missed the boat. So what's new? Bless their hearts, they're all still in the tuppence to make a shilling stage. Put it on the back burner.'

As in all the best works of fiction (especially historical ones), the characters in here naturally do not have any resemblance to anyone, living or dead. It's been a fun whimsy by someone who loves his Army, warts and all. They and we have, on the whole, done our best as we saw it at the time. Any hurt relatives – please believe my apologies are not unduly hollow. And don't anybody sue. I'm only on a pension. RSA

Last Word:

Vesper Hymn (At the End of the Day)

IF you measure success by fame and fortune, RSA has achieved the former, even now moving beyond all sorts of boundaries (remarkably, given the limits within which he has chosen to work) – and he has not achieved the latter at all! Not many know that he would also have liked to write for string orchestra, which medium he loves. However, in his view and in our view and, we believe, in God's view, success is measured in lives that will never be the same again because they have been introduced, through RSA's pastoral and musical ministry, to a God who transforms, a God with a heart and a purpose and a face and the name of Jesus Christ. Success like this is immeasurable. Who can ever know who will be one of the myriad in the new Jerusalem because of RSA? It is the unknown and the innumerable that make RSA's story crackle with life. This is not just a history or a harmony, it is the chronicle of a living and ongoing ripple that has been on the move ever since he set pen to paper, under the good hand of God.

However, it's not just about the influence his music has had, whether inspirationally to other composers and performers or spiritually. This story has illustrated the inherent nature of music itself to transform when crafted from a heart of integrity. Ray's has been a lifetime of seeking after truth, of expressing it masterfully and with integrity – in manuscript and word. Ray's creative spirit has been a gift that he has offered to us all generously and humbly, not just in music and word (we have sat in endless meetings hearing him and my mother preach eloquently and passionately, not least the memorable sermon Dad preached once on Absalom – King David's anguish as a father is forever imprinted on our memory and we can't have been very old), but in the gift of himself in everything.

When God created the world, he left an imprint of himself in it (Romans 1:20). It's true of every creative artist – you write something, you offer it to the public space and, in a way, it is no longer yours, it's theirs, to interpret as they like, to use as they wish, even to misunderstand and murder, but it bears your mark. We appreciate Dad being able to talk dispassionately about his own work with others. It is the mark of the truly creative mind – not holding on to a work, but letting it go and moving on. It is music for the joy of craftsmanship and excellence.

Our deepest thanks to all who have contributed with such affection and careful consideration to this collection, and to Dad for his extraordinary ability to record autobiographical detail and willingness to share his perspective on life.

This is our best shot at recognising RSA, who has embraced and enjoyed all that he has done and let his work fly free to accomplish its purpose – and it just goes on and on. On behalf of us all, thank you, Ray, and thank you, Joy!

Barbara and Rosemary Steadman-Allen

Appendix

Further Analysis – Dudley Bright

IN his defence of 'The Holy War', Brian Bowen quotes Hubert Parry, who suggests that music of value is likely to require repeated hearings in order to be appreciated. In-depth consideration (with its necessary employment of technical terms) is not for everyone and the unwary reader is warned to proceed no further, if there is a risk that their enjoyment of the chosen works might consequently be impaired. However, deeper knowledge of a work can enhance the listening experience and clarify the composer's intentions. It is hoped that these notes may provide a further fascinating insight into the art and skill of Ray Steadman-Allen.

In the chosen works, RSA displays both common and diverse approaches to compositional technique. Ideally the reader may have a full score available but it is strongly advised that the following recordings are to hand for which timings are given in the text.

'Fantasia for Piano and Band' – *Royal Albert Hall Highlights Vol 1*, SPS 251
'The Holy War' *Legacy*, International Staff Band, SPS 280
'The Lord is King' (3 tracks) *Essays for Brass Vol 1*, QPRL 080D
All available through World of Brass.

Much of the focus will relate to the thematic and motivic derivations of the material. Broadly speaking this can be classified in four orders or levels:

1. Easily recognisable, direct quotation with or without slight changes to rhythm and pitch.
2. Fragmentation into smaller motifs but still with clear derivation.
3. Further removed but with discernible origins, sometimes inverted or in reverse.
4. Remote, obscure relationships sometimes of contestable origin.

It is fascinating to consider to what extent material can be transformed and still be related to its source. It will be seen that fragmentation of pitch, rhythm and interval can all be varied but still retain identity. Creatively speaking, these techniques provide diversity while preserving unity, but merely employing them does not produce work of value. There remains the composer's skill, good taste and innate artistic expression that ultimately produces artistic work.

In 'Fantasia for Piano and Band' virtually all the music can be heard to be derived from the distinctive lines of Colonel W. Maltby's song 'Christ is the Answer'. The overall design, after an introduction, consists of a lively allegro wrapped around a central reflective section featuring the band singing.

The bold unison opening bar from the band suggests music of substance and import followed by some flourishes from the piano and band immediately introducing the most significant motif of the piece based on the chorus:

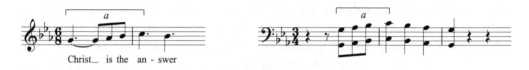

This can easily be recognised all through the piece by its four rising notes:

The little known minor verse of the song, presented dolefully in 4/4, asks serious questions [0.59].

With an uplift in tempo the answer comes – 'Christ is the Answer' – and a joyful mood is established and maintained for much of the piece [1.27].

The harmonic structure of the chorus becomes the framework for a playful cornet solo (no doubt with Derek Smith, then solo cornet of the New York Staff Band, in mind) [1.44].

278

A change of key to the major inspires the solo piano's own skittish comment on the verse, significantly with a modal flavour. It is worth pointing out that it is solely the repeated G and the rising fourth that identifies it to its origins [2.02].

The band responds with another derivation of (a) [2.08].

A tempo e gajamente

The dialogue continues with thematic ties becoming less clearly defined but somehow quite recognisable. The rhythm continues with the now distinctive missing down beat and the third phrase of the chorus provides the melodic shape: an example of third order development [2.22].

(problems of life   my   spi-rit may a - sail)

It is not possible to highlight every instance of the music's logical progression but suffice it to say there is hardly a bar which does not draw on (a) or (b) in some way. As the music moves towards the central section we hear (b) in augmentation [3.19].

(Augmentation)   *cresc.*

After a short piano cadenza, the reflective central section is principally a male voice rendition of Maltby's well known chorus [4.49], cast in 4/4 rather than 6/8, each phrase being commented on by the piano soloist, always incorporating the rising four-note motif (a).

This section is framed by lyrical solo cornet and euphonium interjections always built on (a).

There is now a fairly faithful recapitulation of the preceding *tempo e gajamente* modified in key and leading to a wonderfully grandiose interlude based on (b) [7.25].

279

Grandioso ♩ = 84

And as the vista fades the band resumes the allegro with a purposeful homeward march [8.35]:

Vivace Marziale ♩ = 144

Almost every bar has the (a) motif with its inversion added as counterpoint. When the piano presents the chorus in augmentation [9.00] the band maintains the march momentum interjecting fanfares based on (a), the last phrase breaking up into a dialogue between band and piano [9.28].

Vivace ♩ = 144

The onward motion is halted by a few reflective piano moments before plunging headlong towards the conclusion. In so doing the original opening statement (x) returns for the first time [10.29].

Vivace ♩ = 168

One would suggest that (x) might be an isolated example in this piece of fourth-order development achieved by taking the penultimate note and the preceding four pitches of the chorus and reversing their order. Of course, this makes sense at the close of the piece, with the associated words – 'Christ is the answer *to my need!*'

Christ is the ans - wer to my need

Characteristic of RSA is his proclivity, before concluding the piece, to make a nifty eight-bar excursion through a flurry of remote keys (motifs (a) and (b) being entirely absent) before finishing solidly in C major.

'Fantasia' is in essence a fine example of doing a great deal with very little. The principal motifs are always unmistakable, tonality is stable and the style is always inventive but direct and accessible. Possibly because of the presence of a harmonically active solo instrument, the band scoring is highly transparent, throwing colours into relief rather than using the traditional brass band values of blending and mixing.

In 'The Holy War' the structures are more demanding, tonality is strained and developmental orders three and four abound. We move from a reassuring, joyful Salvationist chorus in the 'Fantasia' to an austere, Lutheran chorale 'Ein Feste Burg' [4.25] which at the time did not appear in the Army tune book and doesn't itself appear in the work until nearly half-way through. There are more frequent tempo changes coupled with a wealth of angular thematic derivations making the overall design complex and challenging to follow. Lest any reader still be under the impression that RSA's music is a product of 'a very mixed up mind' we shall find that it is, in fact, highly organised and tightly developed. For behind the wealth of invention is a surprisingly limited source.

Once passed the introduction 'Mansoul' is depicted thus [0.44]:

Allegro vivace $\bullet$ = 176

Characterised by its wide-leaping motif (m), at first sight it might appear to be an entirely original theme. On closer inspection it is intrinsically derived from the second and final phrases of Luther's chorale (y). Consisting of a downward scale, beginning on the last beat of the bar, there is a simple deviation of one step up and then two down (a) [5.31].

It can now be seen that the four notes (a) are a constituent part of the 'Mansoul' theme and, furthermore, the single upward step is implicit in (m). In addition, the accompaniment is a downward scale incorporating the characteristic shape (a) [0.44].

Over the next dozen or so bars RSA displays masterful handling of his material, never becoming a slave to his motifs; (m) itself appears in slightly differing versions, always at the service of the musical flow and focus. After a few repetitions of 'Mansoul' the accompaniment changes to an upward scale and the melody develops fluently. It should be noted that this music is by no means discordant or atonal but firmly diatonic, having already passed through a variety of related keys.

Having come to some conclusions, it is worth returning to the work's opening. It can be seen that the initial presentation by cornets and trombones begins with (m) and goes on effortlessly to imply elements of the chorale. Even the opening bass statement can be construed as 'Mansoul' inverted [0.04]!

Andante maestoso

Then the link to the *allegro vivace* is made up of three contractions of the (y) with the emphasis on the first note, building to a splendid A major statement suddenly resolving to the Db major of the 'Mansoul' theme! [0.41]. If the foregoing analysis seems a little intense, it goes to show how taut and focused is the construction of the music and how brilliant and fluent is the composer's technique.

When the trombones take over the 'Mansoul' motif they add three notes to the end (x1) [1.10].

On its own this has little significance but it will become apparent that RSA takes the intervals of a second and a third in (a) and uses them in three-note patterns; sometimes the interval of a second relates to the next but one note. Hence the following permutations can be found at various pitches with free chromatic alterations.

This idea of permutation can be classed as fourth-order development with the risk that its analysis is debatable. However, as the music progresses it is quite clear that this flexible three-note pattern does in fact permeate the rest of the piece.

Another permutation quickly follows [1.32]:

With an augmentation of (y) [1.47]:

The mood now changes with the first new idea of the second subject group [1.56]:

This subtly deceptive, tonally unstable music depicts the wiles of Satan and by virtue of its wide downward intervals obviously relates to the 'Mansoul' theme in inversion. The tonality slips unstably between indeterminate keys, slithering and wriggling [2.09].

The falling third (x) is derived from the permutation (x1) – the flugel horn being left holding this fragment (reminiscent of 'Go Down, Moses') [3.55].

As initial skirmishes begin, one more of the three-note permutations (x1) becomes more prominent as (x5). Standing unadorned in the face of mounting opposition is Luther's chorale [4.26], serene and prayerful, the central section solemnly scored for trombones. The prayer is rudely interrupted by an apparently new figure [5.40]:

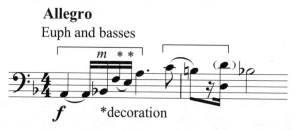

However, it is but a decoration of the 'Mansoul' motif (m) and an inversion of (x1). Tension continues to build with these two ideas added to the arsenal of weapons to be deployed in battle [5.56] [6.15]:

With chorale fragments [6.31] a final blessing is given and battle commences. It is important to appreciate that the ensuing chaos is not in any way haphazard but the initial battle sounds seem to have little in common with preceding music. Family motifs, permutations and fragments are then hurled into battle in a highly organised structure: developing, progressing and building [7.38].

Without any slackening of tempo, a memory of the march-like first subject returns [8.32] before all is engulfed in disintegrating tonality [8.45]:

Each trombone exclamation (x5) deploys nearly all 12 notes of the chromatic scale as the infamous, discordant cascade ends the battle with a roar [9.00].

Suddenly all is still! As the smoke of battle clears, the victor emerges (augmentation of the 'Mansoul' theme) and faith's victory is affirmed with recapitulation of suitable ideas. Then, to use the composer's own words, there is an 'Aftermath of battle – the grey dawn with dim shapes tiptoeing amongst the heaps of slain and wounded'. A high lyrical baritone sings a high lament (b) while cup-muted cornets recall the chorale [10.10].

Gradually getting up and dusting itself off, 'Mansoul' hears the bells ring out [11.11].

The music is now tonally extremely stable in the key of C major, throughout the triumphant restatement of the chorale [11.32] and 'Mansoul' theme [12.35] almost to the end of the piece. But true to form, RSA characteristically senses the need to strengthen his finale with four bars of chords in distant tonality [12.59] before the bass end restores C major with a reprise of the (y) [13.04].

'The Lord is King'

As has been shown, 'The Holy War' is closely unified in its material, which appears in many guises and permutations. In a similar way, Ray Steadman-Allen composed 'The Lord is King' using mainly the Welsh hymn tune 'Llangollen' as material for his trademark thematic transformations. Although it is indeed possible to trace the origin of most of his material to this tune, sometimes this is merely speculation. Nevertheless, the outworking of the musical scheme results in a masterpiece which is at once closely unified and widely diverse. In 'Llangollen', RSA has chosen a tune that is in itself fascinating.

Its lines, strong and recognisable, are for the most part pentatonic and capable of considerable development. The theme appears three times in its entirety, twice in the first movement and once in the last and, unlike 'The Holy War', is present from the very first bar. None of the movements is particularly formalised (as in sonata or binary form) but they aptly illustrate RSA's ideal for logical progression from one idea to the next. Interspersed between the phrases of the initial statement of 'Llangollen' are two toccata-like interventions, the second incorporating a motif which becomes significant [0.18].

286

Superficially unrelated to the theme, it could be considered to be either a reversal of (c) in inversion or possibly based on the shape of (d). Either way this motif becomes a motto theme. In appending the subtitles of 'My Joys', 'My Toils' and 'My Craftsman's Skill' to the movements, the composer has suggested a biographical element. Whether the possessive adjective is the composer, the listener, or both, remains to be seen but one might suggest that the motto stands for 'The Hero'.

Whereas 'The Holy War' presided over the disintegration of tonality, 'The Lord is King' is tonally stable, sometimes simple (not simplistic) in language but quite profound in expression. As the initial statement of the theme concludes, its penultimate bar is extended by repeating shape and rhythm, if not the exact notes [0.29].

This can be classed as second-order development. The motto fragment (w) is also present in counterpoint and the tempo increases. A jubilant, playful idea incorporating the motto is introduced, which might be considered a decoration of (a) (fourth order) [0.36].

With another increase in tempo comes a dotted rhythm figure possibly derived from (g) [0.52].

This reaches a climax before dissipating through a calming gesture fashioned from (j) [1.06].

287

The second appearance of 'Llangollen' is simply stated in the mellow instruments over a walking bass flowing out into an arching phrase, achieved by repeating the rhythm and joining with the calming gesture (j2). This phrase is then repeated by a trombone quartet [1.40] to a point that may be considered the end of the exposition; (y), (j2), and (z) now vie for attention, precipitating a brief pompous march [2.17] which recalls the opening toccata-like figures building to a tutti climax with the syncopations of (z) [2.35] combined with (f). As the texture thins, solo cornet and baritone toy with (y) weaving in the motto, before mounting excitement (x) builds to an affirmation of (a) in the home key of Db major before the movement concludes in a blaze of Bb major.

The second movement pitches us from jubilation to darkness with haunting chord sequences almost bereft of melody. If there is a thematic link, it might be found in the last two notes of the third phrase and the first two of 'Llangollen'.

Moderato espressivo

As this dies away a strong, one-bar statement (q), a reversal of the preceding line, seems to cry out – 'The Lord *is* King' [1.23].

Now, first on solo cornet and then full band, a long, elegant melody is spun from the motto (w) [1.37].

Woven into the line is a simple crotchet and two semiquaver fragment (k) [3.07] whose origin will soon become apparent. Coming to rest in D major the flugel horn plaintively intones (a). A solo euphonium sings the motto theme whose cadence figure

is first repeated by pairs of cornets, horns and trombones, finally becoming a countermelody to the old chorus 'He Died of a Broken Heart for Me' [4.18], intoned by a blending of horns and emotively high euphonium.

Now the origin of the (k) fragment is clear. A further return of the motto is short-lived and darkness again descends [5.11]. Subdued at first, the bass pedal 'D' becomes more and more insistent, trombones plead 'He died of a broken heart' [5.42] and out of the tension bursts forth (q) the affirmation 'The Lord *is* King' [6.04]. Without doubt, this is one of the most profound moments in all Salvation Army music.

The long elegiac melody (w) now returns and is drawn out by pondering the fragment (k) [7.05] – 'he died, he died for me'. In conclusion muted cornets and trombone whisper – 'The Lord is King'. To recall the movement's title 'My Toil', one is inclined to regard it less as drudgery but akin to a Christian's identification with Christ's passion.

Energetic and muscular, the last movement's links with 'Llangollen' are ever more remote. Is it too pedantic to point out that the opening 'Be-dum-dum', said to be Leslie Condon's drumming, might be (e1) or even a corruption of the motto theme?

There is also some second order development of (a) [0.21]:

Allegro energico

The music is lively and tumultuous with ever-increasing complexity.

Allegro energico

An augmentation of 'He died…' introduces a motor figure as an accompaniment to a warm flowing appearance of (a) [0.57].

One must point out that repetition is rarely a feature of RSA's music and deduce that here it has a specific function. Can it be that here the composer wants to say that, regardless of skill and inspiration, the role of an artist involves an awful lot of hard graft? Building to an interim climax the music again falls back on the motor figure which then builds and builds, giving way to a clamorous fugato [1.33] possibly based on the motto. Wave upon wave of energy surges forward until 'Llangollen' bursts forth in glorious praise [2.20], with counterpoints drawn from across the entire work.

As if to affirm our suspicions, the penultimate bars of the tune recall the dotted rhythm of the first movement [2.50] (z). A short, energetic codetta calls forth the trombones alone declaring 'The Lord is King' and the lower band suddenly recalls, in the dark key of F♭ major, 'He died of a broken...'. But at the point where one expects '...heart for me', the motto (w) replaces the word 'me', surely confirming all along this motto theme has stood for 'The Hero'. Truly a masterwork with a message [3.07].

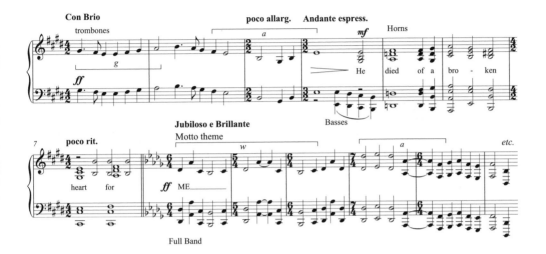

Index

Joy Steadman-Allen herself is not indexed because, with Ray, she is integral to the whole book